THE
BLACK CHURCH

ALSO BY HENRY LOUIS GATES, JR.

Stony the Road:
Reconstruction, White Supremacy, and the Rise of Jim Crow

100 Amazing Facts about the Negro

Finding Your Roots, Season 1:
The Official Companion to the PBS Series

Finding Your Roots, Season 2:
The Official Companion to the PBS Series

The Henry Louis Gates, Jr., Reader

Life Upon These Shores

Black in Latin America

Tradition and the Black Atlantic

Faces of America

In Search of Our Roots

Lincoln on Race and Slavery

Finding Oprah's Roots

America behind the Color Line:
Dialogues with African Americans

The Trials of Phillis Wheatley

Little Known Black History Facts

Wonders of the African World

Thirteen Ways of Looking at a Black Man

Colored People

Loose Canons

Figures in Black

The Signifying Monkey

WITH EMMANUEL K. AKYEAMPONG

Dictionary of African Biography

THE
BLACK CHURCH

This Is Our Story,
This Is Our Song

HENRY LOUIS GATES, JR.

PENGUIN PRESS
NEW YORK
2021

PENGUIN PRESS
An imprint of Penguin Random House LLC
penguinrandomhouse.com

Illustration credits appear on pages 265–266.

Photo research by Toby Greenberg

LIBRARY OF CONGRESS CATALOGING-IN-PUBLICATION DATA

Names: Gates, Henry Louis, Jr., author.
Title: The Black church : this is our story, this is our song /
Henry Louis Gates, Jr.
Description: New York : Penguin Press, 2021. |
Includes bibliographical references and index.
Identifiers: LCCN 2020042098 (print) | LCCN 2020042099 (ebook) |
ISBN 9781984880338 (hardcover) | ISBN 9781984880345 (ebook)
Subjects: LCSH: African American churches—History. |
African Americans—Religion—History.
Classification: LCC BR563.N4 G295 2021 (print) |
LCC BR563.N4 (ebook) | DDC 277.30089/96073—d c23
LC record available at https://lccn.loc.gov/2020042098
LC ebook record available at https://lccn.loc.gov/2020042099

Printed in the United States of America
1   3   5   7   9   10   8   6   4   2

Designed by Amanda Dewey

In memory of
Congressman John Robert Lewis
(1940–2020)

Prayer is one of the most powerful—well, I don't want to call it a weapon, but it's a tool, an instrument, a way of reaching out that humankind has. We can and do use it to deal with problems and the things and issues that we don't understand, that we don't quite comprehend. It's very hard to separate the essence of prayer and faith. We pray because we believe that praying can make what we believe, our dreams and our visions, come true.

Amen.

There is an old African proverb: "When you pray, move your feet." As a nation, if we care for the Beloved Community, we must move our feet, our hands, our hearts, our resources to build and not to tear down, to reconcile and not to divide, to love and not to hate, to heal and not to kill. In the final analysis, we are one people, one family, one house—the American house, the American family.

—JOHN LEWIS, *Walking with the Wind:*
A Memoir of the Movement

CONTENTS

Never confuse position with power. Pharaoh had a position, but Moses had the power. Herod had a position, but John had the power. The cross had a position, but Jesus had the power. Lincoln had a position, but Douglass had the power. Woodrow Wilson had a position, but Ida B. Wells had the power. George Wallace had a position, but Rosa Parks had the power. Lyndon Baines Johnson had a position, but Martin Luther King had the power. We have the power. Don't you ever forget.

—THE REVEREND OTIS MOSS III

PREFACE

Heart of what slave poured out such melody
As "Steal away to Jesus"? On its strains
His spirit must have nightly floated free,
Though still about his hands he felt his chains.

—JAMES WELDON JOHNSON,
"O Black and Unknown Bards"

In a recent essay, the writer Darryl Pinckney notes that
"[Ralph] Ellison opposed the notion of black life as a 'meta-physical condition' of 'irremediable agony' because that made
it seem as though it either took place in a vacuum or had only one
theme."[1] No cultural institution formed within the African American experience gives the lie to such a simplistic, despairing view
more than the Black Church. Political activists—including Malcolm X, of course, but especially the Black Panther Party in the
latter half of the 1960s—have debated whether the role of the Black
embrace of Christianity under slavery was a positive or negative
force. There were those who argued that it was an example of
Marx's famous indictment of religion as "the opium of the people"
because it gave to the oppressed false comfort and hope, thereby
obscuring the causes of their oppression and reducing their urge to

overturn that oppression. But I do not believe that religion functioned in this simple fashion in the history of Black people in this country.

As a matter of fact, although Marx was no fan of religion, to put it mildly, this statement, which the Panthers loved to quote, was part of a more complicated assessment of the nature and function of religion. The full quote bears repeating: "Religious suffering is, at one and the same time, the expression of real suffering and a protest against real suffering. Religion is the sigh of the oppressed creature, the heart of a heartless world, and the soul of soulless conditions. It is the opium of the people."[2] Karl Marx could not imagine the complexity of the Black Church, even if the Black Church could imagine him—could imagine those who lacked the tools to see beyond its surface levels of meaning. James Weldon Johnson, in his lovely poem about the anonymous authors of the sacred vernacular tradition, "O Black and Unknown Bards," put this failure of interpretive reciprocity in this memorable way:

> What merely living clod, what captive thing,
> Could up toward God through all its darkness grope,
> And find within its deadened heart to sing
> These songs of sorrow, love and faith, and hope?
> How did it catch that subtle undertone,
> That note in music heard not with the ears?

The role of Black Christianity in motivating our country's largest slave rebellion, Nat Turner's Rebellion in Southampton County, Virginia, is only the most dramatic example of the text of the King James Bible being called upon to justify the violent revolutionary overthrow of the slave regime. But we need only look at the brilliant use of the church in all of its forms—from W. E. B. Du Bois's triptych of "the Preacher, the Music, and the Frenzy" to the use of the building itself—to see the revolutionary potential and practice of Black Christianity in forging social change. What most intrigues me about Marx's full quote is his realization that it is at once "the expression of real suffering and a protest against real suffering," a crucial part of the quote that seems to have fallen away.

People, of course, pray and worship for all sorts of reasons. Despite what Marx and the Black Panthers thought, despite its share of bad actors and practitioners of bad faith; its undeniable and inexcusably long history of sexism, homophobia, and anti-Semitism; its unforgivable occasions of child abuse; the sheer greed of scandalous, shameful manipulators of what's become known as the prosperity gospel—all voluminously documented and rightly so—the importance of the role of the Black Church *at its best* cannot be gainsaid in the history of the African American people. Nor can it be underestimated. It isn't religion that keeps human beings enslaved; it is violence. Most normal human beings don't need an elaborate religious belief system to resist the temptation to sacrifice their lives in the face of overwhelming odds and the certainty that they will be brutally suppressed and killed. That would be unreasonable.

The "failure" of African Americans to overthrow their masters, as the enslaved men and women did on the island that became the Republic of Haiti, can't be traced to the role of the church per se, as Nat Turner's decision to act based on his interpretation of prophecy attests. Early on, the church and Christianity played a role both in Black rebellions and in the preparation of Black people for leadership roles. Following Denmark Vesey's alleged slave insurrection, Emanuel Church in Charleston, South Carolina, was burned to the ground; at the end of the Civil War, the Reverend Richard Harvey Cain left his congregation in New York to go south, to resurrect Mother Emanuel, and then, during Reconstruction, was elected to the U.S. House of Representatives. (Other churches would be the subject of deadly attacks and explosions carried out at the hands of white supremacists, most notably the bombing of the Sixteenth Street Baptist Church in Birmingham, Alabama, in 1963, in which four little girls were killed, another was blinded, and more than a dozen people were injured.) Nat Turner knew his Bible. Frederick Douglass, too, was thoroughly grounded in the church, having attended the Methodist church on Sharp Street in Baltimore while enslaved and then delivering his first public speeches—sermons—at the AME Zion Church ("Little Zion") on Second Street in the whaling city of New Bedford, Massachusetts. It has long been assumed that Douglass miraculously "found his voice" at an abolition meeting on Nantucket Island in 1841, three years after he escaped from slavery in Maryland, spontaneously rising to his feet in front of a roomful of white strangers. Not so, and he was even "ordained" in a way at Little Zion when he was about twenty-one or twenty-two years old.[3] Like his father, the Reverend Adam Clayton Powell, Jr., pastored at Harlem's Abyssinian Baptist Church; unlike his father, he ran for political office and served his Harlem constituents in the U.S. House of Representatives. Powell effectively led the civil rights movement in the North until Montgomery, Alabama, emerged as the epicenter of the movement and the Reverend Dr. Martin Luther King, Jr., became its most recognizable face and voice. I could provide many other examples. The Black Church has a long and noble history in relation to Black political action, dating back at least to the late eighteenth century. Again, the failure of enslaved African Americans to overthrow the institution of slavery, as their Haitian sisters and brothers would do, cannot be traced to the supposed passivity inbred by Christianity; rather, it can be traced to the simple fact that, unlike the Black people enslaved on Saint-Domingue, African Americans were vastly outnumbered and outgunned. Violent insurrection would have been a form of racial suicide; insurrection meant death.

What the church did do, in the meantime, as Black people collectively awaited freedom, was to provide a liminal space brimming with subversive features. To paraphrase one of the standard phrases from the Christian tradition, one should never underestimate the power of prayer. Just ask Bull Connor or George Wallace. Without the role of the Black Church, the Civil Rights Act of 1964 and the Voting Rights Act of 1965—signed into law by President Lyndon Johnson, with King by his side at both, and the future congressman John Lewis, himself an ordained Baptist minister, present in 1965—would never have been enacted when they were. There is no question that the Black Church is one of the parents of the civil rights movement, and today's Black Lives Matter movement is one of its heirs.

This is a truth made manifest in the mourning of Representative Lewis this summer. In a season of pain marked by the ongoing coronavirus pandemic and the murder of George Floyd, John Lewis's funeral included a service at Brown Chapel AME Church in Selma and his final crossing of the Edmund Pettus Bridge. For Lewis, voting was sacramental, and he shed his blood for us to exercise this most fundamental of rights. In revisiting these sites and reflecting on his many marches for justice, "we, the people" once again bore witness to the deeper historical reality that faith has long been the source of the courage of those toiling on the front lines of change. As Lewis himself once put it, "The civil rights movement was based on faith. Many of us who were participants in this movement saw our involvement as an extension of our faith."[4] Generations to come will honor Lewis by casting their ballots, a secular communion to strengthen our democracy.

One of the greatest achievements in the long history of civilization, as far as I am concerned, is the extraordinary resilience of the African American community under slavery, through the sheer will and determination of the men and women within the community to live to see another day, to thrive. The number of Africans dragged to North America between 1526 and 1808, when the slave trade ended, totaled approximately 388,000 shipped directly from continent to continent, plus another 52,430 through the intra-American trade.[5] That initial population had grown to some 4.4 million free and enslaved people by 1860. How was this possible? What sustained our ancestors under the nightmare of enslavement to build families and survive their being ripped apart and sold off in the domestic trade (the dreaded "Second Middle Passage"); to carry on despite not being able to ward off the rapacious sexual advances of their masters (a verity exposed by DNA, which shows that the average African American is more than 24 percent European); to acquire skills; to create a wide variety of complex cultural forms; to withstand torture, debasement, and the suffocating denial of their right to learn to read and write; and to defer the gratification of freedom from bondage—all without ever giving up the hope of liberty, as one enslaved poet, George Moses Horton, put it, if not for themselves, then for their children or grandchildren, when slavery had no end in sight? What gave them a belief in the future, and by that I mean the future not just in the clichéd "world to come" in heaven, but *here, in this world to come on earth*—the future that their sacrifices enabled us to occupy today? What empowered them with "hope against hope"? Darryl Pinckney, in the essay referred to earlier, notes that "if a person cannot imagine a future, then we would say that that person is depressed." To paraphrase Pinckney's next line, if a people cannot imagine a future, then its culture will die.

And Black culture didn't die. The signal aspects of African American culture were planted, watered, given light, and nurtured in the Black Church, out of the reach and away from the watchful eyes of those who would choke the life out of it. We have to give the church its due as a source of our ancestors' unfathomable resiliency and perhaps the first formalized site for the collective fashioning and development of so many African American aesthetic forms. Although Black people made spaces for secular expression, only the church afforded room for all of it to be practiced at the same time. And only in the church could all of the arts emerge, be on display, be practiced and perfected, and be expressed at one time and in one place, including music, dance, and song; rhetoric and oratory; poetry and prose; textual exegesis and interpretation; memorization, reading, and writing; the dramatic arts and scripting; call-and-response, signifying, and indirection; philosophizing and theorizing; and, of course, mastering all of "the flowers of speech." We do the church a great disservice if we fail to recognize that it was the first formalized site within African American culture perhaps not exclusively for the *fashioning* of the Black aesthetic, but certainly for its *performance*, service to service, week by week, Sunday to Sunday.

James Weldon Johnson, writing at the height of the Harlem Renaissance, feeling a certain urgency to valorize Black vernacular forms, put it this way: "In truth, the power to frame the poetic phrases that make the titles of so many of the Spirituals betokens the power to create the songs. Consider the sheer magic of 'Swing Low Sweet Chariot,' 'I've Got to Walk My Lonesome Valley,' 'Steal Away to Jesus,' 'Singing With a Sword in My Hand,' 'Rule Death in His Arms,' 'Ride On King Jesus,' 'We Shall Walk Through the Valley in Peace,' 'The Blood Came Twinklin' Down,' 'Deep River,' 'Death's Goin' to Lay His Cold, Icy Hand on Me,' and confess that none but an artistically endowed people could have evoked it."[6]

The Black Church was a cultural system, a system of symbols and signs. And navigating its multiple levels and nebulous contours demanded a sophisticated degree of cultural literacy, the training for which began in Sunday school, ranging from ways to dress and comport oneself on narrow wooden benches in stifling heat during even the most tedious and boring sermon, to the creation of uncommonly original modes of composing, singing, and playing sacred music and its remarkably brilliant reinterpretations of King James English through entirely new lyrics and imagery, generating and mastering and passing down a genre of oratory and sermonizing hitherto unknown in Christendom, keeping their African heritage alive by engaging in rhythmic call-and-response interactions with the preacher, and experiencing the multifarious manifestations of the frenzy, especially receiving possession by the Holy Ghost, perhaps the most sublime of all of God's gifts to the pure and faithful.

The Black Church was the cultural cauldron that Black people created to combat a system designed in every way to crush their spirit. Collectively and with enormous effort, they refused to allow that to happen. And the culture they created was sublime, awesome, majestic, lofty, glorious, and at all points subversive of the larger culture of enslavement that sought to destroy their humanity. The miracle of African American survival can be traced directly to the miraculous ways that our ancestors—across a range of denominations and through the widest variety of worship— reinvented the religion that their "masters" thought would keep them subservient. Rather, that religion enabled them and their descendants to learn, to grow, to develop, to interpret and reinvent the world in which they were trapped; it enabled them to bide their time—ultimately, time for them to fight for their freedom, and for us to continue the fight for ours. It also gave them the moral authority to turn the mirror of religion back on their masters and to indict the nation for its original sin of allowing their enslavement to build up that "city upon a hill." In exposing that hypocrisy at the heart of their "Christian" country, they exhorted succeeding generations to close the yawning gap between America's founding ideals and the reality they had been forced to endure. Who were these people? As the late Reverend Joseph Lowery put it, "I don't know whether the faith produced them, or if they produced the faith. But they belonged to each other."[7]

Henry Louis Gates, Jr.
Cambridge, Massachusetts
November 1, 2020

THE
BLACK CHURCH

INTRODUCTION

No pillar of the African American community has been more central to its history, identity, and social justice vision than the "Black Church."* To be sure, there is no single Black Church, just as there is no single Black religion, but the traditions and faiths that fall under the umbrella of African American religion, particularly Christianity, constitute two stories: one of a people defining themselves in the presence of a higher power and the other of their journey for freedom and equality in a land where power itself—and even humanity—for so long was (and still is) denied them. Collectively, these churches make up the oldest institution created and controlled by African Americans, and they are more than simply places of worship. In the centuries since its birth in the time of slavery, the Black Church has stood as the foundation of Black religious, political, economic, and social life.

For a people systematically brutalized and debased by the inhuman system of human slavery, followed by a century of Jim Crow racism, the church provided a refuge: a place of racial and

---

* Although there is no monolithic "Black Church," just as there is no monolithic "Black vote" or "Black perspective," for clarity throughout this book, I will use the phrase the "Black Church" as a way to acknowledge the importance of institutions of organized religion to African Americans over time.

individual self-affirmation, of teaching and learning, of psychological and spiritual sustenance, of prophetic faith; a symbolic space
where Black people, enslaved and free, could nurture the hope for
a better today and a much better tomorrow. For a community disenfranchised and underserved by religious institutions established
by and catering to the needs of white people, it served both secular
and spiritual needs. Its music and linguistic traditions have perme-
ated popular culture, and its scriptural devotion to ideas of liberation, equality, redemption, and love have challenged and remade
the nation again and again, calling America to its higher self in
times of testing and trial.

The Black Church has influenced nearly every chapter of the
African American story, and it continues to animate Black identity
today, both for believers and nonbelievers. In that sense, the Black
Church functions on several levels, as a spiritual center—a place of
worship—and as a social center and a cultural repository as well, a
living treasure trove of African American sacred cultural history
and practice: literally the place where "the faith of the fathers and
mothers" is summoned and preserved, modified and reinvented
each Sunday, in a dynamic process of cultural retrieval and transformation, all at the same time.

Call-and-response exchanges between congregation and pastor; at its best, the seamless interplay between the rhythms of the
sermon and the harmonies of song, both reflecting the pastor's
biblical exegesis of "the text for today"; modes of prayer, both formal and informal; and possession by the omnipresent Holy Spirit:
all are really links in a chain of cultural continuity that connects
Africa to Black America. They are repetitions with brilliantly

improvised differences within a received "frame," a discursive frame, a sacred cultural "language" in which worshippers are so thoroughly fluent and literate that they can riff within that frame freely and creatively. They are echoes of sermonic and musical formations of the past fashioned by our ancestors over successive generations of creation, repetition, revision, and, most importantly, improvisation, quite probably since the first hundred years of American slavery.

We see it in jazz, with musicians riffing upon standards in the jazz tradition and in popular culture. John Coltrane did it with "My Favorite Things," and Louis Armstrong did it with "La Vie en Rose," to take just two of countless examples. We see it in the work of performers today, this living chain of Black cultural signifiers imbibed and internalized, respectfully acknowledged yet sublimely transformed. Daring and defiant artists, ranging from Thomas A. Dorsey, with his experiments in gospel, to Kirk Franklin, with his fresh fusions of hymns with hip-hop, risked the opprobrium of the more conservative keepers of the tradition by daring to alter and infuse the sacred with borrowed techniques from the scandalously secular: that long and controversial tradition of Saturday night sneaking into the church on Sunday morning.

With a language all its own, symbols all its own, the Black Church offered a reprieve from the racist world, a place for African Americans to come together in community to advance their aspirations and to sing out, pray out, and shout out their frustrations. It was the saving grace of both enslaved Black people and of the 10 percent or so of the Black community that, at any given time before the Civil War, were ostensibly free; the site of possibility for the liminal space between slavery and freedom, object and subject, slave and citizen, in which free Black people were trapped. The church fueled slave rebellions, nurtured and sustained the Underground Railroad, and was the training ground for the orators of the abolitionist movement, and for ministers such as Richard Harvey Cain who emerged as powerful and effective political leaders during Reconstruction. It powered antilynching campaigns and economic boycotts, and formed the backbone of and meeting place for the civil rights movement. Rooted in the fundamental belief in equality between Black and white, human dignity, earthly and heavenly freedom, and sisterly and brotherly love, the Black Church and the religion practiced within its embrace acted as the engine driving social transformation in America, from the antebellum abolitionist movement through the various phases of the fight against Jim Crow, and now, in our current century, to Black Lives Matter.

The Black Church, in a society in which the color line was strictly policed, amounted to a world within a world, providing practical physical and social outlets and economic resources for local African American communities. Even in the antebellum period, the Black Church was the proving ground for the nourishment and training of a class of leaders; it fostered community bonds and established the first local, regional, and then national Black social networks. It was under the roofs of these churches that African Americans, in the heyday of Reconstruction—especially in that magical summer of 1867, when Black men in the former Confederacy got the right to vote—also learned of the opportunities and obligations of citizenship and the sanctity of the franchise.

(It is a shocking fact and disgrace of American history that even free Black men—with the exception of those living in five of the six New England states plus New York, *if* they satisfied an onerous property requirement—could not vote until the ratification of the Fifteenth Amendment in 1870.) The story of religion in African American culture carries us into almost every corner of the African American experience. As the Reverend Al Sharpton puts it, "The Black Church was more than just a spiritual home. It was the epicenter of Black life."

The church also bred distinct forms of expression, maybe most obviously its own forms of music. Black sacred music, commencing with the sacred songs the enslaved created and blossoming into the spirituals (which W. E. B. Du Bois aptly dubbed the "Sorrow Songs"), Black versions of Protestant hymns, gospel music, and freedom songs, emerging from within the depths of Black belief and molded in repetitions and variations in weekly choir practice and Sunday worship services, would eventually captivate a broad, nonsectarian audience and influence almost every genre of twentieth-century popular music. The blues, jazz, rock and roll, soul and R&B, folk, rock, and even hip-hop bear the imprint of Black sacred music. It is evident in the sound of such a wide array of legendary artists that it is difficult to limit a list, but there are some names that simply cannot go unspoken: Ella Fitzgerald, Sarah Vaughan, and Dinah Washington; Aretha Franklin, Little Richard, and James Brown; Sam Cooke and Marvin Gaye; Donny Hathaway and Teddy Pendergrass; Curtis Mayfield and Jerry Butler; Tina Turner; Whitney Houston; Patti LaBelle; practically all of Motown, all the way to Mary J. Blige, John Legend, Jennifer

Hudson, and Kirk Franklin, whose talents were nurtured in church pews and choirs. Mahalia Jackson, Dr. King's sacred soul mate and private muse, is, of course, in a class of her own, stubbornly resisting the extremely lucrative financial lure of "going secular" but nevertheless influencing the styles of a plethora of Black singers ranging over a host of genres. "The church is our foundation," Hudson says. "Somehow to me it relates to our culture. I noticed when I was in Africa how the music wasn't just music; it was a message. Well, it's the same in the church. When you're singing a song, it's not just a song; it's your testimony. It's your story. You're singing with purpose and to God."

One can also hear the music of the church in its range of preaching styles and their emanations in the broader public square, constructed out of the magical poetic diction of the English of the King James Bible, the silent second text of both African American sacred culture and the African American literary tradition. Its cadences, rhythms, and allusions ring most familiarly through the soaring rhetoric of Martin Luther King's spellbinding, iconic calls for civil rights and economic justice, but also in the riveting oratory of his Muslim brother, Malcolm X. Dr. King, of course, was drawing on a very long tradition of resonant masters of the pulpit, tracing all the way back to the published sermons of formerly enslaved preachers, such as John Jasper's canonical "De Sun Do Move," first published in 1882, and including the great Black preachers whose sermons he actually heard, starting with his grandfather and father but including Howard Thurman, Benjamin E. Mays, Vernon Johns, and Gardner C. Taylor especially.

Dr. King's indelible, supremely inspirational delivery, as powerful as I always find it, was part of a truly awesome, perhaps unparalleled tradition of artistry and master craftsmanship that characterizes Black sermonizing in the Christian tradition. The oratorial genius of Black women and men—in the pulpit and out of it—is, without a doubt, one of the principal and most abundant legacies of the Black Church. For my PBS film and for this book, I interviewed an amazing cohort of pastors who are themselves beneficiaries of and contributors to this powerful tradition: Dwight Andrews; William J. Barber II; Traci Blackmon; Charles Blake; James Bryson, Jr.; Calvin O. Butts III; Michael Curry; Kelly Brown Douglas; Michael Eric Dyson; Yvette Flunder; Cheryl Townsend Gilkes; Victor J. Grigsby; T. D. Jakes; Vashti Murphy McKenzie; Otis Moss, Jr.; Otis Moss III; Brianna Parker; Yolanda Pierce; R. Janae Pitts-Murdock; Stephen G. Ray; Eugene F. Rivers III; Cheryl J. Sanders; Al Sharpton; Martha Simmons; Thurmond N. Tillman; Eboni Marshall Turman; Jonathan L. Walton; Raphael G. Warnock; Jeremiah Wright; and Andrew Young.*

In the canonical works in the African American literary tradition, no text is more resonantly foundational, more unmistakable, than the King James Bible. We need only think of the speeches and writings of Frederick Douglass, both before and after the Civil War, or of the Harlem Renaissance classic *God's Trombones* by James Weldon Johnson, among many other examples. But this tradition reaches its zenith in the prose of James Baldwin, especially in his essays, which we might think of as truly "Jamesian,"

---

* We conducted a poll among these spiritual leaders, as well as scholars, activists, and writers interviewed for the series and book, and asked who, for them, ranks among the greatest preachers and orators in the tradition. That list can be found in the appendix of this book.

reflecting the twin influences of the King James Bible and Henry James. Baldwin's literary legacy, in fiction, reached its most sublime extension in Toni Morrison's mythopoeic fictional universes. But even in these written works, we "hear" the printed word striving to imitate the power of the spoken word, just as Zora Neale Hurston's fictions mimic secular Black vernacular forms and Langston Hughes's and Sterling A. Brown's poetry sought to make a formal poetic diction out of jazz and the blues.

But the grand legacy of the spoken-word tradition, starting in slavery, without a doubt reached its crescendo in the Black Church, where it continues to this day. In Black music, the past is ever present. "Even if they aren't singing the old Negro spirituals," says the Episcopal bishop the Most Reverend Michael Curry, "you hear the idioms of those spirituals. It's where when you begin to speak in a certain way, or better yet, when somebody starts singing in a certain way, folk inside, they start reacting and responding, and eventually there may be some shouts and there may be silence. Something is moving. That's where the Black Church is found. It's in those heartbeats." Bishop T. D. Jakes, himself a master orator, speaks to this history: "The singing on the wounded soul goes all the way back to the soils of Africa. We have always been people that have sang out into the wind and exhaled what hurt us." Jakes is describing the "music" and rhythms inherent in the language of the Black spoken sacred word, but it's in the Black Church where the language of music and the music of language meet to create one grand, inimitable, irresistibly powerful form.

The power generated by the sound and feeling of the music during a service is so astounding as to be virtually indescribable.

As the gospel singer Yolanda Adams puts it, "It sets the tone for how you will feel when the word comes forth." Its importance has traveled down through generations. "It's such a distinct flavor of music," says the musician John Legend. "It is its own thing. It's a very American thing. It's a very Black American thing." "We tell our story with music," Bishop Yvette Flunder of the City of Refuge, United Church of Christ, says. "We forget sermons, but we can remember songs." The genius of Black sacred music was probably the very first cultural attribute that even racist slave owners could, if begrudgingly, attribute to Americans of African descent. The popularization of the "slave songs" by the Fisk Jubilee Singers following the war led to Antonin Dvorak's claim, published in 1893, that not only was Black sacred music America's sole original contribution to world culture, but that the only truly "classical" American music must be constructed on its foundation. Du Bois would echo this claim a decade later in *The Souls of Black Folk*.

Always, the Black Church has included a spectrum of beliefs and voices. The simplified idea of the "Black Church" traditionally refers to a group of seven major historical Black denominations in the Methodist, Baptist, and Pentecostal traditions: the African Methodist Episcopal Church (AME), the African Methodist Episcopal Zion Church (AME Zion), the National Baptist Convention, USA (NBC), the National Baptist Convention of America (NBCA), the Progressive National Baptist Convention (PNBC), the Christian Methodist Episcopal Church (CME), and the Church of God in Christ (COGIC). A Pew Research Center study lists the following as the ten most popular religious denominations:

Other Baptist (historically Black Protestant tradition)	15%
National Baptist Convention	12%
Catholic	5%
Church of God in Christ	4%
Southern Baptist Convention (evangelical tradition)	3%
Missionary Baptist (historically Black Protestant tradition)	3%
AME	3%
Other Pentecostal (historically Black Protestant tradition)	3%
Nondenominational (historically Black Protestant tradition)	3%
Nonspecific Protestant family (historically Black Protestant tradition)	3%

These denominations, of course, do not represent the totality of Black religious affiliation or experience. They barely constitute a majority; indeed, a third of respondents claimed no religious affiliation at all.[1] There have always been, and are increasingly, Black members of a wide variety of denominations, including but by no means limited to Seventh-day Adventists and Jehovah's Witnesses, Roman Catholics and Episcopalians, Mormons and Muslims, Buddhists and Jews, Baha'i and Jains. Sometimes the facts defy preconceived notions about Black Church membership: for example, there are more African American Roman Catholics than there are Black Muslims and Jehovah's Witnesses combined, and more Roman Catholics than members of the Church of God in Christ. There are African Americans who practice Hoodoo, Obeah, Vodou, Ifa, Santeria, Candomblé, and other religions born from and nurtured by African people in the Caribbean, in South America, and throughout the American South. Today, many African American Protestants attend services in interracial congregations or belong to Black congregations that are part of otherwise predominantly white denominations.

Like the "Black experience" itself, the Black Church is diverse and contested. Tensions that showed from its birth and the denominational splintering that soon followed—surrounding doctrinal matters, personality clashes, "proper" modes of worship during church services, respectability politics, activism, integration, Black nationalism—speak to broader fault lines in Black thought and identity.

Today, African Americans, like all Americans, are increasingly moving away from organized religion. Yet in nationwide surveys, roughly 80 percent of African Americans—more than any other group—report that religion is very important in their lives. This is hardly surprising when we understand just how central faith institutions have been in the history of Africans and African Americans and their cultures and social institutions in this country. For centuries, these religions—primarily but not only many denominations of Christianity—have served as a lifeline for African Americans. Whether that lifeline will remain as vigorous and vital in the twenty-first century is an open question. At a moment when the Black community and the nation overall seem to be at a crossroads in the future of race relations, it is more important than ever to illuminate the Black Church's past and present, both to appreciate what Black religion has contributed to the larger American story and to speculate about the role it will play as race relations transform in this society.

A ndrew Young, the civil rights icon, former mayor of Atlanta, and U.S. ambassador to the United Nations in the Jimmy Carter administration, understands that faith and a sense of identity go hand in hand. "Your personhood didn't depend on the government or the social order," he says. "It depended on God and your own spiritual bloodlines." Another civil rights activist, Vernon Jordan, uses a vivid example to illustrate the point: "If you're working downtown in Atlanta in 1942, white boys called you 'boy.' And you did not have the best kind of job nor a job consistent with your capabilities, and you were looked down upon and frowned upon. But you put on your Sunday go-to-meeting clothes, and you walked in the St. Paul African Methodist Episcopal Church, you not only were somebody, you felt like you were somebody." Otis Moss, Jr., a friend of Martin Luther King, Jr., and his father, echoes this sentiment: "In that Black worship experience, somebody called you sister, brother, mother, Mr., a whole community of dignity and recognition and somebody-ness." Oprah Winfrey sums it up succinctly. The church, she says, "gave people a sense of value and of belonging and worthiness. I don't know how we could have survived as a people without it."

Worthiness. Personhood. Somebody-ness. Religion has fed generations of African American souls in this country, through the brutal trials of slavery to a new hope within a new nation, through the struggle for liberation, economic freedom, education, and the fight for full citizenship in the country we helped build. "We had to have some individual and institutional armor," says Cornel West, "in order to preserve our sanity."

I've spent my career exploring stories about Black life, but there's one story I've never told on its own. Especially as our society experiences what some have called the twin pandemics of a life-threatening virus whose mortality rates have been colorized and the obscene and revolting racism exemplified in the murder of George Floyd and other victims of police brutality, it might be the most timely and, hence, the most important one of all. It's the remarkable history of the Black Church, the story of the world of belief that enslaved people of African descent created in the face of their enslavement and its concomitant, unrelenting, and morphing white supremacy. Systemic racism may be a new concept to many, but it has deep roots.

This book is my attempt to share the reflections of believers, nonbelievers, musical artists, pastoral leaders *in* the church, and scholars *of* the church who so graciously allowed me to interview them over the past two years. The book ends with a confession of sorts, of my own first encounter with the Black Church, and a deal, a bargain, that at the age of twelve I made with Jesus in a desperate attempt to save my mother's life.

One

THE FREEDOM FAITH

We implore thy blessing, O God, upon the President, and all
who are in authority in the United States. Direct them by thy
wisdom, in all their deliberations, and O save thy people from
the calamities of war. Give peace in our day, we beseech thee,
O thou God of peace! and grant, that this highly favoured
country may continue to afford a safe and peaceful retreat from
the calamities of war and slavery, for ages yet to come.

— ABSALOM JONES, "Thanksgiving Sermon on Account of the
Abolition of the African Slave Trade," January 1, 1808

You profess to believe "that, of one blood, God made all nations
of men to dwell on the face of all the earth" and hath
commanded all men, everywhere, to love one another; yet you
notoriously hate (and glory in your hatred) all men whose skins
are not colored like your own.

— FREDERICK DOUGLASS, Fifth of July Speech
at Rochester, New York, 1852

Religion without humanity is a poor human stuff.

— SOJOURNER TRUTH, *Narrative of Sojourner
Truth* ("A Memorial Chapter"), 1884

In the Africa of our ancestors, the gods had a thousand faces
and a thousand names. Of the African ethnic groups represented in the slave trade to North America, according to the
historians Linda Heywood and John Thornton, it was the Igbo,

Mandinka, Fulbe, Kongo, Akan, and Wolof that were most numerous, and each brought with them their own belief systems. Out of this marvelously diverse blend of customs, religious faiths, and practices, the African American people arose. So perhaps it should not surprise us that enslaved Africans in North America did not accept Christianity—when finally offered a chance to embrace it—exactly as white Americans practiced it or pictured it. Instead they reshaped it in their own images, to satisfy their own spiritual and practical needs. "It's a mistake to think that enslaved Africans came to North America tabula rasa; that is to say, that they came with nothing," says Anthony B. Pinn, a professor of religion at Rice University. "That is not the case. They came bearing a rich cultural heritage, and this cultural world got filtered through Black churches." "African Americans adopted Christianity, but I also think they adapted Christianity," explains the Reverend Yolanda Pierce, dean of the Howard University School of Divinity. "They made it their own. They created it so that it could provide for them something that was nurturing, something that provided catharsis, something that provided hope." The Princeton University scholar Eddie S. Glaude, Jr., agrees: "Wherever African peoples find themselves in the diaspora, they're bringing with them ways of knowing, frames of reference, cognitive schemes to make sense of the world."

Jason Young, a historian of art, religion, and folk culture at the University of Michigan, raises another important point: "We often think of religious identity as an either/or. You're either a member of this religious group or you're a member of that. Religious practice in West and West Central Africa was much more open, and there was a wide and broad network of ritual that people could participate in, and people would move in and out of those religious zones."

The relationship of the first generations of Africans in North America to the Christian religion varied dramatically in the Spanish colonies and the British colonies. We tend to forget that the first enslaved Africans actually arrived in North America long before the much celebrated 1619 arrival of the "20 and Odd Negroes" from the kingdom of Ndongo, in modern Angola, at Old Port Comfort on Hampton Roads at the tip of the Virginia Peninsula. Enslaved Africans had been living in the Spanish colony of Florida at least since 1526, when they were taken as laborers to the failed Spanish colony of San Miguel de Gualdape, near Sapelo Island off the coast of Georgia. Other enslaved Africans followed in 1528, 1539, and 1565, when the first Africans arrived at St. Augustine.

After 1619 and until around the time the Great Awakening reached the South in the 1750s, many of the first generations of enslaved Africans in the British colonies do not seem to have been especially interested in Protestant forms of Christianity, the religions practiced by their white captors. This may have been at least in part a reaction to the fact that Protestant Christians weren't especially keen on converting them either, worried as they were at that time about the relation between conversion, the saving of souls, and the right to be free.

But this was not the case in Spanish Florida or in the Roman Catholic Church. By this time, the Catholic Church had a long history of allowing Africans, both on the continent and in Europe, full admission to the church. The most notable example is the conversion of the King of Kongo and his kingdom to Roman Catholicism in 1491, thus establishing a continuous relationship between the kingdom and the Vatican throughout the sixteenth and seventeenth centuries, including the ordination of its own bishops.[1] But the pattern of openness of the Catholic Church to Black people extends much further back, at least to the medieval period, as the historian Jane Landers notes, and as represented by the image of a thirteenth-century baptism, seen on the facing page.

Landers describes the extensive presence of Black religious confraternities from the late Middle Ages to the Renaissance in Spain, where the Catholic Church worked diligently to convert Africans. "Once Africans accepted the 'True Faith,'" Landers writes, "they enjoyed both the sacraments and the advocacy of the church." This process evolved over time. "In the fourteenth century, church officials approved the earliest documented religious confraternity or *cofradia* for Africans living in the San Bernardo barrio of Seville. This legally constituted and recognized corporation administered the Hospital of Our Lady of the Angels and provided medical care for its members." These brotherhoods expanded geographically as well as in their offerings, and by the fifteenth century they provided both "fraternal identity for their members and critical social services for their communities in major Spanish cities such as Seville and Barcelona." Landers argues that "through such civic and religious activity, Africans in Spain created an accepted public sphere for themselves."[2]

Accordingly, when the Spanish came to the New World, a long tradition of Black conversion to Catholicism came with them, and these practices continued unabated. "Spaniards and Portuguese

A Woman with Bread Loaves before a Man Holding a Scale; Initial S:
The Baptism of a Muslim, Spain, c. 1290–1310. This illuminated
manuscript is housed in the J. Paul Getty Museum in Los Angeles.

both incorporated everyone into the Catholic Church—converted Muslims, Jews, Sub-Saharan Africans, Canary Islanders—and these patterns were transplanted to the Americas," Landers says. In fact, records of Black Catholics—marriages, baptisms, burial registers—appear in St. Augustine church records dating from 1594.[3]

This openness to the conversion of Africans was not affected by New World slavery; indeed, the Spanish seemingly put it to counterintuitive political uses. To give one example, in 1687, when a group of enslaved persons escaped from Charleston to St. Augustine and sought asylum from the Spanish governor, they were granted their freedom under the condition that they convert to Catholicism. In 1693, the Spanish king, Charles II, attempting to undermine the economy of Spain's rivals in the British Carolinas, issued a cedula, or royal decree, establishing the practice of granting Black people religious sanctuary in Florida. The decree came in response to a query from Governor Diego de Quiroga, who asked what he should do about incoming runaways from Carolina who were requesting baptism into the true faith. A subsequent royal decree required four additional years of service before the fugitives gained their freedom. Charles's proclamation declared that he was giving "liberty to all . . . the men as well as the women . . . so that by their example and by my liberality others will do the same."[4] Virtually overnight, conversion to Roman Catholicism became an unprecedented route to freedom south of the British colonies, enticing Africans to flee their British masters by escaping *south* across the St. Mary's River, where they were promised freedom both in this world and the next. The first century of the presence of Black people in North America saw two distinct religious traditions unfold in relation to Christianity, in addition to those who continued, as best they could, to hold on to the Muslim religion.

Eventually, Black people entrapped in slavery in the British colonies in North America saw in conversion to Protestant forms of Christianity a chance to improve their status, to learn to read and write, and, ultimately, to escape the bonds of slavery, albeit in the afterlife. Many also heard in the scripture a different message than that preached by their captors. Ringing through the words of the Bible was a narrative of coming deliverance, heavenly salvation, and God's love for all God's children that spoke directly to their desperate circumstances.

The roots of African American religion run deep on the African continent. The human beings ensnared in the nightmare of the transatlantic slave trade practiced a wide variety of religions, including traditional ancestral worship; Islam, which had come to West Africa by the tenth century; and Catholicism, which had taken root in Central Africa by the fifteenth.[5] Enduring the horrors of the Middle Passage, enslaved Africans brought these myriad ways of worshipping with them, along with their beliefs in the supernatural and their own protective deities.

Over time, in the Caribbean and Latin America, Yoruba- and Kongo-based religions mixed with Roman Catholicism to create new systems of belief: Vodou in Haiti, Santeria in Cuba, and Candomblé in Brazil. Here in the United States, religious practices such as Hoodoo, Obeah, and conjuration reflected the continuity of African beliefs, often in "underground" forms, or transmuted into Black Christian practices (forms such as the ring shout, for instance, and possession rituals), since they were denounced by dominant Protestant Christian faiths as forms of devil worship. W. E. B. Du Bois explains this mysterious, fascinating first century or so of Black religious formation in the United States in this way: "This church was not at first by any means Christian nor definitely organized; rather it was an adaptation and mingling of heathen rites among the members of each plantation, and roughly designated as Voodooism. Association with the masters, missionary effort and motives of expediency gave these rites an early veneer of Christianity, and after the lapse of many generations the Negro church became Christian."[6]

While slave owners in the British colonies were largely resistant to converting these African peoples in the first century of the trade for fear it would cause them to press for their freedom, the goal of evangelical preachers after the start of the First Great Awakening became to convert as many souls as possible—even Black souls.

REMNANTS OF MUSLIM RELIGIOUS PRACTICE IN THE AMERICAN SOUTH

Incredibly, of the approximately 388,000 Africans shipped directly to North America, 210,000 of them were brought to the Carolinas and Georgia, and nearly 50 percent of all Africans imported arrived through the port of Charleston. Accordingly, some have termed Charleston the Ellis Island of the Black enslaved experience. And though scholars disagree about the actual numbers, which are impossible to ascertain, a large percentage of those hailing from Senegambia, especially, were practicing Muslims. This is a startling and long-buried fact about the religious history and practices of the enslaved Africans who came to America. These practicing Muslims did their best to maintain their religious faith and its rituals for as long as they could, sometimes at great cost. Centuries later, when prominent African Americans such as Malcolm X, Muhammad Ali, and Kareem Abdul-Jabbar converted to Islam, the press heralded it as something new, a major departure in the history of Black religious practices in this country. The opposite was true. These converts embraced a religious tradition with long roots in African American religious history, roots that ran deep into the experience of slavery and trace back to the very origins of African people in North America. This history has been almost entirely unknown to the broader American public.[7]

Today, off the Georgia coast, we find some of the deepest traces of Islam and other traditional African religions in places like Sapelo Island, home to the Gullah Geechee people. Islam's strong roots persisted here in ways that creolized Black Christianity. Melissa Cooper, a Rutgers University historian descended from Sapelo Island Muslims, explains that during the 1920s and 1930s, scholars and writers traveled to the island to find the "missing link," "the African origins of Black culture." This influx of interested researchers gave Sapelo Island residents the chance to tell their own history. "The stories that they told about their Muslim ancestors," Cooper says, "contributed to a wealth of knowledge about the existence of Black Muslims on Georgia's coast."

One of the most significant of these interviews occurred in the fall of 1937, when Mary Granger, the supervisor of the Savannah unit of the Georgia Writers' Project, arrived via oxcart at the home of Katie Brown, one of the oldest women living on Sapelo Island. Brown discussed her great-grandfather, Bilali Mohammed, with Granger:

Belali an he wife Phoebe pray on duh bead. Dey wuz bery puhticluh bout duh time dey pray and dey bery regluh bout duh hour. Wen duh sun come up, wen it straight obuh head and wen it set, das duh time dey pray. Dey bow tuh duh sun and hab lill mat tuh kneel on. Duh beads is on a long string. Belali he pull bead an he say "Belambi, Hakabara, Mahamadu." Phoebe she say, "Ameen, Ameen."[8]

The spelling in this transcription reveals Granger's attempt to replicate Katie Brown's speech, but it also drips with cultural biases: after all, why spell *when* as *wen*—the words are pronounced identically—unless you're trying to illustrate cultural and educational "difference" in such a way as to connote backwardness and illiteracy?[9] In her book *Making Gullah: A History of Sapelo Islanders, Race, and the American Imagination*, Cooper writes, "The deep significance of Brown's precious remembrances would be lost on the white woman who walked up to Katie Brown's back step that sunny day." Instead, when the interviewer "offered her an old pair of shoes that did not fit, and pipe tobacco in exchange for her cooperation, Granger had already decided that coastal Georgia blacks were, and had always been, slaves to a primal African impulse that predisposed them to engage in primitive spiritual rites and superstitions."[10]

And yet, says Cooper, reading interviews like this one, which was published in Granger's book *Drums and Shadows: Survival*

Katie Brown with her dog, from
Mary Granger's *Drums and
Shadows*, Georgia Writers'
Project, Savannah Unit, 1940.

Stories among the Georgia Coastal Negroes (1940), can yield crucial
information in spite of the interviewer's biases. For instance, Granger's interview led to the creation of Katie Brown's family tree. "It's
from her memories of the names of Bilali Mohammed's daughters,"
Cooper says, "that we can go back to the census of 1870 and see
where these women are, and see their sons and their children."

Cooper is a descendant of Bilali Mohammed (c. 1760–1855), one
of the many devout Muslims captured and enslaved in Senegambia
and brought to the island in the early 1800s. Remarkably, a quarter
of the ancestors of all enslaved African people arriving in North
America came from this region of West Africa, forcing us to reas-
sess the complexity of the African religious experience in the New

World, and especially in North America. Bilali—pronounced "Blali," according to the New York University scholar Michael A. Gomez—lived on Thomas Spalding's Sapelo Island plantation, where he arrived from Futa Jallon (modern-day Guinea) by way of the slave trade to the Bahamas.

Bilali's biography illustrates the intricacies of life under slavery, which can be difficult for descendants of enslaved individuals to reconcile. Bilali was of course held in bondage by and subject to the whims of his master, but that same master endowed him with responsibilities that elevated him above and therefore pitted him against other men and women owned by Spalding. "There are some historians who suggest in their examination of Bilali Mohammed's life that he may have been Thomas Spalding's [slave] driver," Cooper recalls. "That wasn't necessarily the way that I wanted to imagine having found that African ancestor." The historian Allan D. Austin writes that Spalding trusted Bilali to the point of giving him guns to guard his four-thousand-acre property while he was away. With few exceptions, Black males—enslaved or free—were prohibited from owning or using firearms prior to and during the Civil War; after Reconstruction, bans were put in place that either outright or effectively prevented gun ownership among African Americans.[11]

The folklorist Joel Chandler Harris, of Uncle Remus renown, wrote of Bilali as "Old Ben Ali" in two books, *The Story of Aaron, the Son of Ben Ali* (1896) and *Aaron in the Wildwoods* (1897). He depicted Bilali and his descendants as independent and resourceful, describing them as Arabic people who did not oppose slavery.[12] Bilali was reportedly buried with his prayer rugs, prayer beads, and Koran. He even kept a thirteen-page leather-bound book of religious teachings, written in his own hand, in Arabic, for his *umma* (the Arabic word for community).[13] He was clearly determined to preserve this aspect of his identity.

Bilali's grandsons, Cooper says, helped found the First African Baptist Church on the island. "I like to think about Sapelo and the history of Blacks in coastal Georgia and even coastal South Carolina as a window through which we can see almost the totality of the Black experience," she states, "from enslavement to the cultural negotiations that resulted in the creation of new religious institutions, the Great Migration, people leaving, people fighting in wars, and even to the contemporary struggles that Sapelo Islanders face: their efforts to hold on to their lands and to keep places like Behavior Cemetery sacred and to hold on to their traditions, but at the same time, make sure that they can move forward into a future where they're not sort of stuck in an earlier time in the imagination of everyone around them."

Estimates of the percentage of enslaved Africans who were Muslim arriving in North America vary widely, from 8 percent to 20 percent to a stunning 43 percent.[14] Between 8 and 20 percent is a reasonable estimate, I believe. Through interviews with formerly enslaved people conducted after emancipation and also analysis of ship passenger lists, advertisements seeking runaways, and other plantation documents, as well as such cultural evidence as records of "saraka" cakes, which were associated with Ramadan, historians have shown that thousands of enslaved Muslims lived in the Sea Islands.[15]

Job Ben Solomon (c. 1702–1773), born Ayuba Suleiman Diallo, was of the Fulbe ethnic group and from Bundu, located in modern-day Senegal. An educated man, he was also involved in the slave trade. In February 1730, he attempted to sell two Africans to an English captain, who refused Ayuba's terms. Shortly thereafter, he himself was captured by Mandinka slave traders who in turn sold him into slavery to the same English captain who had rejected his deal. As Gomez puts it, "Everyone was involved in this. No one's hands were clean." Ayuba endured the Middle Passage and arrived on Kent Island, near Annapolis, Maryland.[16]

Stories of Ayuba's Muslim religious practices—running away to find private spaces in which to say his daily prayers—led to his imprisonment. While imprisoned, he received a visit from a white lawyer named Thomas Bluett, who was intrigued by Ayuba's fluency in Arabic and his capacity to write. During his captivity, Ayuba wrote a letter in Arabic to his father in Africa, explaining the desperation of his situation and pleading for help. The letter made its way into the hands of James Oglethorpe, the founder of Georgia, which began as an antislavery colony. Oglethorpe had the letter translated by John Gagnier, the Laudian Professor of Arabic at Oxford. Shocked to learn of Ayuba's royal lineage, Oglethorpe arranged for the Royal African Company to purchase him and send him to its London offices, where he would go on to meet King George II and Queen Caroline and other English royalty and sit for a portrait painted by William Hoare of Bath. After Bluett published a book in 1733 about Ayuba's exploits under the title of his English name, Job Ben Solomon, Ayuba finally returned to Senegal as an employee of the Royal African Company in 1734, where he quickly purchased two horses and a slave of his own.[17] Job Ben Solomon had literally written his way out of slavery, and in the

Arabic language. The splendid portrait of him now hangs in the National Portrait Gallery in London.

Umar ibn Said (c. 1770–1863), also known as Omar Ben Said, hailed from Futa Toro in modern-day Senegal. He practiced Islam in Africa and taught the faith to others. Captured around 1807, he arrived in Charleston, South Carolina, and was sold into slavery not long before the official closing of the Atlantic slave trade. After he escaped to Fayetteville, North Carolina, he was once again captured and jailed. Said wrote in Arabic on the wall of his prison cell. James Owen, the brother of the future North Carolina governor John Owen, purchased him after learning of his writing skills in Arabic and his Islamic faith. He continued to practice Islam, though he also attended Presbyterian meetings and read the Christian Bible. Some scholars have interpreted Umar ibn Said's writings and beliefs as a conversion to Christianity, while others point out that, to his death, he continued his Muslim practices and considered Allah his God. Aside from his writings on Islam and his translation of Christian prayers, he also wrote a memoir, which was translated by the ethnologist Theodore Dwight, who published parts of it in 1864. The original manuscript was discovered in 1995 and is now housed at the Library of Congress.[18]

CONVERSION TO CHRISTIANITY

In Britain's New World colonies, such as Virginia and South Carolina, many Anglican missionaries passionately attempted, but failed, to persuade slaveholders of the merits of converting enslaved people with the full message of Christianity. Masters were determined to reinforce docility, illiteracy, and blind obedience in a rigid, systematic effort to perpetuate the institution of slavery by breeding generations of human beings to believe that they were less than human, fit by nature, or by God, to be enslaved forever.

"There's a troubled relationship between enslaved Africans and the Christian faith," says Pinn. "Slaveholders weren't quite certain what the involvement of enslaved Africans in Christianity would mean." Young points out the intellectual dishonesty: "It had been a long-standing tradition in British common law that Christians couldn't hold other Christians in slavery. At the same time, one of the key justifications for slavery was that it took Africans out of the continent and introduced them to the light of Christianity."

Katharine Gerbner, a University of Minnesota professor and author of the book *Christian Slavery: Conversion and Race in the Protestant Atlantic World* (2018), elaborates on this deep, shifting relationship between slavery and Christianity. Most seventeenth-century European colonists, she argues, believed that enslaved people could not become Christians. In fact, planters based their own superiority on their being Christians, an ideology she calls Protestant Supremacy. Virginia even passed a law in 1667 stating that "the Conferring of Baptisme doth not allow the Condition of the slave as to his Bondage or freedome." Thus, when Anglican missionaries arrived in Britain's New World colonies in the 1670s with the intent to convert those enslaved on plantations, they faced opposition and even violence from white colonists who wanted to keep Christianity exclusive to free white people. They argued that religious equality would breed social equality and that Christianity would only motivate enslaved persons to rebel. Another danger: a mandate of Christianity was the capacity to read the Bible.[19] (The irony here is that as early as 1565, Anglican records show that a Black man—"John the Blackamoor"—had been baptized back in England. The practice of allowing people of African descent membership in the Anglican Church in England had had a long history well before missionaries arrived in America.)

Anglican missionaries therefore had to articulate a vision of Christianity that brought religion to enslaved men and women while at the same time placating their owners. They centered it on race rather than religion; Gerbner calls this Christian Slavery. Missionaries sought to convince planters that Christianity would not foment rebellion. Instead, it would make the enslaved docile, hardworking, and easier to manage.

"Missionaries also convinced slave owners that slave conversion is not threatening," Gerbner explains. "They say race is actually the reason that some people can be enslaved and other people cannot. A concept of whiteness and white supremacy becomes the new way to justify enslavement."

Though it would take until the nineteenth century for this idea to spread across the American South, Christianity from then on would protect and support the idea of slavery. Free men were free not because they were Christian, but rather because they were white. Conversely, Africans and their descendants were enslaved because they were Black, Christian or not.[20]

The Anglican minister Morgan Godwyn led this charge in the final decades of the seventeenth century. He viewed enslaved people as heathens and believed the Anglican Church had a duty to

Christianize them. But upon his arrival in Virginia in the 1670s, Godwyn found an unreceptive audience among masters and enslaved persons alike. Between 1672 and 1675, he worked on the book *The Negro's and Indians Advocate*, published in 1680. Building on the work of the Quaker missionary George Fox, who also yoked slavery to Christianity, Godwyn argued for "the necessity and benefit" of baptizing enslaved people, without any equation with freedom—a lead that would be followed.[21]

Godwyn's experience in Virginia, as well as his time spent in Barbados, convinced him that enslaved Africans were educable. In his 1681 tract "Proposals for Carrying on the Negro's Christianity," he directly refuted planters' justifications for denying Christianity to them. Owners claimed that African Americans resisted Christianity; that Christianity "would make them less governable"; and that people who were enslaved were too ignorant to learn. "As to their (alike pretended) *Stupidity*," wrote Godwyn, "there is as little truth therein: divers of them being known and confessed by their *Owners*, to be extraordinary *Ingenious*, and even to exceed many of the *English*. And for the rest, they are much the same with other People, destitute of the means of knowledge, and wanting *Education*."[22] This rationale would lead to the invention of a new genre of literature, commonly known as slave narratives, exemplified by the two autobiographies published by Frederick Douglass in 1845 and 1855, but including more than one hundred other full-length autobiographical indictments of the institution written by fugitives from slavery between 1760 and 1865. It would also become central to the branch of the American abolitionist movement founded by William Lloyd Garrison in Boston in 1831.

Godwyn's writings taught other missionaries that the first step to Christianizing enslaved people was convincing white planters of its benefits. In 1701, members of the Anglican Church formed the Society for the Propagation of the Gospel in Foreign Parts (SPG) to strengthen the religion among southern whites and also to convert enslaved persons and Indians. The clergyman Francis Le Jau had a solution: following Godwyn's lead, he made the African people he converted swear to their owners that they would not use their baptism to justify seeking freedom.[23]

Gerbner summarizes in her book how what she calls Christian Slavery further oppressed African people: "The irony is dark and yet unambiguous: the most self-sacrificing, faithful, and zealous missionaries in the Atlantic world formulated and theorized a powerful and lasting religious ideology for a brutal system of plantation labor." Gerbner again turns to Godwyn's words, that Christianity would "presseth *absolute* and entire *Obedience to Rulers* and *Superiours* . . . [and] establisheth the *Authority of Masters*, over their Servants and Slaves."[24]

Those enslaved persons who accepted Christianity found ways to make the new religion their own, infusing the religion of their captors with their own African spirituality. There is no Black Church without music and dancing—never was, never will be—and the drum and dance would be unifying forces of Black forms of worship, expressing adulation and exaltation, signifying inheritance and belonging. One example of a carryover that enslaved Africans incorporated from their religious lives in Africa is the ring shout. "The body remembers," says Pierce. "The body remembers how to worship. The body remembers how to do ritual. The ring

An Old-Time Midnight Slave Funeral, W. L. Sheppard,
from Hamilton W. Pierson's *In the Brush*, 1881.

shout is an African practice that comes across the ocean and is practiced by free and enslaved African Americans."

The composer, jazz musician, and Emory University music professor the Reverend Dwight Andrews elaborates on this particular practice. "The ring shout," he explains, "really becomes the cornerstone for understanding the nexus between African religion and emerging African American religion. It's the foundation of singing, worshipping, and praising, getting filled with the Holy Spirit in this circle, which is a way of also identifying the cycle of music, the cycle of life." Many other cultural practices, such as east-west burials, likely resulted from a mixture of Christianity and traditional African practices, including Islam.[25]

In addition to "creolizing" Christianity with their traditions from the Mother Continent, enslaved Africans and African Americans also suffused their adopted religion with radical ideas of justice and equality. Occasionally, enslaved Black Christians did attempt to use their religion to political ends, exactly as early white opponents of conversion had feared. In 1723, an enslaved mulatto person in Virginia, likely writing on behalf of a group, petitioned an Anglican bishop for the group's freedom, arguing that they were modern examples of the Old Testament Israelites.[26]

As the Bible was shared in spaces of worship, enslaved Africans learned of a God much different from the one about whom many white men preached to their discerning ears. "It's this Exodus motif of God, siding with those who are enslaved, a God who rises up," says the Reverend Jonathan L. Walton, the minister and dean of the Wake Forest University School of Divinity, "a Moses that with moral courage and clarity declares, 'Let my people go.' From the earliest Christians, Africans who were converting to Christianity are gravitating to this message, because they see themselves. This isn't a spiritual reality; this is life for those who are living in shackles, living as chattel property."

Missionaries were determined to bring new followers into Christianity, even if it meant withholding the freedom of the Gospel from the enslaved population. Antiliteracy laws were passed to ensure that enslaved people could not legally learn to read or write English, and missionaries excised key stories of the Bible so the enslaved wouldn't be exposed to them. Gerbner explains: "Exodus? Take it out. This is about slaves claiming their freedom."

Parts of the New Testament that challenged imperial power and social hierarchy were ignored in favor of passages such as "Servants, obey your earthly masters." Forgiveness, obedience, and piety informed the heart of the master's message to the enslaved. "Slaveholders truly believed that this would imbue a spirit of complacency within enslaved people," says Pierce, "by encouraging them to follow an example of Jesus as a very meek, mild servant."

But it was the sacrificial suffering of the carpenter from Nazareth that would ultimately resonate most with enslaved Black people. "There's something liberating about the message of the cross, particularly about persecution," Walton says, "to those who are unjustly persecuted, those who are forced to suffer at the hands of an evil empire, those who are forced to deal with nails and the whips of an old rugged cross, just like our enslaved who are feeling very acutely the suffering of society can identify with that Jesus." The Episcopal bishop the Most Reverend Michael Curry concurs: "They knew there was something about this Jesus that was different, that he was oppressed and put down like they were, and he got up from the grave."

The good news of Jesus Christ began to spread across the plantation. At the same time, however, there was white resistance, such as in South Carolina's Negro Act of 1740, which made it illegal to teach enslaved people to read, severely limited their ability to assemble, and even outlawed the keeping or loud playing of horns and drums in places where they were allowed to gather. The Negro Act was passed in response to the Stono Rebellion, which was organized in 1739 by Jemmy, an enslaved man from Catholic Kongo. On September 9, the rebels attempted to reach Spanish Florida. That date may have been significant, coming just one day after the day the rebels celebrated the Nativity for the Virgin Mary. In New York, white Protestants feared potential alliances between Catholic priests and enslaved Black Catholics, blaming what became known as the Great Negro Plot of 1741 on enslaved individuals and Catholics.[27]

White Protestants constructed very restricted forms of worship and religious participation for the Black enslaved. "Under very controlled circumstances were whites willing to allow Blacks to participate in the life of the church," says Larry G. Murphy, professor emeritus of the history of Christianity at Garrett-Evangelical Theological Seminary. "In any gathering of Blacks, there had to be a white person present who could monitor and see to it that there are no things being told or taught or being instigated."

Barbara Savage, a path-breaking scholar and professor of Africana studies at the University of Pennsylvania, explains the absurdity enslaved people must have recognized at these church services. "In some cases, Black people were expected to attend the same churches that whites were controlling and to listen to sermons that were designed to continue to deny the humanity of Black people and certainly to argue for the continued enslavement of Black people."

Despite the suffocating confines of slavery, African Americans found surreptitious ways to create sacred spaces in which they could worship God in their own voices and in their own image. The church they created was known as "the invisible institution." "It could be in the cabins of the enslaved at night," Murphy says. "It could be in makeshift structures with branches and brushes. It could be down by the riverside here in that song, 'Gonna lay down my sword and shield, down by the riverside.'"

Savage explains the importance of the invisible institution: "Black people are able to be among themselves and with themselves and to invent and create a spiritual world that would be sustaining to them, though it needed to be kept secret." The scholar of African and African American religion Albert J. Raboteau, describing the religious life of the enslaved as "hidden from the eyes of the master," writes, "In the secrecy of the quarters of the seclusion of the brush arbors ('hush harbors') the slaves made Christianity truly their own."[28]

Thanks to the Works Progress Administration in the 1930s—which recorded Katie Brown's story of Bilali Mohammed and many others'—we have a wealth of oral histories in which people who lived through slavery look back and tell us their remembrances. Emma Tidwell, who had been enslaved in Arkansas, explained the consequences of open worship. "Black preachers couldn' preach tuh us," she told a WPA interviewer. "Ole boss would tie em tuh a tree an whoop em if dey caught us eben praying. We had er big black washpot an de way we prayed we'd go out an put our mouths to der groun an pray low an de sound wud go up under de pot an ole boss couldn' hear us."

Plantation no. 6, Rockville Plantation Negro Church, Charleston, South Carolina,
stereograph, Osborn & Durbec, 1860.

Nor could enslaved people read the Bible. "My Uncle Ben he could read de Bible," John Bates remembered, "and he allus tell us some day us be free and Massa Harry laugh, haw, haw, haw, and he say, 'Hell, no, yous never be free, yous ain't got sense 'nough to make de livin' if yous was free.' Den he takes de Bible 'way from Uncle Ben and say it put de bad ideas in he head, but Uncle gits 'nother Bible and hides it and massa never finds it out."

That said, Black people braved the consequences to bring the word of God to their people. Clerical training was impossible and, in reality, unimportant. "De preacher I laked de bes' was name Mathew Ewing," Clara Young told a WPA interviewer. "An' he sho' could read out of his han'. He neber larned no real readin' an' writin' but he sho' knowed his Bible an' woul' hol' his han' out an' mek lak he was readin' an' preach de purtiest preachin' you ever heered."[29]

The invisible institution—this was the real Black Church: people who couldn't read memorizing passages from the King James

Bible, interpreting it for themselves, and creating sermons. These "black and unknown bards," as James Weldon Johnson put it so eloquently, set the Bible to music of their own making.

AWAKENINGS AND THE METHODIST CHURCH

The religious earthquake that shook up Britain's North American colonies in the 1730s and 1740s was a soul-saving message exalting Jesus's gospel of blessed redemption and heavenly salvation in a fallen world. A forerunner of the American Revolution, it introduced an ecstatic and passionate style of worship to Protestant Christian churches. Today we refer to it as the First Great Awakening. Methodist and Baptist preachers held fiery revival meetings where both white and Black, free and enslaved, could gather and participate in the energetic services. These revivalist gatherings were full of dramatic preaching, shouting, dancing, fainting, ecstatic trances, and baptism rituals that evoked the religious celebrations of the African ancestors of the enslaved. Conversion in these traditions didn't require lengthy formal instruction, only inner communion with the Holy Spirit. Many Africans and African Americans "caught" that spirit. By 1790, there were nearly ten thousand Black Methodists and twenty thousand Black Baptists.

One of the most influential voices of the First Great Awakening was an evangelist from England, George Whitefield, whose theatrical preaching style was legendary and infectious. The Reverend Martha Simmons, the associate minister at Rush Memorial United

Church of Christ in Atlanta, explains that "Whitefield preaches in ways that make Black folks say, 'OK, now that was interesting; that was powerful; that sounds like what we would do.'" Pinn says the Great Awakening "provided a context in which Black Christians could be themselves. They could worship in public in a way that made sense to them." "If you caught the spirit," says Glaude, "and the enslaved were sitting right next to some white folk and they caught the spirit together, and you found a transformative space right there, white/Black integrated in the way in which they encountered God."

The Great Awakening democratized religion in new ways. "There would be a call to the altar," Pierce says. "Men and women could come forward to give their testimony, to proclaim that they had received salvation, and that was a radically egalitarian space. . . . Sometimes they would be allowed to offer a word of testimony that was sort of really a sermon. This was a space in which they felt a freedom that they traditionally had not felt within white churches."

This process fundamentally reshaped Black churches and Black religion as a whole. "It was during that period that Africans started converting to Christianity en masse," says Walton. It was also, he notes, the time of "the rise of the African exhorter, Black preacher." He imagines the scene: "People chiming in, letting him know that he's hitting the mark. The music comes in, begins to frame the worship experience as we all get caught up in something greater than ourselves. It's not that people are running around, they've lost their minds. No! Actually, people are in their minds, and they're connected spiritually to one another."

"In revival meetings, you had musical formats in which the

Preaching to a Crowd, W. L. Sheppard, *Harper's Weekly*, 1889.

leader would sing the first line, and the congregation would sing it," Murphy explains. "No hymnbooks, and so you had to do the lining out of the hymns. Blacks also had a tradition from the African past of call-and-response singing. So this was not something newly introduced to them but appropriating that into Christian hymnody, creating their own types of hymns." These spirituals were not about hellfire and brimstone but rather, as Andrews puts it, "about a saving God, a redemptive God, a God who even in the fiery furnace can rescue you."

As the machinery of slavery churned on with no end in sight, enslaved Black people found their first glimpse of heaven on earth in the praise house. In the Lowcountry of South Carolina, praise houses provided African Americans with a space for worship, fellowship, and community. The Gullah expert Mary Rivers Legree says the praise house served religious and social purposes: "In slavery, you couldn't go down the road and visit anyone. Gathering here, they not only prayed, but after the services were over, they could talk to each other about who might have had a baby up the road, who might have died, who was sold. And finally, it was a place of transition from the praise house into now a big church that they were able to build."

As the free Black community had slowly begun to grow in the years before the Declaration of Independence, the first institutions that they, along with their enslaved sisters and brothers, created were houses of worship. One of the earliest was in Savannah, Georgia. Today it is known as the First African Baptist Church.

Entering the building, one can't help but feel in the presence of Black religious history. The Reverend Thurmond N. Tillman provides background on the church: "The church actually had its beginnings in 1773," he says, "when George Liele, who is a slave, was granted permission to preach up and down the Savannah River." Liele had been baptized by the Baptist Church, and he quickly earned a following. He organized a congregation in Savannah in 1773 and was officially ordained on May 20, 1775, one month after the Battle of Lexington and Concord ignited the Revolutionary War. By this time, his exhortations had already led to the founding of the Silver Bluff Baptist Church in Silver Bluff, South Carolina, about fifteen miles away on the Savannah River. Silver Bluff's first pastor, David George, an enslaved man who lived on the plantation of George Galphin at Silver Bluff, had been baptized by Liele in Savannah.[30]

In any field, the precise identification of "firsts" is often something of a guessing game. But there is no doubt that over the course of the next decade, other, similar congregations were taking root, including but not limited to First Baptist Church in Petersburg, Virginia, which, like the churches in Savannah and Silver Bluff, was organized by Black congregants with the help of white patrons; First Baptist Church in Williamsburg, Virginia, which was possibly the first congregation constituted independently by African Americans; and Springfield Baptist Church in Augusta, Georgia, which claims a shared lineage with Silver Bluff.[31]

George Liele would ultimately end up far from his first church in Savannah. His owner, Henry Sharpe, was killed fighting on the British side during the American Revolution. He had freed Liele before going to war, but Sharpe's heirs attempted to re-enslave him and had him jailed. Upon the British evacuation of Tybee Island, Georgia, in 1782, Liele fled to Jamaica, as did many of his followers, who went on to form new churches in Nova Scotia and Sierra Leone.[32]

Liele may have departed, but his mission in the United States continued without him. Just before Liele immigrated to Jamaica, he baptized Andrew Bryan, born in slavery in South Carolina, who then took over the Savannah congregation. Bryan's master, Jonathan Bryan, was a New Light Presbyterian who allowed him to preach. Other local white people were less accepting; they feared a slave rebellion, and Bryan and his brother Sampson were whipped and jailed twice for holding meetings after dark in defiance of city law.[33]

In January 1788, the white Baptist minister Abraham Marshall ordained Bryan and recognized his First Colored Church, which would later be renamed the First African Baptist Church. By 1790, the church counted 225 full communicants and 350 converts, and they assembled at Yamacraw, Georgia, in the shed of a white man named Edward Davis. In 1794, they moved to a permanent building in Savannah. Upon Jonathan Bryan's death, Andrew Bryan purchased his freedom from his former master's heirs. As the Great Awakening swept the South, and overall church membership increased, his congregation grew to more than eight hundred members by 1800 and spawned two additional Black Baptist churches in Savannah.[34]

First African Baptist's Tillman explains that Bryan's nephew and successor, Andrew Cox Marshall, played a key role in creating a permanent structure. "This sanctuary actually would not have been built if it had not been for Andrew Cox Marshall, who preached for forty-four years about how he wanted to build a brick church, not just a temporary wooden building that had been built."

The First African Baptist Church continues to hold services to this day, on Montgomery Street in Savannah. Whenever I go into a Black church, I look to see what color God is. What color are the angels? What color is Jesus? Tillman says his saints are his predecessors who founded and perpetuated the tradition. "When we think about those who built the church, they are definitely of recent African descent." He continues: "This building has so many symbols in it that are codes for various things, in the windows, in the ceiling, on the side of the pews."

After long days of labor, the free and enslaved members of First African Baptist worked at night to create a home in which to worship their God. The people who built these pews paid homage to Christ but also left a surprising trace of their African Muslim past. In examining the church, Boubacar Diakite, the preceptor of the African language program at Harvard University, points out what he describes as an "Arabic type of writing." "Those who also wrote these things," he says, "they may be Christian themselves. But for them, religion is a continuity" of Abrahamic religions. In his view, there "may be different ways of worshipping, but it's the same God, the same principle. It was written to be a legacy for future generations."

In the early 1800s, the Second Great Awakening would bring an even greater influx of African Americans to both the Baptist and Methodist Churches, but it would be Methodism that would profoundly change the face of worship. "The Methodist Church declared itself opposed to slavery," says Murphy. "And it was because of that antislavery stance that Blacks were drawn to it." In the South, African Americans joined in droves. According to Michael P. Johnson, a historian at Johns Hopkins University, "In Charleston, the number of whites in the church in 1817 is around three hundred and fifty, and the number of African Americans is about fifty-four hundred, a gigantic difference. So on one hand it is a white church in its sort of umbrella, but it's a Black church in its membership, more than ten to one."

Influential itinerant preachers carried their evangelism and distinct oratory styles far and wide. Harry Hoiser, known as Black Harry and who was formerly enslaved, was considered one of the greatest orators of his time, despite being unable to read or write. He traveled with prominent white Methodist ministers and preached to crowds of white and Black listeners, often moving them to tears.

In the North, the freedom faith would convert an enslaved young man named Richard Allen at a Methodist revival meeting. Allen worked hard to purchase his freedom. In 1786, three years after America won its revolution, he joined St. George's Methodist Episcopal Church in Philadelphia, and in political petitions outside of the church began to advocate a message of liberty and justice. A popular preacher, Allen was inspired by the same ideals that sparked the American Revolution. As the Rochester Institute of Technology professor of history Richard Newman puts it, Allen believed "that hope will prevail; that the Black struggle for freedom will combine with the white struggle for freedom, and this will be the blueprint for the new United States in both secular and sacred terms. It doesn't happen."

Even as Black people played significant roles in white-led churches, including as preachers, they continued to experience discrimination, leaving some worshippers to wonder if they had a place in the Methodist Church at all. Allen and Absalom Jones, also a lay minister in the church, co-founded what is considered to be the first Black mutual aid society, the Free African Society, in 1787. At St. George's, these issues came to a head sometime around 1792, when Jones, according to Glaude, was unceremoniously "told to go to the 'nigger pews,'" a humiliating act that provides "a sense of how deeply segregated American Christendom was."

Allen and Jones led the Black congregation out of the building, and Jones founded the African Episcopal Church of St. Thomas shortly thereafter. Through Allen, an independent Black Christian denomination would soon be born. Allen and his congregants called their sanctuary the Bethel Church. Vashti Murphy McKenzie, who in 2000 became the first woman elected to the role of bishop in the history of the AME denomination, explains why it was important for the founders to include the word *African* in the name of their church. "Because that's where we came from," she says. "It's the motherland. So Africa and African Methodist Episcopal denotes our African descent, our African heritage. It's to honor our African heritage."

Richard Allen initially maintained his affiliation with the Methodist Church and in 1799 became its first Black deacon, but in time he tired of white Methodists' ongoing efforts to control his increasingly popular church. In 1816, after beating back an attempt by the Methodist Church to sell Bethel out from under him, and surviving a lawsuit as well, Allen took full legal claim to his church in court. He then broke from the Methodists and co-founded and became the first bishop of the independent African Methodist Episcopal Church. Over the next six years, the AME Church spread its message, growing to about ten thousand members, predominantly in northern cities.[35]

Not long after the founding of the AME Church, history repeated itself in New York City. Frustrated about being forced to sit in the rear of the building and not allowed to preach, African Americans there established a second Black denomination independent from the Methodist Church. Parishioners formed an African Chapel in 1796, a Black Methodist church in 1801, and then the independent AME Zion Church (AMEZ) in 1821. Active in the antislavery effort, helping enslaved persons, including Frederick Douglass, find safety in the North, the AME Zion Church also counted Sojourner Truth and Harriet Tubman as members. These abolitionists were believers who framed their powerful arguments for freedom and equality in the language of scripture and an uncorrupted Christianity.[36]

Bishops of the A.M.E. Church, J. H. Daniels, Boston, c. 1876.

"The African Methodist Episcopal Church was really not founded on theological differences," McKenzie points out. "It was founded because of racial differences. People wanted to be able to worship in dignity." "For Richard Allen," Newman says, "the Black Church is a freedom church. It's a vehicle for the civil rights struggle. It's a fellowship. So in that sense, it's more than a denomination or a community of worshippers. It's a way of looking at the world."

The freedom to preach had limits, even in the Black churches. Women made up the majority of many AME congregations, and they were crucial to establishing new congregations as the church expanded and to creating missionary and mutual aid organizations within the church. But women had no place at the pulpit, as Jarena Lee found out in the early 1800s when she asked Richard Allen to allow her to preach. "I went to see the preacher in charge of the African Society, who was the Rev. Richard Allen," Lee wrote in her memoir, "to tell him that I felt it my duty to preach the gospel. . . . He said that our Discipline knew nothing at all about it— that it did not call for women preachers."[37]

"There's a great scene," the Johns Hopkins University historian Martha S. Jones says, "in which she describes listening to a man give a sermon. He does a lousy job, and she springs out of her seat and holds forth." Lee later described that moment: "I sprang, as by altogether supernatural impulse, to my feet, when I was aided from above to give an exhortation. . . . During the exhortation, God made manifest his power in a manner sufficient to show the world that I was called to labor. . . . I now sat down, scarcely knowing what I had done, being frightened. I imagined, that for this indecorum, as I feared it might be called, I should be expelled from the church."[38]

She was not. And Allen, who heard Lee speak, changed his mind and in 1819 named her the AME Church's first woman preacher. Nearly two hundred years later, in 2016, she was posthumously ordained.[39]

"The church has two identities," the Harvard University historian Evelyn Brooks Higginbotham explains. "It has the identity of being oppressive of women. And it's interesting, because when you look at slavery, the church of the slave master, it's that same kind of message that would go to the slave. So when women begin to demand empowerment, they call out this dual contradiction. And I think for them to give up to women was in many ways, in their heads, emasculation. And then they had the Bible. They had the Bible to tell them that they were supposed to be on top. It's just that the women had the Bible, too. They could say to the men, 'The Bible's saying more than that, dear.'"

The challenges women faced in the church had long reflected the challenges they faced in broader society, and being Black only added to these difficulties. "I think for any woman to step out of a traditional role and walk into what is perceived as nontraditional is tough," McKenzie says. "Especially to be Black and female, you have to work harder than everyone else. You have to be the best person in the field even to be considered, let alone elected or appointed or selected." The bishop reflected on the groundbreaking path Lee had started down two centuries earlier, one that she herself followed. "Jarena Lee is an extraordinary woman," she says. "She walked thousands of miles and preached, I think it was like one hundred and forty-seven, one hundred and fifty sermons in a year. That's unimaginable. I can't imagine preaching that many sermons. She just kept doing the work. Do the work. The Bible says your gifts will make room for you. And they do."

The church, McKenzie says, is slow to move—and that's all right with most parishioners. "The church is the last place to change," she explains. "We want church to stay the same." McKenzie recalls, "The night when I was elected a bishop in the AME Church, I said I stood here for all the women who were called but never ordained. The word was just in them—it's like the prophet says, 'The fire shut up in my bones. It shut up, and it can't get out.' And so they preached wherever they could preach, however they could preach, whenever they could preach—never recognized, never ordained, never affirmed, never supported, but yet they preached anyhow. And because they did, I am." But, she concludes, "It ain't about me; it's all about God."

ABOLITION

As northern states followed the slow process of emancipation, free Black Christians took a leading role in the abolition movement, becoming the tip of the spear. The abolitionist and essayist Maria Stewart, for instance, published essays in *The Liberator* on the connection between religion, morality, politics, and abolitionism. She believed that the Bible could show the way to equality for African Americans as well as for women.

Meanwhile, the notion of emancipation met with stiff resistance in the South. The liberating momentum that came out of the Revolutionary War was no match for King Cotton. The cotton gin, invented in 1793, would dramatically transform the economy of the South and lead to a massive expansion of the international slave trade until, per the Constitution, it was banned in the United States in 1808. With the international slave trade closed, Glaude says, "the reproduction of the slave population shifts to a domestic industry." The Bible became even more important as a justification for slavery; at the same time, the freedom faith preached by Richard Allen and his colleagues increasingly threatened the slavery regime.

The Methodist Church had to confront the issue of slavery. Paul Harvey, a historian at the University of Colorado, Colorado

Oblate Sisters of Providence, St. Francis Orphan Asylum, Normandy, Missouri, late 1880s.

Springs, explains, "There was a substantial antislavery movement in the South, and there were people freeing slaves, and churches faced the question, Are we going to take a position against slavery or not?" Murphy speaks of the rupture in the church. "In 1844," he says, "the Methodist Church divides into the Southern Methodist Church and the Northern Methodist Church over the issue of slavery, specifically as to whether or not a bishop in the church could be an owner of enslaved persons."

The Roman Catholic Church took a side as well. During the 1830s, it rejected slavery, although Catholics in the southern United States continued the practice. In 1831, Pope Gregory XVI recognized the Oblate Sisters of Providence, a Baltimore order organized by Mary Elizabeth Lange, a Black woman who had fled the Haitian Revolution and arrived in the United States in the mid-1810s. In 1843, free and enslaved Black people organized the Holy Family Society of Colored People in Baltimore. The church ordained three Black priests before the end of the Civil War: the brothers James Augustine Healy (1854), Alexander Sherwood Healy (1858), and Patrick Francis Healy (1864).[40] Patrick Healy would go on to become the twenty-ninth president of Georgetown University, serving between 1874 and 1882.

Nevertheless, the Jesuits and Georgetown played a scandalous role in the history of American slavery. Jesuits in Maryland had turned to enslaved labor when the number of white indentured servants decreased. By 1765, they owned 192 enslaved Black people, and the number would grow to over 200 in the nineteenth century. "The idea was that the Jesuit plantations manned by enslaved people would essentially subsidize the Jesuit educational mission," says Adam Rothman, a Georgetown historian. As their struggling plantations failed to keep the college out of debt, the Jesuits took a fateful next step. In 1838 the Reverend Thomas F. Mulledy and the Reverend William McSherry, both former Georgetown presidents, sold 272 enslaved people for $115,000 (about $3.3 million today) to two Louisiana planters, Jesse Beatty and Henry Johnson. The profits from the sale helped put the college on solid financial footing—so much so, says Rothman, that "the university itself owes its existence to this history."[41]

Despite the willingness of Roman Catholics to accept Black people as converts both in Europe since the late Middle Ages and in the New World (long before the Anglican Church consented to Black membership), European nations in which Roman Catholicism was the official religion played an active and diabolical role in the transatlantic slave trade, from its beginnings and throughout much of the nineteenth century. Ships sailing under the Spanish flag alone were responsible for 1,061,524 Africans being transported across the Atlantic, the fourth highest of any country. Of the top five nationalities of the vessels bringing Africans across the Atlantic, according to the invaluable website Slave Voyages, four were from Roman Catholic nations, including, in order:

Portugal and Brazil: 5,848,266

Great Britain: 3,259,441

France: 1,381,404

Spain: 1,061,524

Netherlands: 554,336[42]

Clearly there was a wide and stark gap between official church doctrine and the commercial practice of individual Roman Catholics through the life of the slave trade. According to the historian David Eltis, "The Roman Catholic Church was the largest single owner of slaves in the Americas."[43] And the Jesuits' sale of the 272 enslaved people at Georgetown was not an exception but rather the rule. As Eltis notes, "The Jesuits, perhaps the largest corporate slave owners in the Americas (after the Catholic Church itself), relied almost exclusively on slave labor to work farms, cane lands, mines, vineyards, and textile mills, as well as ranches for cattle, sheep, and mules. The largest Jesuit estates were in coastal Ecuador, Peru, and Córdoba in modern Argentina, most of which supplied urban centers from Guayaquil to Potosí."[44] The church's role in the slave trade was hypocritical, riddled with inconsistencies, and deeply, darkly shameful.

REVOLUTION!

"Let's be very clear," Glaude explains. "To tell the story of American religion is to tell a political story. So all of the splits, all of the divisions, all the contradictions that define this grand experiment of democracy are evidenced in America's religious life."

"Black people had an existential and political reality that says they were a minority who could be wiped out without legal redress or moral compunction," says the writer and preacher Michael Eric Dyson. "And their religion helped them sustain themselves long enough. You've got to survive long enough to rebel."

Rebellion, of course, occurred on a clandestine, small-scale basis. But, according to Simmons, "In the South, things were so bad that a lot of it was, Just make sure your soul is saved so you can get to see Jesus. Most of the sermons, they're just about holding on to hope. Preachers helped people live another day, so if things didn't get better for them, they got better for their children and their grandchildren."

South of the South, however, revolution burst into the open. In 1791, a Black religion played a key role in sparking the battle cry for freedom in the fabulously profitable French colony of Saint-Domingue. During a now legendary Vodou ceremony, men and women made a pact to end their enslavement no matter the cost. The result would be the most successful slave uprising in the history of the world. The year 1804 saw the birth of the very first independent Black republic, which the revolutionaries named Haiti. The Haitian Revolution sent shock waves through the United States. "It inspires African Americans to be more proactive in the protest initiative," says Newman. "But of course, the Haitian rebellion also inspires a great wave of fear among white masters, particularly in the South."

Denmark Vesey, a Charleston, South Carolina, freedman who was one of the founders of the second largest AME congregation in America, would come to embody the planters' worst nightmare. African Americans organized what was first called the Hampstead Church around 1817, and its independence and support of abolitionism alarmed local white residents. Vesey, a lay preacher, taught congregants to read and write, in flagrant violation of South Carolina law. In June 1818, white people arrested 140 "free Negroes and slaves" at the church and warned its leader, Morris Brown, to shut down the school. In 1822, Charleston authorities accused Vesey of planning an uprising to murder white citizens and rape white women, with plans to flee to the independent Black nation of Haiti.

"The white account from that era," Harvey explains, "was that Denmark Vesey was this radical Black minister who's going to lead this huge slave uprising, and then one of his followers basically turned him in, and that prevented the uprising from happening. But was there going to be a rebellion at all? That's a matter of some controversy."[45] Vesey and roughly thirty-five other Black men were executed, and the church was demolished. It would not be the last attack on this congregation, which regrouped after slavery ended.

"We typically think about Black Christianity along two lines," Pinn says, "one that is concerned with spiritual renewal and isn't very concerned with what is taking place in the world. Then there's a this-worldly orientation that understands the Christian faith as demanding social transformation, as demanding political change. And some of the more vibrant, attention-grabbing episodes of this-worldly Christianity would involve the slave rebellions."

Enter Nat Turner.

Turner was a charismatic preacher in Southampton County, Virginia, who, though enslaved, was sometimes allowed to preach at a local, predominantly white Methodist church. "Whites wanted Blacks to read scripture in a way that reinforced slavery," Pinn reminds us. "But Nat Turner and others understood themselves as being linked to the children of Israel in the Hebrew Bible. And God demanded the freeing of the children of Israel. And that freeing required bloodshed." "I had a vision," Turner said, "and I saw white spirits and black spirits engaged in battle, and the sun was darkened. The thunder rolled in the Heavens, and blood flowed in streams and I heard a voice saying, 'Such is your luck, such you are called to see, and let it come rough or smooth, you must surely bear it.'"[46]

On August 21, 1831, Turner led approximately forty other enslaved men from plantation to plantation, murdering as many as sixty white men, women, and children. Fifty-five alleged conspirators were executed by the state. Two hundred more were murdered by vigilantes. As the Haitian Revolution had done, Turner's rebellion shook the foundations on which white people justified slavery. "For many, it pointed to what they feared all along," says Pinn, "that Christianity would damage a delicate social balance in which

Nat Turner and His Confederates in Conference, John Rogers, in
Orville J. Victor's *History of American Conspiracies,* 1863.

whites were on top, Blacks on the bottom." Savage explains the
significance: "All of a sudden, the dangers of independent Black
religious thought, Black religious theology, were really brought
home to whites."

At a gathering of the National Negro Convention in Buffalo,
New York, in 1843, male representatives of the free Black community argued fiercely over the best way to end slavery. They were
keenly aware that their fates were bound up with those still in
chains in the South. "The initial approach of abolitionists was that
of moral suasion," Murphy says, "that because we are a Christian
nation, founded on Christian principles, we are all created equal,
so the notion that people are fundamentally good, and if they're
doing wrong, the corrective of that is to show them they're wrong."

Frederick Douglass and Henry Highland Garnet, both of whom had escaped slavery in Maryland, led opposing camps on the question of whether violent slave uprisings were necessary to advance the abolitionist cause. Says Harvey, "Douglass takes the position that you have to fight it within the American constitutional system. Garnet holds the view that you must strike a blow; violence must be used."

In 1843, Garnet, a Presbyterian minister, delivered what became known as the Call to Rebellion:

> It is your solemn and imperative duty to use every means, both moral, intellectual, and physical, that promises success. . . . The Pharaohs are on both sides of the blood-red waters! . . . Brethren, arise, arise! Strike for your lives and liberties. . . . Let every slave throughout the land do this, and the days of slavery are numbered. Rather die freemen than live to be slaves.

Glaude points out that Garnet was challenging the hopeful idea of Exodus, the promised land: "That's an attempt to interrupt an interpretation of the story that is awaiting God's intervention. We can't wait to get on the other side for freedom because there's no other side."

Douglass, with the mix of conviction and political pragmatism that would make him the most influential Black leader of the century, surmised that Garnet's suggestions would antagonize northern white allies, ultimately bringing harm to the abolition movement.

When the convention finally voted on whether to publish Garnet's address, Garnet lost—but only by one vote.[47]

Soon Congress would appease the South by passing the Fugitive Slave Act in 1850, which strengthened a provision in the Constitution that stated that individuals who had escaped from bondage must be returned to their owners. As the nation fractured over the issue of slavery's expansion, Douglass became reconciled to the fact that slavery must end violently: "Action! Action! not criticism, is the plain duty of this hour. . . . I now for the first time during this war feel at liberty to call and counsel you to arms."[48]

On April 12, 1861, defenders of slavery in South Carolina cheered as Confederate guns opened fire on federal troops stationed at Fort Sumter. The Civil War had begun. There was no longer a question as to whether violence would be used to bring an end to slavery at last. Black Christians believed their Exodus moment was finally at hand. "The African American experience had always been one that they were looking to prophecies for freedom," Harvey says. "And of course the Civil War was the fulfillment of that prophecy."

Two

A NATION WITHIN A NATION

Every race of people since time began who have attempted to describe their God by words, or by paintings, or by carvings, or by any other form or figure, have conveyed the idea that the God who made them and shaped their destinies was symbolized in themselves. . . . We do not believe that there is any hope for a race of people who do not believe that they look like God. God is a Negro.

— THE REVEREND HENRY McNEAL TURNER,
The Voice of Missions, 1898

Thus one can see in the Negro church to-day, reproduced in microcosm, all the great world from which the Negro is cut off by color-prejudice and social condition. . . . Practically, a proscribed people must have a social centre, and that centre for this people is the Negro church.

— W. E. B. DU BOIS, *The Souls of Black Folk*, 1903

No church should be allowed to stay in a community that does not positively improve community life.

— NANNIE HELEN BURROUGHS, 1914

During slavery, praise houses—the forerunners to brick-and-mortar churches, the physical loci of Black spirituality and religion—operated in the shadows, becoming incubators of African American culture in the South and resilient sites of resistance to various forms of white supremacy. But as the Civil War raged, African American people and the "peculiar institution" that had kept them in chains for centuries were at a crucial turning point. Freedom could at last be glimpsed on the horizon. By the end of the nineteenth century, throughout the former Confederacy, where 90 percent of all African Americans lived, freedpeople would transform these small, simple structures into something much larger. Black houses of worship would shelter a nation within a nation, gradually becoming the political and spiritual centers of local Black communities.

"There had always been in Black Christianity a notion that God is a delivering God," Larry G. Murphy says. "So it was out of that kind of biblical, scriptural context that Black clergy interpreted what was happening in this cataclysmic event which had erupted in the nation. There is this narrative of a person who upon hearing the cannon fire in the distance exclaims: 'He is coming. My deliverer he is coming.'"

By the summer of 1862, after more than a year of bitter and brutal fighting, slavery began to unravel in the Confederacy as African Americans fled behind Union lines. In the North, Black and white abolitionists, liberal congressmen, and Black congregations kept pressure on President Abraham Lincoln to transform the North's focus in the Civil War from preservation of the Union alone to union and emancipation combined. But the man who would become known as the Great Emancipator was not initially interested in Black and white people living together peacefully as equals.

"Lincoln is of the view that slavery may end, slavery will end, but people of color, people of African descent will never be full citizens," Martha S. Jones says, "that instead, the vision is one that would have former slaves removed or deported from the United States in the wake of their emancipation."

To persuade Black people to go along with his plans, President Lincoln believed he had to convince their spiritual leaders. In August 1862, he invited a delegation of five free Black clergymen to the White House to discuss emancipation. In effect, he said that Black people could be free as long as they left the country. Lincoln, at this time at least, favored a colonization program that would relocate freed slaves to territories in Central America. These Black leaders and the congregations to whom they reported back strenuously rejected Lincoln's proposal; Frederick Douglass, who had not been invited to the meeting, was outraged. America—the country they had done so much to build, overwhelmingly the land of their birth, since the international slave trade had ended in 1808—*was* their home. Their future was here, as had been their recent past. As Harriet Tubman had said in 1859, at the New England Colored Convention at Boston's Tremont Temple, "They can't do it; we're rooted here, and they can't pull us up."[1]

Despite Lincoln's initial resistance, the African American clergymen and their congregations, Black journalists throughout the North, and a dedicated, tireless coalition of white abolitionists such as William Lloyd Garrison and Black abolitionists such as Douglass had an effect. Within a month of the meeting at the White House, Lincoln would issue the Preliminary Emancipation Proclamation. In its final form, it would abandon mention of colonization and enable Black men to fight in the war. On New Year's Eve 1862, Northern Black congregations held Watch Night

Watch Meeting, Dec. 31, 1862—Waiting for the Hour, Heard & Moseley, Boston, 1863.

services, desperately praying for Lincoln to make emancipation a reality. In Boston, leading lights from the abolitionist struggle filled the pews at Tremont Temple. Garrison, Douglass, and Harriet Beecher Stowe were all there, singing, nervously waiting for the hour of freedom.

With Lincoln's signature on New Year's Day, the Emancipation Proclamation stated that "all persons held as slaves" in the rebel states "shall be then, thenceforward, and forever free." Reginald Hildebrand, a professor of African American studies and history at the University of North Carolina at Chapel Hill, says that, to the enslaved, "this is a confirmation that their prayers have been answered, that God has heard. The story of the deliverance of the Israelites is being played out again." He quotes W. E. B. Du Bois: "'The magnificent trumpet tones of Hebrew Scripture, transmuted and oddly changed, became a strange new gospel. All that was Beauty, all that was Love, all that was Truth . . . free, free, free.'"

Come and Join Us Brothers, published by the Supervisory Committee for
Recruiting Colored Regiments, printed by P. S. Duval & Son, c. 1863.

The news inspired an estimated half million enslaved people to
flee plantations with only the clothes on their backs to find freedom
behind Union lines. Lincoln's proclamation also made it possible
for nearly two hundred thousand Black men, three-fifths of whom
were formerly enslaved, to join the Union army.[2] While soldiers
were liberating bodies, churches were eager to liberate souls. "Black
ministers will organize to recruit young men who will serve during
the war. Black women in their church communities are going to
do the work of war relief, initially among refugees as former slaves
migrate behind Union lines," Jones explains.

Henry McNeal Turner, an outspoken freeborn pastor in

Washington, D.C., joined the Union army as one of more than a dozen African American chaplains who provided spiritual guidance to Black soldiers fighting and dying for their country. As Turner wrote in a so-called Chaplain Letter from Harrison's Landing, Virginia, published in *The Christian Recorder* on September 24, 1864, "There is quite a religious element in our regiment. Last Sabbath we had church three times . . . and our membership is rapidly increasing. . . . Some of my brave soldiers wish baptism by immersion. Their wish shall be granted."[3]

During the Civil War, hundreds of thousands of Union and Confederate soldiers converted to Christ in mass river baptisms and religious revivals. "Both sides saw it as a kind of trial that God had given them because of the death and destruction of the Civil War," Paul Harvey says. "And of course God's people have to be tried."

As the war became increasingly deadly and prolonged, the Christian religion and its sacred music provided a release from fear and terror. Around campfires in the Sea Islands of South Carolina, Black soldiers found solace in what Du Bois called the "Sorrow Songs" of slavery.

Colonel Thomas Wentworth Higginson was sitting around those same campfires. As the Massachusetts-born white commander of a Black regiment in South Carolina (although Black men were allowed to fight in the war, they could not be in command of their own troops), he scribbled in his diary about watching "dusky figures [move] in the rhythmical barbaric dance the negroes call a 'shout,' chanting, often harshly, but always in the most perfect time, some monotonous refrain." A former associate of the abolitionist John Brown, Higginson captured the sublime music of the Black Church for posterity, writing in his 1869 book *Army Life in a Black Regiment*, "These quaint religious songs were to the men more than a source of relaxation; they were a stimulus to courage and a tie to heaven." Hearing these soldiers celebrating life in the field through song provided new insight to Higginson and many in his milieu. "Really what you see in the Civil War," Harvey says, "is northern whites awakening to the fact that there's this deep religious culture, and they understand that this has to do with the freedom movement of African Americans."

Robert Darden, a Baylor University professor and expert on Black religious music, references a quotation from the great blues musician W. C. Handy to illustrate the impact of the spirituals on African Americans during the Civil War, as freedom neared. In a radio broadcast in 1931, Handy said, "I think these spirituals did more for our emancipation than all the guns of the Civil War."[4] Through the spirituals, Darden believes, enslaved people "were conjuring out of nothing the manhood that had been stripped away from them for four hundred years, and they used the spirituals as that catalyst." To singers and listeners, the spirituals, ideally, projected a common humanity. "It's hard to hate somebody if you can hum their music," Darden says. "And you can feel it. And that's what the great spirituals still do and why they're still sung today."

These spirituals, these Sorrow Songs, reflected enslaved people's melding of African religious cultures and white Protestant evangelicalism. In West Africa, music and worship were holistic, and the Africans who were captured and shipped to America in the seventeenth century brought their singing with them. The spirituals emerged as enslaved people fused Protestant hymns with African musical styles into songs they could safely sing during work or prayer. The songs gave expression to their suffering, cloaking their yearning for freedom in the stories of the Bible. In a world of utter instability, where African American families could be torn apart at a moment's notice, the enslaved found a rock in the religion and practices they developed in communion with one another outside of the backbreaking work of the plantation system. Du Bois's characterization of the spirituals is classic: "The Music of Negro religion is that plaintive rhythmic melody, with its touching minor cadences, which, despite caricature and defilement, still remains the most original and beautiful expression of human life and longing yet born on American soil. Sprung from the African forests, where its counterpart can still be heard, it was adapted, changed, and intensified by the tragic soul-life of the slave, until, under the stress of law and whip, it became the one true expression of a people's sorrow, despair, and hope."[5]

The spirituals shared similar important traits: group participation, improvisation, spontaneity, and lyrics rooted in religious deliverance. The songs and performances represented enslaved people filling the religious vacuum created when their masters forbade them from openly expressing their spirituality. White planters used the Bible to justify slavery; Black people, held in bondage, used the spirituals to express their own beliefs in God, justice, and freedom. Frederick Douglass called the songs "a testimony against slavery, and a prayer to God for deliverance from chains."[6]

Their lyrics were biblical in nature, riffs on and profoundly moving reformulations or translations of passages from the King James Bible, focusing on the power and martyrdom of such mighty figures of transcendence as Moses, David, and Jesus. They typically emphasized justice, retribution, redemption, sorrow, joy, hope, and faith. In many cases, such as in "Blow Your Trumpet, Gabriel," the songs depicted Satan in the form of the African conjurer: "O Satan is a liar, and he conjure too / And if you don't mind, he'll conjure you."[7] With stories like those of the Israelites' escape from slavery in Egypt, certain songs alluded to opposition to slavery, as did others like "Steal Away to Jesus": "Steal away, steal away home / I ain't got long to stay here."[8]

Lyrics printed on a page will never tell the entire story; the spirituals were a performance. The vocals, the melodies, the repetition, the ring shout—all were as distinct from white American music and worship as Black people were from white people. Musicians and singers used repetition as a basis for improvisation, like a jazz soloist breaking away from the beat. Call-and-response vocals reflected the African influence. Enslaved people sang "blue notes," which the Harvard University musicologist Ingrid Monson defines as "a chromatically altered pitch (generally b3, b5, b7) that in melodies is often bent, slid, and extended to create an unforgettable palette of feeling."[9] As many contemporary observers noted, white people did not recognize these so-called blue notes because they existed between notes on the Western scale—in the interstices, as it were, perfectly symbolizing in sound the formal gaps between Black and white American cultures.[10] The great novelist and critic Albert Murray refuted any notion that the spirituals were lacking or primitive in any way. "You can put the spirituals

Queen Quet Marquetta L. Goodwine, chieftess of the Gullah Geechee Nation,
Pete Marovich, St. Helena's Island, South Carolina. Goodwine stands at one of the
three remaining praise houses built during slavery that survive to this day.

right in there against the stained windows of the great cathedrals
without a drop in aesthetic sophistication or profundity," he said.
"I'm proud of that. I want to stake our claim to that."[11]

Today, these songs are being preserved by an older generation
in South Carolina's Sea Islands. Eric Crawford, a musicologist of
Gullah music and its echoes, considers the idea that, of all the
things a subjected people would create, it would be these amaz-
ingly beautiful, sublime, sacred songs. "They were born from frustration and from tragedy and from a terrible life," he says, "and
when you are chained in a ship, you long for movement and for
freedom. And for them, all of these songs speak of a better day."
Gracie Gadson, a Gullah praise house singer on the Georgia Sea
Islands, agrees: "A lot of people might have a burden or are going

through something. And when they come to the church, and then you sing that song, said, 'Glory, glory, hallelujah.' Said, 'Since I laid my burden down, I feel better, so much better, since I lay my burden down.'"

STAKING THEIR CLAIM

By the fall of 1864, the South was in shambles. After conquering Atlanta, the Union general William Tecumseh Sherman began his famous March to the Sea, trailed by thousands of formerly enslaved women, men, and children. With the end of the war quickly approaching, General Sherman needed a plan for the tens of thousands of Black refugees grappling with their newfound freedom. He used Lincoln's blueprint from three years earlier. On January 12, 1865, on the second floor of a house in Savannah, Georgia, General Sherman and the U.S. secretary of war, Edwin Stanton, met with another group of trusted leaders of the Black community: twenty Baptist and Methodist ministers.

More than half of these ministers had been born in slavery and were leaders of prominent congregations. They chose the mighty Garrison Frazier as their spokesperson. "Garrison Frazier is articulate; he's imposing," says Charles Elmore, a prolific writer on jazz and his home city of Savannah. Frazier had purchased his and his wife's freedom for a thousand dollars, and he had served in the ministry for thirty-five years. He made clear to Sherman and Stanton what African Americans wanted: "The way we can best take care of ourselves is to have land, and turn it and till it by our own

The Sanctuary, Edwin Forbes, 1876.

labor—that is, by the labor of the women and children and old men; and we can soon maintain ourselves and have something to spare."[12] Elmore explains why this was so. "Black people were so deprived of rights. You were a slave, you worked on a plantation, and the land wasn't yours. So they said, you know what? If I had my own land, I could be self-sufficient, and having your own land meant that you don't have to be under the yoke of the white oppressor." Finally, the freedmen had a voice: "The preachers went in and demanded it."

Frazier's words were persuasive, illuminating for Sherman and Stanton the pressing need for land ownership among the freedmen. For Sherman, the redistribution of Confederate land had tactical advantages as well. Not only would it hurt the Confederate military and Confederate property holders, it would also allow freed Black people and those who had escaped slavery a place to settle away from Union lines. The goals of Frazier and Sherman dovetailed: both recognized the need for Black people to own land, if for varying reasons. Two days after the meeting, Sherman issued Special Field Order No. 15, declaring that all abandoned rebel lands stretching from Charleston, South Carolina, to the St. John's River in Florida—some four hundred thousand acres in all—would be distributed to the formerly enslaved in parcels of forty acres. Forty thousand Black people settled on this so-called Sherman Land by June 1865. The Baptist minister Ulysses Houston, who had attended the Savannah meeting, established a community of one thousand Black people at Skidaway Island, Georgia. Tunis Campbell, who served as a Georgia state senator during Reconstruction, worked for the Freedmen's Bureau to settle freedpeople on the Georgia Sea Islands of Ossabaw, Delaware, Colonel's, St. Catherine's, and Sapelo.

The distribution of forty-acre lots also led to rumors that the government would provide freedpeople with "forty acres and a mule" to begin their lives in freedom.[13] "This had been some of the richest land in the country prior to the Civil War," Harvey says. "The masters flee, and so this idea of forty acres and a mule is understood by the freedpeople as a promise that they will have this land, because they had been the ones working it all along, after all." The promise was an empty one. In the chaos that followed Lincoln's assassination in April 1865, President Andrew Johnson pardoned thousands of white planters and reversed General Sherman's field order. The promised land was restored to those who had declared war on the United States.

Although ownership of land would be elusive, one part of Garrison Frazier's requests would come to pass. With their newfound freedom, African Americans living in the South began to exert control over the one thing within their power: their faith.

"One of the first things that free Black people do," Barbara Savage says, "in addition to being able to marry and to go in search of relatives, is that they want to build—and they do build—their own churches. I was raised in one of those churches, and these are family-run churches, and they're formed with great pride, with the kind of religious independence and power that comes from having our own church."

Before the war, a number of Black-led churches had been suppressed or violently destroyed. By the late 1860s, no longer forced to worship underground or under white control, thousands abandoned segregated slave pews for their own churches.

Brick Baptist Church's deacon Joseph McDomick recounts the history of the church, the oldest on St. Helena Island in South Carolina's Sea Islands, which predates the end of the Civil War by ten years. "Brick Baptist Church was built by the slaves for their slave masters," he explains. "The master that was over here needed a place to worship, so they took the slaves who made the bricks and came and built a church for them so they could worship there. What the slave master would do is to bring down slaves, the house slaves, here with him to the church and put them up in the balcony, so they could just sit up in the balcony, but they couldn't see anything." Black parishioners were also expected to be silent.

The Brick Baptist Church has a fascinating history, not least because much of that history was made *during* the Civil War.

When the U.S. Navy captured the Sea Islands following the Battle of Port Royal in 1861 and white planters abandoned their lands, newly freed African Americans took control of the church. One Sunday, Brick Baptist was white. The next Sunday, it was Black. It housed a school that in 1862 got its first African American teacher, the abolitionist Charlotte Forten (later Grimké), who worked alongside white missionary teachers. In January 1865—still before the war's end—the school expanded. It later became known as the Penn School, officially the first school in the South established to teach formerly enslaved individuals.[14]

With the end of slavery, "eleven o'clock on Sunday morning," Martin Luther King, Jr., famously commented on *Meet the Press* in 1960, "is one of the most segregated hours, if not the most segregated hour, in Christian America."[15] One of the first blossoms of Reconstruction was the flowering of independent Black churches all over the South. "They didn't believe that we could do it," Vashti Murphy McKenzie says. "When you think a person is less than a man, less human, three-fifths, as it says in the Constitution, then the opinion is you can't think, you can't talk, you can't write, you can't read, you can't do."

Yet the church grew, and the people who built those churches prospered. "The immediate impact that emancipation had," Harvey explains, "was that it made the independent Black Church in the South possible, and it allowed Black people to exercise the freedom of choice in religious matters." At church, Black congregants answered to nobody but God.

SAVING THE SOULS OF BLACK FOLKS

The independent Black Church gave African Americans—all of them now free—freedom of expression, freedom of movement, freedom of prayer. The Reverend Al Sharpton speaks to that freedom: "I think the Black Church was an incubator because it was the thing we were totally in charge of. We didn't have any external forces that had to give us permission. Whatever we wanted to do, it was up to us. It was ours."

In the first decade after the Civil War, thousands of independent Black churches sprouted across the South to unify and uplift a community that had been divided and degraded in bondage. "Here are people who need freedom, need education, and they need the tools of citizenship," says Harvey. "The idea is to Christianize and to civilize people who had not been given true Christianity."

Black religious leaders wasted no time. Across Georgia, the veteran military chaplain Henry McNeal Turner was planting churches, recruiting ministers, and leading revivals with support from the African Methodist Episcopal Church. The fervor with which he led Black troops to religion during the war continued after it. "No one had entered the South with greater optimism, a greater energy," Hildebrand says. As Turner himself put it, "Every man of us now who has a speck of grace or bit of sympathy, for the race . . . is called upon . . . to extend a hand of mercy to bone of our bone and flesh of our flesh." After the war, he worked for the Freedmen's Bureau. He established AME churches in rural areas of Georgia and even won election to the Georgia House of Representatives. He became an AME bishop in 1880, and the following decade he established AME churches in Africa.[16]

Another leader in this effort was the AME bishop Daniel Payne, who in the spring of 1863 had given an address before an audience that included Turner and Richard Harvey Cain, both of whom played critical roles in AME efforts in the South. Payne was an educator who had run a school in Charleston from 1829 until 1835, when the state outlawed the teaching of African Americans. (The British colony had outlawed the teaching of enslaved people to read a year after the Stono Rebellion of 1739.) Literacy, in the minds of white slave owners, was far too powerful a tool with which to equip the enslaved. Payne moved to the North, established a school in Philadelphia, and joined the AME Church. In 1852 he became a bishop. In this capacity he worked to organize postwar missionary efforts, which were largely local in nature.[17]

Northern missionaries, both Black and white, flooded the South seeking to save the souls of Black folk. But Black denominations such as the AME and the AME Zion Churches proudly took the lead in seeking converts while building national organizations. Culturally, Black missionaries had an edge with the formerly enslaved.

"The Civil War gives the Black denominations an opportunity to traverse the Southern landscape and radically increase numbers," Anthony B. Pinn says. "The church not only provided an opportunity for spiritual renewal, but Christian faith also provided enslaved and free Africans with a way to rethink themselves. Why not worship with people who look like you? Why not be involved in denominations that are run by people who look like you?"

Thirteenth General Conference AME Church Photo, 1868.
Bishop Daniel Payne is seated in the front row, second from the right.

Before long, differences of class and culture threatened to fracture this community.

The four million individuals who emerged from the shadows of slavery carried their culture and customs into freedom. The traditional beliefs and styles of worship they practiced in the time of slavery would sometimes encounter stiff resistance from the formal church brought down by the northern missionaries, who, in Harvey's words, sought to instill "a much more nineteenth-century, proper, Victorian idea of respectable spiritual expression." This was true regardless of whether the missionaries were Black or white.

Still, one Black pastor at an AME church in Brooklyn, New

York, was eager to get into the action. Richard Harvey Cain headed south to Charleston because, according to Hildebrand, "He just doesn't want this historical moment to pass without him putting his mark on it." In Charleston, once the heart of the slave trade in the United States, racial tensions ran deep. But Cain believed the southern port city was fertile ground for this independent Black denomination.

McKenzie outlines Cain's motivations: "You don't go away from danger; you don't go away from the center of oppression to try to turn the tables of oppression. You go into the vortex. You go into the center of things, and the Deep South was the center of things."

More than forty years after Denmark Vesey had been executed to assuage fears among whites of a slave revolt, Cain started to rebuild the church that Vesey had founded and mobs had destroyed. It would become the flagship of the AME Church in South Carolina, ironically located on a street named for that staunch defender of slavery, former senator and vice president John C. Calhoun. Christened Emanuel, a Hebrew name meaning "God is with us," the beloved southern church known as Mother Emanuel to its parishioners would again become the site of horrific racist violence in the twenty-first century.

Cain understood the history and significance of the church. Hildebrand explains that he "hired the son of Denmark Vesey as the architect for that church, symbolically making a statement. He took great pride in saying that every nail hammered in Emanuel was driven in by a Black hand. And the people responded to this symbol of what was happening. At a time when money was very scarce, people contributed to the building of Emanuel church as a symbol of their freedom."

On September 25, 1865, a crowd of some three thousand people gathered to witness the laying of the cornerstone. Cain became the church's first pastor. "The sun has lit up the horizon . . . ," Cain declared the following year. "The time has come for the black man to take his place as a free man."[18]

THE WORD OF GOD, THE WORK OF GOD

With nearly 95 percent of freedpeople unable to read, education became a critical means of uplifting the Black community in the years after the Civil War. "Remember, during slavery, it was illegal to teach slaves to read and write," says Evelyn Brooks Higginbotham. "So that denial, the illegality of it, made the people even more desirous to want to read and write, because they understood that education was power."

The newly freed, holding deeply felt religious convictions, were especially eager to learn to read the word of God. Anthea Butler, a professor of religious studies and Africana at the University of Pennsylvania, explains, "In the Reconstruction period, acquiring a Bible was one of the first things people would do in a home because it showed that you were being settled, that you have a place to live, you had a little bit of money, and then also that you could study that Bible. You would know scriptures just as well as your pastor did."

Most early schools for the freedpeople were housed in Black

Freedman's Village, Arlington, Virginia, adults and children
reading books in front of their barracks, c. 1865.

churches. In rural areas of the Deep South, where schools were rare, northern missionaries used the Bible to encourage literacy among Black churchwomen. Describing women's Bible study groups, Butler says, "Bible Bands worked this way: There would be a reading for the day. If somebody didn't know how to read, you would teach them the words that were in that scripture for the day, and you'd ask them to also memorize it."

As Bible Bands expanded across the Deep South, women like Virginia Walker Broughton, a Baptist missionary, became community leaders by organizing their own Bible study groups. Born free in Nashville (her father had purchased the freedom of both himself and his wife), she graduated from Fisk University in 1875 and then moved to Memphis. Seven or so years later, she joined her first Bible Band.[19] According to Higginbotham, Broughton's husband was displeased. "She's from Tennessee, and she's meeting with women, and she is causing quite a stir. Her own husband is saying, 'You need to stay home.' And she tells her husband, 'I've had a talk with God. God has told me this is my calling. I have to do this. So you and God work this out.'"

Broughton's work saw immediate results. "Soon, Bible Bands were organized throughout the city of Memphis," Broughton wrote, "and the women of our churches took on new life. Every Monday afternoon women could be seen in all sections of the city with Bibles in their hands, going to their Bible Band meetings." Broughton continued her work over the following decades, traveling across the state as missionary and organizer. Higginbotham says that her theology, which Broughton summarized in the 1904 book *Women's Work, as Gleaned from the Women of the Bible*, offered "biblical precedents for gender equality."[20]

Black churches viewed education and literacy as paramount to the success of the African American community. Wilberforce University in Ohio, the oldest of the nation's private Historically Black Colleges and Universities founded by African Americans, actually predates the Civil War. It was founded in 1856 by the AME Church in conjunction with the Methodist Episcopal Church to teach African American youth and support abolition. After the outbreak of the Civil War disrupted Wilberforce's enrollment and funding and forced it to close its doors, Bishop Daniel Payne was so determined to see it survive that he convinced the AME Church to buy the school outright. Wilberforce reopened in 1863, making it the first Black-owned and -operated university in the nation.

"The vast majorities of HBCUs were founded to be seminaries and divinity schools, training grounds for ministers and teachers," says Yolanda Pierce. "These schools understood themselves to be religious organizations, that they had a calling and a value higher and beyond just the individual. They understood themselves to be doing the work of God." Indeed, schools in church basements evolved into HBCUs: Morehouse College arose from the basement of Springfield Baptist Church in Augusta, Georgia; Spelman College, from the basement of Friendship Baptist Church in Atlanta; and Tuskegee Institute, out of a room near the local AME Zion church.

Further promoting Black self-representation and pride and drawing on precedents such as the *A.M.E. Church Magazine*, which was initially published in the 1840s and then resurrected in 1884 as the highly influential *A.M.E. Church Review*, other Black churches launched publishing arms and Black-owned ventures in the late nineteenth century. The Reverend R. H. Boyd, a Baptist minister who had spent the first two decades of his life in slavery, unable to read or write, founded the National Baptist Publishing Board in 1896 to create Black-authored magazines and church materials. His efforts to empower the Black community did not stop there. In 1904, Boyd co-founded the Citizens Savings Bank, enabling poor Black clients to open their first bank accounts, and in 1908 he established the Negro Doll Company, offering young Black girls toys that eschewed caricature at a time when racist paraphernalia was all too easy to come by.

As the institutional Black Church was maturing, conflicting visions emerged within different denominations about an educated ministry. "The more people that are getting educated," Higginbotham says, "they're losing some of the old style of worship, the old style of speaking. They're losing a lot of what was initially African American culture."

In the years since the Civil War, charismatic former slave preachers like John Jasper had created Baptist churches across the South. In his most famous sermon, "De Sun Do Move, de Earth Am Squared," Jasper said, "I take my stand by de Bible and rest my case on what it says. I take what de Lord says bout my sins, bout my Saviour, bout life, bout death, bout de world to come and I take what de Lord say bout de sun and moon and I cares little what de haters of my God chooses to say."

"Everybody everywhere was talking about that sermon," says Martha Simmons. "Even people who knew it didn't make sense scientifically were drawn to the way that John Jasper could paint a picture."

The new churches appealed to African Americans on many levels. "In part, the genius of this growing Black Church is the way in which it doesn't require that kind of formal education in order to access leadership opportunities," Pinn says. "Their commitment to their faith, the ability to articulate that commitment without the written word was enough." "Baptist churches are congregational," Harvey explains. "And you don't have to have an educated minister. You don't have to have a structure. If you want to form a Baptist church and you have ten people, you just decide to do it."

The AME Church, however, made formal education a requirement for becoming a minister. Hildebrand explains why: "Someone like Henry McNeal Turner would ridicule preachers who thought you didn't have to prepare a sermon, you could just go with the spirit. He is saying that day has passed. If you are going to

De Sun Do Move, book cover. The preacher John Jasper
first delivered this sermon in 1878.

be ministering effectively to the people who are trying to make a big leap forward, you're going to have to symbolize what the new Black man and woman is going to be. And that means you have to model discipline, productivity, education, respect for learning, all those sorts of things. This isn't just a cultural debate for them; this is about the survival and advance and progress of the race." Pinn concurs: "Church involvement would give African Americans an opportunity to prove their worth to a larger white society. And proving this worth meant African Americans reflecting the values and the sensibilities of the larger white world."

The AME bishop Daniel Payne strongly disapproved of the singing, dancing, and excessive emotionalism characteristic of the worship of the formerly enslaved. He dismissed spirituals as "cornfield ditties" and insisted on traditional hymns in all his churches. Payne and others preached honesty, thrift, temperance, hard work, and discipline—"respectability" that would support Black claims to equal citizenship. As Higginbotham notes, "Bishop Payne felt duty bound to rid his denomination of the vestiges of slavery. Through admonishment and the threat of excommunication, he sought to stamp out the ring shout, spirituals, and other folk beliefs." Payne unabashedly recounted one such experience:

> After the sermon they formed a ring, and with coats off sung, clapped their hands and stamped their feet in a most ridiculous and heathenish way. I requested the pastor to go and stop their dancing. At his request they stopped their dancing and clapping of hands, but remained singing and rocking their bodies to and fro. This they did for about fifteen minutes. I

then went, and taking their leader by the arm, requested him to desist and to sit down and sing in a *rational* manner. I told him also that it was a heathenish way to worship and disgraceful to themselves, the race, and the Christian name.

Clearly there were two Black churches that spoke in distinct languages and timbres, and the battle over "appropriate" modes of worship were battles in the first Black culture war.[21]

Church music and worship practices became a major battleground. "When we look at the music of the Black Church, there are two distinct cultural traditions at play," says James Abbington of the Candler School of Theology at Emory University, "one that is influenced and adheres to white Protestant denominations. Then there is the second cultural tradition that was developed, created by Black people, that held on to some West African retentions. That tension remains very much alive today."

In 1871, that cultural tension surrounding the spirituals would come to a head at Fisk University in Nashville. Prewar slave narratives often mentioned the importance of singing the spirituals, but the spirituals performed in these "invisible" churches did not gain a wider audience until after the Civil War. In 1867, the abolitionists William Francis Allen, Charles Pickard Ware, and Lucy McKim Garrison published the book *Slave Songs of the United States*. The editors compiled 136 spirituals, including 43 from Ware's own collection, which he gathered personally at Coffin's Point, St. Helena Island, South Carolina.[22]

Despite the publication of this important book, the spirituals were not immediately well-known or popular. At a time when min-

African American Men, Women, and Children outside of Church, from the album *Negro Life in Georgia, U.S.A.*, compiled and prepared by W. E. B. Du Bois, vol. 3, no. 274, 1899 or 1900.

strel shows were dominating the American stage, Fisk's choral director hit on the idea of a concert tour featuring his "colored Christian singers" performing slave songs and spirituals that would appeal to white audiences and raise desperately needed funds. The white missionary George L. White, Fisk's treasurer and music professor, assembled nine students, seven of whom had been born in slavery, to perform. Although the students sang the spirituals together privately, at first they resisted performing them in public, for fear that their white audiences would recognize the songs from minstrel shows, thereby diminishing their beauty and sacredness. They wondered if the spirituals should be left in the past along with slavery. After many months of rehearsing together, however, they decided to perform publicly—and the singers and their spirituals were a massive success. The Fisk Jubilee Singers would bring their respectful performances of the spirituals not only to the North but also to Europe, including a performance before Queen Victoria and Prime Minister William Gladstone in 1873.

The first African American scholar to compile and publish Black spirituals was John Wesley Work, Jr., who taught at Fisk University. Beginning around 1898, he organized touring groups based on the original Fisk Jubilee Singers. Work argued that the spirituals reflected "the Negro's inmost life, both intellectually and spiritually, they are the only true course of our history. If any man would read the Negro's life, let him study his songs." He collaborated with his brother Frederick Jerome Work to publish the 1901 book *New Jubilee Songs as Sung by the Fisk Jubilee Singers*, and in 1907, the brothers published *Folk Songs of the American Negro*. He would perform and record with a new Fisk Jubilee Singers quartet until 1917.[23]

Dwight Andrews describes the spirituals' origins: "The spirituals were really melodies, without accompaniment, and then over generations, we adapted them, adopted them, arranged them. The Fisk Jubilee Singers, the Hampton Groups, all of those arranged melodies, which were quite beautiful in and of themselves, but they were quite different from the simple folk songs that had a single melody and repeated over and over."

These changes were intentional, designed to appease—and appeal to—a white audience. They were trying to "clean up" the folk tradition in a way, to dress it up in a suit and tie, metaphorically.

"Those internal machinations of class division and warfare

were there from the very beginning," Michael Eric Dyson says. "The respectability politics was born in a good way when Black people were trying to adjust to the new situation for us to win and curry favor morally. But the irony is, we're trying to convince white people to see us as human, who enslaved us. They don't see you as human. Dressing nicely can't do it. Speaking the king's English to the queen's taste is not going to flip a switch."

THE VOTE

Frederick Douglass once said that "slavery is not abolished until the black man has the ballot." The Fifteenth Amendment gave Black men the right to vote, even though it left out half the Black population: women, who, like most of their white sisters, would have to wait until 1920 for a suffrage amendment to the Constitution. In reality, these amendments were not strong enough to stand against racism during the Jim Crow era, and it would be several decades before the right to vote for southern Black people, male or female, was secure. The postwar years were hopeful, however, and once the Fifteenth Amendment was ratified in 1870, it opened the door for Black men to exercise their political power nationwide.

Black churches became sites where Black men and women could worship, hold political meetings, debate issues, and get out the vote. During Reconstruction, approximately two thousand Black men held public office at the federal, state, and local levels, including at least 243 ministers.[24] As the Reverend Calvin O. Butts III of

Harlem's Abyssinian Baptist Church points out, "In our experience as a people, there is no separation of church and state. Our political strength, our forward movement in this nation has always been led by people of deep spirituality." "You have ministers who are moving into politics, who are being sure enough involved in the political life of the nation," says Pinn. "You have churches that are supporting this, and you have a growth in terms of Christian obligation having social and political impact."

Richard Harvey Cain, the AME minister from Charleston, had used his power base at Mother Emanuel to become the first Black clergyman to serve in the United States House of Representatives, elected in 1872. (Two other African American ministers served in the U.S. Congress during Reconstruction: In 1870, Hiram Revels became the first Black man to serve in the U.S. Senate, filling a vacant seat for Mississippi; and in 1874, Jeremiah Haralson of Alabama was elected to the House.) On the Capitol floor, Cain eloquently appealed for civil rights: "I do not ask any legislation for the colored people of this country that is not applied to the white people. All that we ask is equal laws, equal legislation, and equal rights throughout the length and breadth of this land. . . . I appeal to you in the name of God and humanity to give us our rights, for we ask nothing more."

For many white southerners, it was too much, too soon, a claim that would become depressingly familiar. Throughout American history—including extremely recent American history—Black progress has been met with an intense white backlash. Southern Black preachers and their churches increasingly became targets of racially motivated violence.

Hildebrand shares a horrifying story, sadly only one of many like it: "Benjamin Randolph, a Black minister in South Carolina, got involved in Republican politics, was standing on the platform of the railroad station in Orangeburg, and some men ride up, knowing who he is as a minster and politician, and shoot him, and ride off, and nothing happens." For African Americans, Hildebrand says, there "is the ever-present danger and reality of violence, of death."

With the effective overthrow of Reconstruction in 1877, the last remaining federal troops were removed from statehouses in the former Confederacy. This period bore the name Redemption, the era characterized by the South's quest to "redeem" southern governments from "Negro rule." Emboldened former Confederates immediately sought to roll back all the gains that Black southerners had achieved following the Civil War. "Larger white society is suspicious of what's taking place within these independent Black churches," Pinn says. "And the key word there is *independent*. These churches were symbols of rebellion, symbols of protest, symbols of Black folks striking against the status quo. And white backlash took a variety of forms—church burnings, lynchings."

Dyson addresses the significance of white supremacists targeting these sacred symbolic spaces in the history of the Black community. "What these supremacists understand, they know, without sophistication, that's the height and depth and breadth of our existence. The church is a refuge. It's our sanctuary, literally. The very nature of the Black Church is what makes it so powerful and yet so vulnerable at the same time."

Richard Harvey Cain, who had reached great heights as the

pastor of Mother Emanuel in Charleston and as a member of Congress, died in the midst of the growing racial violence seizing the country. Hildebrand explains: "Cain died in 1887, but he lived long enough to see much of what he worked for become unraveled, and that's the tragedy of this story. It accentuates just how great and exhilarating the moment was when all things seemed possible, but that also makes it even worse when things fall apart."

After Reconstruction, in state after state of the former Confederacy, African Americans were stripped of voting rights and abandoned by Congress and the Supreme Court. They were left to make their own way in a segregated world. In their darkest hour, they retreated to the safe space that had always helped them survive oppression: the church.

"You have Black churches becoming responsible for so many dimensions of Black life," Pinn says. "They are trying to meet a range of needs: educational needs, social needs, economic needs, political needs. The life of Black folks in some very significant ways is being filtered through these organizations." Or, as Higginbotham puts it, "The church has formed a nation within a nation. The church was, then at least, the single most important institution in the Black community."

A key part of the survival of African Americans during the Jim Crow era was the church's financial independence. Black congregants filled collection plates to support the institution's work. "It was the first place of social cohesion for people of African descent, the first place of economics, where we pooled our resources," says Butts. Adds Higginbotham: "Poor people would give virtually everything they had to their churches to see those churches grow."

"GOD IS A NEGRO" AND OTHER REVOLUTIONARY THOUGHTS

As Jim Crow laws took root and public spaces became increasingly segregated, a burgeoning race consciousness began to percolate within the church. Nowhere was this commitment to empowerment harnessed more powerfully than in the formation of the National Baptist Convention, USA, in 1895. "Determined to create a forum through which black people could voice their spiritual, economic, political, and social concerns, the convention's leaders equated racial self-determination with black denominational hegemony," Higginbotham writes in her classic book of African American religious history, *Righteous Discontent* (1994). "Black Baptists constituted the most numerically significant attempt to counter the debilitating intent and effects of American racial exclusionism." After just over a decade in existence, those numbers told a story of their own, with the National Baptist Convention counting an astounding 61.4 percent of all African American congregants among its membership. According to Higginbotham, "In 1906 it had 2,261,607 members, while the second largest denominational membership, African Methodist Episcopal, had only 494,777." Even more importantly, "by 1916 National Baptists numbered 2,938,579," at which point "the convention was larger than any other black religious group and larger than either of the two major white Baptist groups, namely, the Northern Baptist Convention with 1,232,135 or the Southern Baptist Convention with 2,707,870. . . . In 1916 it ranked as the third largest religious body in the United States—

trailing only the Roman Catholic and Methodist Episcopal church-es." Of the opportunities for self-reliance afforded Black people by the convention, one of its leaders, the Reverend Emmanuel K. Love, said following its creation, "There is not as bright and glorious a future before a Negro in a white institution as there is for him in his own. . . . We can more thoroughly fill our people with race pride, denominational enthusiasm and activity, by presenting to them for their support enterprises that are wholly ours."[25]

Shortly after its founding in the fall of 1895, the AME bishop Henry McNeal Turner, always at the radical edge of Black reli-gious thought, delivered a blistering sermon at the National Bap-tist Convention's first gathering in Atlanta. He asked for those in the room to see God in a radical new way. It did not go over well. "I worship a Negro God," he said. "I believe God is a Negro. Ne-groes should worship a God who is a Negro."

"Henry McNeal Turner comes along, and he says everyone has a God that looks like them," says the Very Reverend Kelly Brown Douglas, who serves as both the dean of the Episcopal Divinity School at Union Theological Seminary and as the canon theolo-gian at the Washington National Cathedral. "And he says, if we are created in the image of God, then God is black."

Harvey says that Turner was "creating what we now call Black theology. He's literally challenging several generations now of a complete kind of universality of the idea of Jesus as this white, blond-haired guy that everyone thinks him to be." Simmons draws on one of Turner's sermons for an example. "He has a line where he says, Lord have mercy on any race of people who do not be-lieve that they look like God. And I think that sums up so much of what the Black Church has fought its way through and has been fighting for, and that is to have its people see themselves as important to God, as not less than. And Henry McNeal Turner, he got that."

The violent end to interracial democracy wasn't just serving to radicalize ministers like Turner. By publishing scathing columns about the church's sexism in the Black press, Black churchwomen, repeatedly pushed to the margins by male church leaders, began to push back on the issues of ordination, preaching licenses, and the power of the purse. Pierce offers numbers to illustrate the uphill battle of Black churchwomen. "The membership of the African American Church is somewhere between 80 to 90 percent women," she summarizes. "But the leadership is 80 to 90 percent male."

Higginbotham explains why, despite this wild discrepancy, the late nineteenth century is referred to as the women's era in Black history. "The women are excited. They have come into gender consciousness. They are saying to the men, 'The churches are the most important institutions in our community. It is out of our churches that we have schools, that we have newspapers, that we have all these things.' And they are making the argument that, according to the Bible, women have the right to preach. Or women have the right to be in their own separate missionary organizations. Or women have the right to raise money for their churches and raise money for schools and be in control of the money that they raise."

In 1894, Julia A. J. Foote, at the age of seventy-one, became one of the first two women to be ordained as deacons in the AME Zion Church. But as Black male influence in the larger world began to shrink, some Black men became even more intent on holding on to their power within the church.

"Unfortunately, the Black Church carries all the anxieties and insecurities born of the dominant society," Jonathan L. Walton says. "Therefore, the church becomes a space where Black men can be that conception of manhood in American society, which is about power."

In the Baptist Church, an outspoken young activist was frustrated that the "sisters were hindered from helping." Her name was Nannie Helen Burroughs. Burroughs was active in the National Association of Colored Women and chaired its antilynching committee. The NACW's motto was "Lifting as we climb," which, according to Pierce, means that "what we're trying to do is uplift a group of people who had experienced oppression for so long that there had to be a concerted effort that was rooted and grounded in spiritual practice." Guided by her faith, Burroughs's vision for social justice encompassed women's equality. She argued for an expanded role for women in the church in her rousing speech at the 1900 National Baptist Convention, "How the Sisters Are Hindered from Helping": "For a number of years there has been a righteous discontent, a burning zeal to go forward in his name among the Baptist women of our churches. . . . Will you as a pastor and friend of missions help by not hindering these women when they come among you to speak and to enlist the women of your church?"

Higginbotham elaborates: "She says, for a number of years now, we have been out here in the fields doing missionary work, trying to get our women educated, trying to get our women jobs. But the key of the righteous discontent is just this sense that it's our time now."

Nine African American Women Posed, Standing, Full Length, with Nannie Burroughs Holding Banner Reading, "Banner State Woman's National Baptist Convention," c. 1905–1915.

In 1901 Burroughs co-founded the Woman's Convention. There, the assembled churchwomen demanded the right to vote as well as equal treatment on public transportation and in courts, equal school funding, an end to lynching, and better treatment of Black prisoners. By 1907, this Baptist women's auxiliary included 1.5 million women. "Nannie Helen Burroughs," Savage explains, "was one of the people who said that Black women within churches were undervalued and overlooked, and invested all of her political and spiritual powers in the Woman's Convention of the National Baptist Convention. She is inside the Black Baptist Church but is a persistent critic of the Black Baptist Church." She went on to found a pioneering school for Black women in Washington, D.C., the

National Training School for Women and Girls, and lived until 1961, passing the torch of church activism to Martin Luther King, Jr., and other civil rights leaders.

Churchwomen like Burroughs, who had been the glue of their denominations, started to seize opportunities to expand their activities beyond church walls. "Some churchwomen, in these debates over power and authority," explains Jones, "raise the specter, even the threat, that perhaps they will leave the church communities if men can't accommodate their ambition."

THE FRENZY AND THE HOLY SPIRIT

Black churchwomen were not alone in lamenting the growing conservatism of Black churches. Around the turn of the century, W. E. B. Du Bois explored the issue in two of his landmark works, *The Philadelphia Negro* (1899) and *The Souls of Black Folk* (1903). Du Bois detailed the church's enduring significance to African American social and cultural life, but he also criticized its excesses and challenged it to address its political limitations.

"Du Bois is very interested in the Black Church," Savage says, "and part of his interest, I think, in African American religion comes from the fact that he was not raised in it. And he especially didn't have experience with southern Black religious expression or southern Black churches." Jason Young observes that Du Bois "saw a real genius and a real gift in rural and African American country folk, in the kind of heart, what we might think of as kind of the salt-of-the-earth folk."

Many rural southern Black people felt that the presence of God and the Holy Spirit manifested itself in what Du Bois called "the Frenzy." Du Bois defined it thusly:

> The Frenzy of "Shouting," when the Spirit of the Lord passed by, and, seizing the devotee, made him mad with supernatural joy, was the last essential of Negro religion [along with the Preacher and the Music] and the one more devoutly believed in than all the rest. It varied in expression from the silent rapt countenance or the low murmur and moan to the mad abandon of physical fervor,—the stamping, shrieking, and shouting, the rushing to and fro and wild waving of arms, the weeping and laughing, the vision and the trance. All this is nothing new in the world, but old as religion, as Delphi and Endor. And so firm a hold did it have on the Negro, that many generations firmly believed that without this visible manifestation of the God there could be no true communion with the Invisible.[26]

Du Bois was writing over a century ago, but the power of the frenzy is alive and present in charismatic Black churches today. "The frenzy goes by many names," Young explains. "In churches where I grew up, it was called 'getting happy,' 'getting touched.' And it's a space of what we might call, for lack of a better term, 'spirit possession.' It's a moment of deep, expressive behavior that happens in and out of the church, in which one's body becomes connected intimately with the divine."

Deep in the Mississippi Delta and in parts of the Southeast,

SPEAKERS OF
THE WORD

This is a collection of portraits and photographs of a small but illustrious sample of the countless preachers, evangelists, and missionaries who have been shaping the Black Church since its institutional beginnings in the eighteenth century. While it is impossible to highlight every major figure in this history, my hope is that the experience of seeing these representative faces across time will underscore the strength, diversity, power, and enduring relevance of Black churches and leaders to the larger African American experience and to U.S. history as a whole.

Absalom Jones

George Liele

Richard Allen

Jarena Lee

Zilpha Elaw

Sojourner Truth

Garrison Frazier

Daniel Alexander Payne

Frederick Douglass

John Jasper

Henry Highland Garnet

Julia A. J. Foote

Harriet Tubman

Richard Harvey Cain

Henry McNeal Turner

Virginia Walker Broughton

Adam Daniel Williams

Charles Harrison Mason

Adam Clayton Powell, Sr.

Lucy Turner Smith

Nannie Helen Burroughs

Father Divine

Charles Manuel
"Sweet Daddy" Grace

J. M. Gates

Benjamin Elijah Mays

Lillian Brooks Coffey

Howard Thurman

Martin Luther King, Sr.

Adam Clayton Powell, Jr.

Pauli Murray

C. L. Franklin

Johnnie Colemon

Gardner C. Taylor

Rena Joyce Weller
Karefa-Smart

Samuel DeWitt
Proctor

C. T. Vivian

Malcolm X

Martin Luther King, Jr.

Barbara C. Harris

Louis Farrakhan

Otis Moss, Jr.

Frederick J. "Reverend Ike" Eikerenkoetter II

James A. Forbes, Jr.

Charles Gilchrist Adams

James Hal Cone

Prathia Hall

Jesse Jackson

Jeremiah Wright

Peter J. Gomes

Vashti Murphy McKenzie

Calvin O. Butts III

Katie Geneva Cannon

Jackie McCullough

T. D. Jakes

Gloria White-Hammond

Dwight Andrews

Cynthia L. Hale

Renita J. Weems

Al Sharpton

Yvette Flunder

Emilie Townes

Claudette Copeland

Kelly Brown Douglas

Eugene F. Rivers III

Suzan Johnson Cook

Juanita Bynum

Otis Moss III

Bernice King

Traci Blackmon

William J. Barber II

Raphael G. Warnock

religious fervor was sweeping church revivals and campmeetings. The Holy Spirit didn't stop at the color line; southern white people and rural Black people alike were drawn to the supernatural healing and ecstatic worship in Holiness churches. Butler says, "In the latter part of the nineteenth century, many African Americans in the South and around the country begin to get involved in this Holiness movement, which would set the stage for the entrance of what would eventually become the Pentecostal movement."

The so-called Sanctified churches emphasized strict moral behavior while emulating the ecstatic style of gatherings of formerly enslaved people. African Americans developed the "genius term 'Sanctified church,'" explains the religion historian the Reverend Cheryl Townsend Gilkes, "to manage their religious identities with reference to Holiness, Pentecostal, Apostolic, and Deliverance congregations and denominations."[27] Adult baptism and possession by the Holy Spirit were central, as was music. These devout worshippers introduced secular instruments like drums, guitars, and piano to church music, setting the stage for the development of gospel. "The whole movement of the Sanctified Church," wrote Zora Neale Hurston, "is a rebirth of song-making!"[28]

Traditional denominations largely ignored the new movement until a Baptist minister from Arkansas named Charles Harrison Mason started to deliver sermons on sanctification. Gilkes provides a brief summary of a complicated history. Between 1895 and 1897, Mason, along with fellow Baptist preacher C. P. Jones, formed the Church of God in Christ as a Holiness church, using their existing congregation in Mississippi. In 1897, their church was "disfellowshipped." "Baptists," she says, "were less elaborate about sanctification."[29] After a decade, Jones and Mason would split, with Jones forming a new church that remained Holiness. Under Mason, following a historic event that would change the face of African American religion, the Church of God in Christ would become Pentecostal.

A debate has ensued over what the scholar Estrelda Y. Alexander calls "the racial birthright of American Pentecostalism." Pentecostal leaders and scholars of both races "place its beginning variably at either New Year's Day in Topeka, Kansas, under the leadership of the white evangelist Charles Fox Parham, or April 1906 in Los Angeles, under the leadership of African American William Joseph Seymour."[30] Robert Mapes Anderson, a renowned social analyst of the Pentecostal movement, credits Seymour with broadening the denomination's reach. "What had been under Parham, a relatively small, localized movement, was to assume international proportions through the Los Angeles ministry of an obscure, chunky black man."[31]

In 1906, the various threads of the Pentecostal movement would converge on Azusa Street in Los Angeles, California, where a diverse gathering of believers—Black, white, and Hispanic; American and European—staged a frenetic street revival that would extend over three years. Seymour presided over the event. Mason was there. It was here, at Azusa, that speaking in tongues went from becoming a feature of ecstatic worship to a doctrinal part of sanctification in the Pentecostal faction of the Church of God in Christ.[32]

"You can see in some of the Los Angeles newspapers and newspapers around the country that people began to talk about the

Myrtle Avenue Revival Tent, Trance, William Gedney,
Brooklyn, New York, c. 1962.

Azusa Street Revival as 'Oh, this is the harbinger of the coming of Christ,' and that makes people flock to Los Angeles," Butler says. Pierce elaborates on the significance of their growth: "These denominations and churches were not in fact an offshoot of white churches. Within the Pentecostal denominations, you have completely independent denominations in which there is Black leadership, and also in which Black women are leaders from the very beginning." Gilkes agrees. "The formation of COGIC was historically significant," she explains, "because COGIC was one of the earliest legally organized Pentecostal denominations, and it ordained ministers of diverse ethnicities." The diversity would fracture, however, as whites ordained by COGIC withdrew and formed Assemblies of God. Gilkes notes, "The complexities and kinships of the Sanctified Church are amazing."[33]

"The Church of God in Christ is the largest African American Pentecostal denomination in this country," Pierce says. "I think that it has such a resonance for people who love the music of the Black experience, who love bodily and ecstatic worship, who believe in the gifts of the spirit, including speaking in tongues."

Even though speaking in tongues and ecstatic worship per se hadn't been present at the inception of the church or been seen previously in its service in any formal way, Bishop Charles Blake of the COGIC intimates that there had been a precedent for both. "The Black Church, no matter what its denomination," he states, "whether it was Methodist or Baptist, they had shouting and praising the Lord audibly with a loud voice"—with, as they say, tongues of fire. The Howard University religion scholar the Reverend Cheryl J. Sanders supports this notion. "Tongue-speaking has been a part of African and African American religious performance. Anywhere there is 'shouting,' there is also likely to be speaking in tongues."[34] The late Howard University professor James Tinney, a leading expert on Pentecostalism and African American religion, also suggested that versions of speaking in tongues had been ever present in African religions.[35] "Students of African religion have long been familiar with the speech event," he wrote. "Throughout Christian history, tongue-speaking never completely died out as an observable event. . . . Even in the U.S. speaking in unknown tongues was sometimes witnessed in connection with shouting, jerking, shaking, dancing, jumping, falling prostrate, and other motor phenomena during unsupervised Black worship, the New England Great Awakening, and the Holiness campmeetings of the Nineteenth Century."[36]

The new century would see the explosion of a new Black movement that transcended race, gender, and geography and marked a new chapter for the Black Church. Within fifty years, the Black community had made a great leap forward from the dark days of slavery to the dawn of a new century, guided by a freedom faith.

After all the exploration, a question still lingers: Would there be an African American people today had there not been a strong Black Church?

Higginbotham isn't sure. "I don't know, because the church is all we had. How would you make sense out of the kind of cruelty that was endured? There's got to be something that gives you hope just to make it, to persevere. And what we had, the message we had, was to keep the faith."

Soon a mass movement of people would radically change the form and function of the Black Church. But this exodus would take place without a Moses, and in the years to come, a preacher from Georgia would be propelled to the forefront of a spiritual movement that would change the world and, while the young man spoke of peace, spark extreme acts of violence against the church.

Three

GOD WILL MAKE A WAY

Sometimes in the midst of our own crises, the midst of our own life-problems, in the midst of the things that we find ourselves involved in, sometimes the power of our deliverance is in our own power and in our own possession. What you need, my brothers and sisters, is within you.

— THE REVEREND C. L. FRANKLIN, "Moses at the Red Sea"

I am many things to many people: civil rights leader, agitator, trouble-maker and orator, but in the quiet resources of my heart, I am fundamentally a clergyman, a Baptist preacher. . . . The church is my life and I have given my life to the church.

— THE REVEREND DR. MARTIN LUTHER KING, JR.

Black preaching, I believe, is more than preaching with a Black face; it is a unique cultural narrative and theological enterprise where African motifs meet diverse Western influences of North America. A beautiful, bold, homiletical voice, poetry, prophetic witness, Southern storytelling, lament, blues, and celebration are born out of this tradition.

— THE REVEREND OTIS MOSS III

As the sun rose on the twentieth century, the Black Church in America, that nation within a nation, extended its reach well beyond the front steps of the sanctuary. Emboldened by the unshakable belief that the liberating God of their fathers and mothers was on their side, a rising generation would deploy the prophetic Gospel in a bold new battle for freedom and civil rights.

"The church has been a powerful force against sin," says the Reverend William J. Barber II, an NAACP activist and pastor of the Greenleaf Christian Church in Goldsboro, North Carolina, "the sin of racism, the sin of oppression, particularly when the focus has been threefold: prophetic social justice, holiness, and spiritual empowerment and worship."

Thrust into a fast-changing world and contending with not only internal conflicts but also external oppression in the form of white supremacy, Black churches confronted a burning restlessness in their members, a restlessness rooted in this world and not in the next, one bent on freeing Black people from the strictures of seg-regation and granting them full participation in the country that their ancestors had built with no remuneration, no gratitude, and no acknowledgment of their humanity.

Stifled in a South that had violently dismantled Reconstruc-tion, Black people began to migrate north in search of economic and political opportunities in what they dreamed would be the land of Canaan. During what became known as the Great Migra-tion, which lasted from the early 1900s through the 1970s, massive numbers of African Americans moved from the South to the in-dustrial North and West, from rural areas to cities, establishing themselves in places like Pittsburgh and New York, Detroit and Chicago, even as far west as Los Angeles. Wherever Black families migrated, they brought with them their social customs, their

Train in Grenada Showing Coaches Filled with Negroes En Route to Chicago,
Gernada [sic], *Miss.,* 1910s.

music, and, most important of all, their faith. Sometimes entire congregations migrated, along with their pastors.

"We are talking about a period in the South that was absolutely awful," the historian Sylviane Diouf states. As Jim Crow laws took hold, African Americans lived under the constant threat of violence and lynching, while state and local laws stripped away their voting rights and forced them to live on their side of the color line. It was in this context that "Back to Africa" movements took root in the church. Some churches sent missions to Africa, believing it was the destiny of the African American people to redeem the souls of their ancestral homeland. Others simply advocated emigration as an escape from America's racism. The AME Bishop Henry McNeal Turner was one of the most influential leaders of his time, having participated in the Civil War and in Reconstruction politics and invested tirelessly in the idea of a racially just America. But, disillusioned by Jim Crow, the man who proclaimed "God is a Negro" came to support emigration to Africa as the means by which Black people could truly be free.

Northern and western cities were indeed no paradise. "There's always this idea that there must be a better life out there someplace," Paul Harvey says. "What happens in World War I really provides the opportunity because it cuts off the flow of European immigrant labor, and you see northern factories explicitly recruiting Black laborers for that reason." The urban environments presented myriad challenges, some that resembled the discrimination of the rural South, others distinct to the city experience. The Princeton University religion scholar Judith Weisenfeld describes "the reality" that awaited Black people in the North. "Southern migrants saw the same kinds of discrimination. It was difficult to find a job. Housing was crowded—conditions that made people think that in some ways it was 'up South' and not the kind of transformative promised land that they had imagined." These conditions, she continues, influenced the Black Church. "People are looking for other sorts of social and economic opportunities, and religion becomes part of that as well. People begin to ask themselves, What is God's plan for us as a people?"

"Being new migrants, many of them had to work in the most menial of jobs," says Sylvia Chan-Malik, a Rutgers University scholar. "They were working in factories; they're working as domestics. And in the South, they had had rural sort of forms of support, where your neighbor could make sure your son or your daughter was OK, your family was supported, whereas in the North, you were off at work, and nobody was watching your children." The Black Church filled these gaps. "Migrants did not have access to minimal services, whether it was health care, job employment," says Jonathan L. Walton. "They would find these things in the church."

According to Barbara Savage, this role of the church had long been important in Black communities. "I think there is a way in which African American churches have always assumed a greater responsibility for the lives of their congregants, something greater than simply meeting spiritual needs on Sunday." Wallace Best, a professor of religion and African American studies at Princeton University, seconds that. "Some churches chose to respond almost aggressively. 'We're really going to make sure these migrants come into our fold.' For instance, Olivet Baptist in Chicago started something that they called the Bethlehem Baptist Association, specifically to address the material needs of Black southern migrants, many of whom arrived with nothing."

Out of that commitment to help their own, Black churches built upon the framework broadly known as the social gospel:

Members of Olivet Baptist Church, Chicago, c. 1925.

Christianity's attempt to address social and economic problems, drawing upon the tenets of the Bible to scale these persistent, seemingly unmovable mountains.

"This is having a profound impact on churches in terms of the numbers," Best says. Walton calls this process "the beginnings of the megachurch movement. We see multiple megachurches in Chicago, or Abyssinian in Harlem, with five thousand, ten thousand members."

Abyssinian's current pastor, Calvin O. Butts III, expands on what was happening with the church during the Great Migration. "Abyssinian's role going into the twentieth century, with a young gospel giant named Adam Clayton Powell, Sr., was certainly responding to a social gospel. He had classes: tailoring, learning how to read. He was working then to cure the ills that were hampering our people, because as much as people think of the North as the promised land, it was hell up here, too."

While southern migrants faced the harsh realities of rebuilding their lives in the North, perhaps surprisingly, they sometimes also faced disapproving attitudes from the old, established Black communities that greeted them. "There's always a difference between the rural and the city," says Larry G. Murphy. "The religious life of the South is much more informal, spontaneous. Somebody could be praying and somebody could raise a hymn while they're praying, the congregation will join in."

In the North, explains the Juilliard School musicologist Fredara Hadley, "that was not welcomed in the mainline churches of the Baptist and Methodist Churches of the late nineteenth, going into the twentieth century. And so you start to see storefront churches dotting the cities of Chicago, Detroit, Philadelphia, and New York, and those spaces become one in which African Americans, particularly working-class African Americans, feel as though they can express themselves musically and religiously most freely."

Class differences were at play as well. "Many of the urban churches across America were trying to get away from that sort of worship experience," says Lerone Martin, a professor of religion and politics at Washington University in St. Louis. These parishioners, adopting a politics of respectability, "wanted a worship experience that was more urbane. They wanted it to be more sophisticated and more staid." Chan-Malik explains how African Americans from the South found the adjustment difficult. "Chicago in the 1920s is a space where there is already a thriving Black bourgeoisie. And at the center of this Black middle-class and upper-class life is the church, and part of the church is this politics of respectability. For these migrants, this can be alienating, if you can imagine coming to a very respectable Black church and feeling out of place, feeling like they're not good enough or their spiritual practices are not up to snuff."

This clash of cultures created an opening for a new way to distribute the word of God. In the very early days of the phonograph, jazz and blues recordings made by African American artists were marketed as "race records," and Black people lined up to purchase them. No genre was more popular than religious race records. "When you had migrants going into these congregations," Walton says, "they weren't hearing a familiar sound. And the record companies took advantage of that by packaging and then selling this southern revivalistic sensibility captured on wax."

"In the twenties, race records channel the very thing that a lot of African American urban migrants have been missing," Martin says. "It includes the African American preacher taking rhythmic breath and the chanted sermon. It includes African Americans in the congregation saying, 'Amen,' 'Preach,' 'All right now,' 'Come on, preacher.'"

LPs hadn't been invented yet, and the technology of the time imposed limitations on what could be recorded. "Now most sermons would be twenty minutes, thirty minutes, an hour, two hours, three hours," says Robert Darden. "And the old seventy-eights, two and a half, three minutes max." Under these circumstances, preaching to the choir, so to speak, was a tall order. "A preacher only had three minutes to sing your introductory song, give the scripture, offer the sermon, and then sing the closing song," marvels Walton.

Darden explains the process: "Most of the time, they're not really live sermons being recorded. What they would do is take a few congregants into a recording studio, and they're almost like little stage plays. One of the fascinating things about these seventy-eights: preachers will be talking about what's going on in the world."

Perhaps the most popular recording artist of this time was the Reverend J. M. Gates (no relation!) from Atlanta, whose charisma and dynamic sermons at his Mount Calvary Baptist Church convinced a talent scout named Polk Brockman to record five of his sermons for release on Columbia Records. Sales of Gates's recording of "I'm Gonna Die with the Staff in My Hands" far outpaced even those of the incomparable blues artists Ethel Waters and Bessie Smith. Insisting on releasing his music on multiple record labels, Gates recorded an astonishing ninety sermons in 1926.[1]

In 1930, Gates released on record the sermon "Manish Women," about women who, in his words, "try to walk and talk like a man." (The spelling of *mannish* is his.) Martha Simmons provides context: "The culture was changing. Amelia Earhart was flying planes. Women were starting to wear pants. And the moralistic side of the church said women are getting out of their place; this is going to hurt homes. So be this type of feminine woman and you'll keep your husband; you'll be thought well of."

"It's a fascinating sermon," says Martin, "both because it gives us some insight into the 1920s but also provides for us a historical line that we see, that some of these battles are still going on in our churches today. We're still dealing with churches who don't

"Death's Black Train Is Coming," advertisement, *Chicago Defender*, August 21, 1926.

recognize women as preachers. We're dealing with a church that's still wrestling with whether or not they will recognize same-sex marriage. So these issues about how one's sex, if you will, should shape the role you're allowed to play in society are still battles we're dealing with."

The influence of this early preaching on wax would extend throughout the twentieth century. One of the most influential pastors to take advantage of the medium was the Reverend Clarence

LaVaughn Franklin, Aretha Franklin's famous father, a legend on the Black Church circuit for the power of his sermons. Known by his initials, C. L., "the man with the million-dollar voice" recorded his enormously popular sermon "The Eagle Stirreth Her Nest" in 1953 at Detroit's New Bethel Baptist Church, his pastoral home. Quincy Jones once told me that if there was one recording that every Black family had in their homes, it was "The Eagle Stirreth Her Nest."

"Franklin was really a southern minister in this huge congregation in Detroit," says Harvey. "When people hear him on the radio, nationwide, and when they buy his records, what they're hearing is generations of Black religious tradition that's reflected in the southern style of sermonizing, singsong style."

Walton describes the sermon's momentum: "It begins like a locomotive getting started. It's like a train. And then it begins to build and pick up steam. And by the conclusion, he's literally singing his sermon."

> *Just as the eagle stirs her nest, fluttereth over her young, and protect them, Yahweh has done that in history for Israel. . . .*
>
> *The question is: is God still stirring the nest? . . . And my great-grandparents were slaves. But oh, look, where her great-grandson stands tonight, oh lord, while God has been stirring the nest, oh lord.*

According to the scholar and gospel music producer Anthony Heilbut, "Most of the famous preachers were very dramatic, and they specialized in a kind of growl that was known as the

Mississippi Whoop." "Whooping is melody," Simmons explains. "And it's cohesive pitches that you shorten."

Darden argues that the history of gospel goes back to one of "the richest of the lavish gifts Africa has given to the world": rhythm. Gospel music is rooted in the spirituals, the slave songs of resistance, uplift, and hope that had remained largely private until the Fisk Jubilee Singers introduced them to an international audience.[2]

The Great Migration was key to the origins of modern gospel, as southern sounds spread into northern cities. "The multitude of denominations that opened those storefront churches during the Great Migration were not just Pentecostal, but were Holiness, Pentecostal, Apostolic, and Deliverance churches," says Cheryl Townsend Gilkes. "To the outsiders, with their tambourines and church ladies in hats and white uniforms, they looked alike, but within, there were deep and sometimes highly contested differences."[3] Sanctified Church preachers and evangelists, among them Pentecostals and lay preachers, integrated the spirituals into music characterized by chanting, clapping, and group participation. Dwight Andrews emphasizes an association between early gospel music and the Pentecostal tradition. "Pentecostals believed that spirit fills you, and you have to praise, you have to move, you have to dance. Gospel music really encourages you to feel the Holy Spirit, and I think that's one of the reasons why it caught fire, because it had a certain truth to it, and it spoke to African Americans, and in an interesting way, it really reflected the church before it became so denominationally influenced by the Methodist and Baptist churches."

Charles A. Tindley published his gospel songs as *New Songs of*

Paradise in 1916. Titles like "Stand by Me" and "I'll Overcome Someday" became classics. By the 1920s, the term *gospel* was known well beyond Pentecostal churches. "When the National Baptist Convention assembled its latest collection of religious songs, *Gospel Pearls*, in 1921," Darden notes, "the term must have been in such widespread usage that the editors felt no need to explain their choice of title."

The Reverend Clarence Henry Cobbs founded the First Church of Deliverance in his mother's house on the South Side of Chicago in May 1929. It was a do-it-yourself launch: he used an ironing board for an altar. Later that year, Cobbs's fledgling church became affiliated with the Metropolitan Spiritual Churches of Christ Inc. (MSCC), founded in Kansas City, Missouri, in 1925. The First Church of Deliverance was Spiritualist, meaning it combined the divine healing and psychic worship of Pentecostalism with Catholic ritualism, including the use of vestments and candles. Cobbs also appointed a woman, the Reverend Mattie Thornton, as his assistant pastor. By 1934, Cobbs and the First Church of Deliverance gospel choir were broadcasting on Chicago radio stations, and church membership topped two thousand by the next decade.[4]

Cobbs was controversial, both in the church and outside of it. His flamboyant lifestyle and vacations with his male secretary led some Chicagoans to charge him with homosexuality. *The Chicago Defender* reported on December 2, 1939, "Rev. Clarence H. Cobbs was this week facing the possibility of questioning by the state's attorney's police concerning widespread rumors of a scandalous nature. These rumors have become so general that the pastor has had to come to his own defense over the air on several of his Sunday night broadcasts. On one occasion, he said: 'I am full man, don't believe any gossip you hear circulated about me.'"[5]

When two MSCC bishops in Kansas City were arrested for sodomy in 1940, accusations of Cobbs's homosexuality intensified. In their 1945 book, *Black Metropolis: A Study of Negro Life in a Northern City*, St. Clair Drake and Horace Clayton wrote, "The Rev. Cobbs wears clothes of the latest cut, drives a flashy car, uses slang, and is considered a good sport. Such a preacher appeals to the younger lower-class people and to the 'sporting world'—he's 'regular.' . . . Brother Cobbs symbolizes the New Gods of the Metropolis. He is the alter ego of the urban sophisticate who does not wish to make the break with religion, but desires a streamlined church which allows him to take his pleasures undisturbed."[6]

Cobbs's church remained vital for decades, attracting a number of "star parishioners," including Redd Foxx and Duke Ellington, during the 1950s and 1960s. He pastored there until his death in 1979, a month after the church's fiftieth anniversary.[7] It was during the church's early years, however, in the late 1930s, that the First Church of Deliverance brought its music to a new level when Kenneth Morris became its choir director. Cobbs's church provided Morris with the funds needed to purchase a Hammond organ, the instrument that would redefine gospel music. Morris also anticipated the increasing commercialization of gospel music and founded one of the first gospel publishing houses.[8]

Shirley Caesar, a powerhouse of gospel music known for her spirit-filled, evangelical performances, shed some light on its history, a history that she herself is part of. Caesar's performances embody in musical form that crucial element that Du Bois called "the Frenzy." As she explained: "I come from a very energetic background. My father was a great gospel singer, and he couldn't stand still. All his brothers and sisters were gospel singers, and they couldn't stand in one place. In the Pentecostal churches, they like to clap their hands and shake their tambourines. It's not so much that I want people to shout; I want them to forget that burden they left behind when they came to the concert. I want to give them a spiritual catharsis."[9]

Caesar, an eleven-time Grammy winner who is known as the first lady of gospel music, exemplifies the long tradition of African American leaders for whom music, politics, and the pastoral have commingled. During her four-year term on the Durham City Council, to which she was elected in 1987, she became a pastor of the Mount Calvary Word of Faith Church in neighboring Raleigh, North Carolina. "I have two separate ministries," she said in 2000. "I'm a gospel singer, and I'm a pastor. They're altogether different. Pastoral work is dealing with the lives of people. A concert is more like evangelizing; you go in and make a connection and run."[10] Throughout her musical career, her lyrics often contained direct references to the civil rights movement, social justice, and problems confronting too many African Americans. In 2013, she sang in "Fighting the Good Fight":

I'm coming out swinging in the name of Jesus . . .

We're fighting against addiction, we're fighting against drugs

Somebody been fighting a cancer, but you're on the winning team

Somebody's fighting with poverty, but you're on prosperity's side

You've been fighting with that sickness,

I come today to speak healing in your body

You've been fighting against hate, but I come to just give you love

Because of Jesus, we are winning the fight. . . .[11]

Music, she says, is integral to the Black Church. "If you take music out of the church, preaching is going to cease. All of this other stuff is going to cease. It's something about those songs that brings joy. It helps you to get over a lot of humps that you're going through in your life, and it might be temporary, but we thank God for that temporary blessing. Somebody in the choir might sing the old hymn 'Amazing Grace' or whatever, but once they sing it and it brings joy in your life, you might get up and go back home and the burden is much lighter." Whether singing or speaking, according to Caesar, "The word is the word, no matter what."

Different styles of delivering the word evolved over time. "When you think about the difference between hymns and gospel and spirituals," Hadley says, "a lot of that has to do with chronology, when things emerge, and also structure. The folk spirituals emerge during the period of enslavement. There's an identifiable structure there, but the words are interchangeable. Then we get into hymns. The hymns have this standard verse-chorus structure, and that comes out of European hymnody. As we get into the blues era, we're taking this idea the blues formed in its lyrical structure and in its melodic structure and marrying that. So when you get to gospel hymns and gospel, you have the merger of all of those things."

As the recording industry blossomed, blues and jazz artists who had been raised in the church inevitably borrowed from Black religious music, cross-pollinating genres to create a brand-new, secular sound. Black churches were doing the same thing in reverse, creating a style of their own with gospel innovators infusing the sacred with popular, secular music. This tug-of-war between the sacred and the secular would drive the evolution of Black music to this day. Within Black churches the battleground was especially fierce, with many religious leaders staunchly believing that singing about God's word using chords from blues and jazz had absolutely no place in God's house. "A lot of people felt that if the music was being played outside of the four walls of the church, it could not be gospel," the artist BeBe Winans says, "where the contemporary listeners felt as if we're obeying what God said because he said, 'Take my word to the highways and to the hedges.' That means take the music everywhere." Andrews also believes that the rise of gospel music threatened to upend denominational traditions and structure. "Gospel music has that kind of reality that denominations couldn't control, and that's one of the reasons that I think some Black denominations were very resistant to the idea of gospel music, because it took the power out of the hymnal and put it in the hand of people composing gospel songs and gospel sheet music."

The legendary gospel singer Rosetta Tharpe exquisitely merged the earthly and the eternal. "Rosetta Tharpe grew up in the Church of God in Christ family," explains Harvey. "In the 1930s, she realizes that she can convey these kinds of messages in

Sister Rosetta Tharpe performing in a nightclub with Lucky Millinder's jazz band, c. 1943.

nightclubs just as much as she can in church services, so she begins a professional musical career, appearing in secular venues but still doing religious music, but also playing what we would think of as rock-and-roll guitar. Rosetta Tharpe's church responds by condemning her, because if you're a member of the Church of God in Christ, you're not supposed to be at a nightclub, simple as that."

Andrews expands on Tharpe's impact. "Rosetta Tharpe is really an example of music of African Americans who have both migrated to the North but brought the South with them," he says. "It's a music that's both blues-influenced and influenced by common practices of the people. It's not so much music that comes out of a learned European tradition, but it really is vernacular music, and it really touched thousands of people."

The former bluesman Thomas A. Dorsey, otherwise known as

Thomas Andrew Dorsey, 1930s. Dorsey is seated at the piano.

Georgia Tom, Ma Rainey's band leader, and later as the father of gospel music, would become one of the most famous songwriters in the history of the genre. One of the key channels for his success was the heavenly vocal instrument of a young Mahalia Jackson, who gave spiritual life to his compositions. "Thomas Dorsey works with singers like Mahalia Jackson to get churches interested in the music that he's creating," Hadley says. "It is both a spiritual imperative for him as well as a commercial one, how you sell music."

Dorsey debuted "Take My Hand, Precious Lord" in 1932 and published prolifically after that, going on to organize the National Convention of Gospel Choirs and Choruses with Sallie Martin and other gospel performers. In 1935 he began to work with Jackson, a collaboration that transformed gospel into the most popular style of Black religious music. As Arna Bontemps described it in 1942, gospel music "was church music that can hold its own against anything on the hit parade." In 1947 Jackson recorded "Move On Up a Little Higher," which Harvey calls the beginning of the Golden Age of Gospel.[12]

"Gospel music has survived in part because there's always been this tension," Darden explains, "that love of improvisation, the beat, those African survivals, and that fact that in its heart, if it's gospel music, it's evangelical."

This tension between Saturday night and Sunday morning reached far beyond the choir lofts. The twentieth century would see a profound expansion in worship practices, both inside and outside the confines of Christian churches. Even as the numbers of congregants in Black churches across the country grew, many looked for new ways to find God, especially in the urban North.

"On the one hand," says Weisenfeld, "there are lots of people who joined churches that are like the ones they came from, to help stabilize them and continue on their religious paths. But there are lots of people who seek new things, and we see the rise of new cultural and political positions and religious formations." Chan-Malik continues: "It is in this moment where you see the rising consciousness around Pan-Africanism through the figure of Marcus Garvey. Garvey actually tells his followers that it might be time to find a religion that critiques some of the white supremacist leanings of the Christian church."

Garvey offered a different vision of God than congregations were used to hearing: "Because if Negroes are created in God's image, and Negroes are Black, then God must in some sense be

· Black." His words harkened back to those of the Reverend Henry McNeal Turner, who preached, "God is a Negro."

Garvey's iconoclastic stance influenced the founding of the African Orthodox Church in 1921 and helped to inspire the creation of the Nation of Islam in 1930.[13] Peniel Joseph, a scholar at the University of Texas at Austin, explains, "Garvey's promotion of black history and culture found new energies in the Nation, but with a twist." The Nation of Islam founder Elijah Muhammad, Joseph writes, "promoted black political self-determination as part of God's design to restore black people to their former glory. In this sense, the NOI's teaching represented the opposite of the Protestant Social Gospel, which insisted that religious faith be tied to worldly deeds. The Messenger predicted doom for whites, who were characterized as 'devils' for crimes against blacks that stretched from slavery to the present."[14]

"We get the emergence of dramatically new kinds of religious claims that reject Black Church theologies and traditions as false, as always having been false," Weisenfeld says. "This is still a period in which white supremacy is the dominant orientation, and African Americans both privately and publicly are being taught that they are inferior," Anthony B. Pinn says. "The Nation of Islam turns the tables. White people are the problem. They are inferior."[15]

"The Nation of Islam explicitly critiques white supremacy through its theology and practice," says the anthropologist Donna Auston. "And this is everything from what the divine looks like to what the divine wants you to look like. In other words, as a Black person, the way God made you is beautiful. Don't perm your hair; don't emulate a standard of beauty that's outside of Blackness."

Chan-Malik agrees: "So much of it had to do with the conscious modes of presentation that Elijah Muhammad and later Malcolm X presented of the Nation. Black men in suits. These were proud Black men, clean-shaven, standing tall. And this created an impression that any person on the street could come and join this organization and emerge strong, empowered, enlightened."

The Nation recruited members in targeted fashion. "They're very active in sort of what in Nation parlance is called 'fishing,'" says Auston. "The Nation of Islam wanted to go after the man in the mud, the person who is really at the lowest point, and those people in most need of this teaching that they understand to be life-giving."

The Nation of Islam was a largely northern and western phenomenon, as Michael Eric Dyson explains. "If you were in Harlem, which is important, revving up the psychology of Black people, Elijah Muhammad was incredibly important to the psychological infrastructure of Black people. But the fight was in Birmingham with the bicuspids and incisors of police dogs ripping at the flesh of Black men and women and children. The fight was against Bull Connor, not in Harlem but in Bombingham."

THE REVEREND DR. MARTIN LUTHER KING, JR.

The political and social progress seen in the Black urban enclaves of the North would not reach Black people in the Deep South, trapped in a racist past, until the modern civil rights movement. One of the greatest struggles of African Americans in the South would be the pursuit of the right to vote, which would reach its apex in the 1960s. Black churches—and one Black Church leader in particular—stood at the forefront of the battle.

"The fifties and sixties and the civil rights revolution and the attention that's paid to it, there's a number of external factors that explain some of that—the Cold War, the advent of television," Harvey says. "But at its core is a freedom that had never been fully realized in American history, and that idea of freedom is fundamentally expressed in the African American religious tradition."

"Many critics from the early twentieth century had been calling for an educated clergy," says Savage, "one who brings the power of intellect, of having studied and learned and critiqued the scriptures, someone who is humble and politically committed to the community rather than toward himself. King is exactly the embodiment of that."

The Reverend Dr. Martin Luther King, Jr., came from a family of preachers who held the pulpit at Ebenezer Baptist Church in Atlanta, which was founded in 1886. His maternal grandfather, Adam Daniel (A. D.) Williams, took over the pulpit in 1894 and was succeeded upon his death in 1931 by Martin Luther King, Sr., "Daddy King," who had married Alberta Williams.[16]

Martin Luther King, Sr., would remain a profound influence on his son, directing Martin, Jr., to attend seminary and then earn a PhD from Boston University before inviting him to co-pastor Ebenezer Baptist Church. The son would share the pulpit at his father's church from 1960 until his assassination in 1968. But it would

Martin Luther King, Sr., and Martin Luther King, Jr., Charles Moore, 1958.

be at the Dexter Avenue Baptist Church in Montgomery, Alabama, where, in 1955 and 1956, a bus boycott would catapult the young King to the center stage of the civil rights movement. "Montgomery came out of the church," says Vernon Jordan, the civil rights activist and adviser to President Bill Clinton, "because that was our one place of freedom. It was a place where we could talk."

While Daddy King guided his son into the ministry, Howard Thurman was one of Martin Luther King's major influences. Thurman was born in the Jim Crow South in 1899, in Daytona Beach, Florida, the grandson of a woman born in slavery, and as a young child he was prone to mystical experiences and deep connections with the natural world. As an adult, he devoted his ministry to writing, teaching, and preaching, not only in this country but abroad. His teachings would profoundly shape King's prophetic ministry and his nonviolent approach to protest.

"For the African American church, Howard Thurman looms large," says Yolanda Pierce. "Years before the civil rights movement formally began, he had an understanding that an interracial cooperation around religious and theological concerns was going to be the key to political and social and civil movements." Thurman's journey to India, where he met with Gandhi as part of a delegation representing the International Christian Student Movement, which sponsored the trip, had been a defining moment in shaping his philosophy. "There are a number of Black ministers who made almost pilgrimages to Gandhi," Reginald Hildebrand explains. "Thurman was enormously impressed by the combination of a spiritual and political movement committed to the discipline of nonviolence that was effective in removing the British colonial power and freeing the people of India."

In 1949 Thurman published *Jesus and the Disinherited*, which, in the words of the psychologist and Thurman scholar Lerita Coleman Brown, "urges people to master the force, the power of love so that you can love another person who may be hateful into knowing that they are also a holy child of God." That text was essential in molding King's own belief system. King's confidant Andrew Young remembers well his friend's belief in Thurman's writings. "Martin Luther King, Jr., always traveled with *Jesus and the Disinherited*," he says. "I mean, clean underwear, shirt, and he'd have

Howard Thurman in his briefcase. And he read Howard Thurman for inspiration."

Another minister critical in guiding the civil rights movement was Gardner C. Taylor of Concord Baptist Church of Christ in Brooklyn's Bedford-Stuyvesant neighborhood. A dynamic minister known as "the dean of the nation's Black preachers," Taylor had an activist side as well, and he was a close ally of Martin Luther King, Jr. In 1961 he and King formed the Progressive National Baptist Convention, which supported the direct-action protests that the mainline National Baptist Convention refused to endorse. Indeed, Chicago's Joseph H. Jackson, president of the NBC, believing that civil rights must be achieved through the court system, argued that King's activism was actually counterproductive.[17]

When it came to fundraising for the movement, one group in particular would help lead the way. They were the Freedom Singers, founded in Albany, Georgia, in 1962 by four organizers from the Student Nonviolent Coordinating Committee, or SNCC. The activists sang freedom songs in a congregational style before mass meetings. Cordell Reagon of SNCC recognized the power of these songs, and he recruited Bernice Johnson (whom he would later marry and who would go on to found the a cappella group Sweet Honey in the Rock) as an alto singer, Rutha Mae Harris as soprano, and Chuck Neblett as bass. The group not only raised fifty thousand dollars for SNCC but also brought the songs of the movement to wider audiences. One can't help but be reminded of the Fisk Jubilee Singers' fundraising efforts at the end of the nineteenth century, which brought the spirituals born in slavery to wider, whiter audiences. Bernice Johnson said the group was "a singing newspaper," that its songs "became a major way of making people who were not on the scene feel the intensity of what was happening in the South." In 1963 Harry Belafonte personally chartered a flight to bring the Freedom Singers to the March on Washington, where they sang "I Want My Freedom Now." The following year, a new, all-male lineup of Freedom Singers performed for activists during Freedom Summer in Mississippi.[18]

Rutha Mae Harris reflects on the relationship between the freedom songs and the songs of the church. "The freedom songs were taken from gospel, congregational hymns. Only thing we had to do was change the lyrics to fit the occasion, whatever it was, like 'I woke up this morning with my mind stayed on Jesus.' The only thing we had to change was, 'I woke up this morning with my mind stayed on freedom.'" This music, she says, was critical to the success of the civil rights movement. "Personally, I feel that without the songs of the civil rights movement, there wouldn't have been a movement, because a song kept us from being afraid. Say you're walking down the street doing a march and this policeman tell you, 'You're gonna be hit,' or whatever. You start singing, 'Ain't gonna let nobody turn me 'round, not even the chief of police, not even a billyclub.'"

Music played a variety of roles in the movement. "Oftentimes I have heard many of the civil rights leaders here in Atlanta say that they sang when they didn't have a strategy," Andrews says. "They had to march, and when they didn't know what they were going to be heading into, they sang. And it's kind of reminiscent of that idea

Mahalia Jackson.

that the spirit will descend on a song, and I think they found that songs gave them power and a sense of safety and security, even in the midst of quite dangerous and treacherous moments."

Prominent gospel artists like Mahalia Jackson offered not only a spiritual foundation to the movement but also a financial one. "Religious music," Pierce says, "is literally what gave the civil rights movement the financial means in order to continue. It was gospel artists like Mahalia Jackson, who would give a concert and raise thousands of dollars. She helped to fund the Freedom Rides and helped to fund King as he traveled."

Darden agrees: "There were so few African Americans who

were financially able to support the movement, but Jackson did it on multiple levels." For instance, Martin Luther King, Jr., was known to turn to Jackson at trying moments, asking her to sing for him—even over the phone, even in the middle of the night—as he fortified himself for the hard road ahead.

Black women, ranging from masterful singers like Mahalia Jackson and echoing through the ranks of every aspect of church life, were the lifeblood of most church congregations. They remain the indispensable and all too often overlooked leaders in the fight not only for salvation but for liberation. "When we think of these women and their social activism, we must recognize the ways in which it emerges from their faith," argues the Reverend Eboni Marshall Turman of Yale Divinity School.

Ella Baker, for one, was raised in Virginia by an activist mother whose missionary association "called on women to act as agents of social change in their communities." Baker would answer the call throughout her life, taking on numerous leadership positions in Black-led activist organizations, including as an assistant field secretary and director of branches for the NAACP in the 1930s and 1940s. She was also the organizer of the Southern Christian Leadership Conference (SCLC), which Martin Luther King had formed in 1957. An advocate of grassroots organizing, Baker, from her position as the SCLC's executive secretary, issued the call to organize SNCC at a conference at Shaw University in Raleigh, North Carolina, in early 1960. She left the SCLC that August and was open in her criticism of what she called its "leader-centered" as opposed to "group-centered" style. In 1968 she famously said of Martin Luther King, Jr., and his work with the SCLC, "To be very honest, the movement made Martin rather than Martin making the movement. This is not a discredit to him. This is, to me, as it should be." Andrew Young recognized her "dissatisfaction all around" with the Baptist Church's dearth of women in leadership roles. Baker remained an outspoken activist until she died in 1986.[19]

Fannie Lou Hamer, a sharecropper in rural Mississippi, was an everyday churchgoer who became one of the movement's most enduring forces. Her life changed forever after a visit to her local church by organizers from the SCLC and SNCC who were seeking volunteers for a voter registration test. From that moment on, Hamer became a fierce civil rights activist and community organizer who endured arrests and beatings to fight for political rights and representation in Mississippi and beyond. Deeply religious, Hamer was a rousing speaker and singer, blending biblical language with firsthand experiences of poverty, racism, and violence.

Another of these women was Prathia Hall, who would become a powerhouse minister. She said of civil rights activists, "They were convinced that God was right now standing with them. That was the faith which burned deeply in the souls of our African American ancestors."

"Prathia was one of many women who has not gotten her just due," says the Reverend Raphael G. Warnock, the pastor at Ebenezer Baptist Church since 2005. "In fact, Martin Luther King, Jr., was a part of a mass meeting one day here in rural Georgia, and while he was in that mass meeting, she began to talk to God aloud about what she desired for the world. And over and over again, she kept saying to God, 'I have a dream.'" Those words that Martin Luther King had immortalized, that were inextricably tied to his legacy, had an origin story of their own, in Terrell County, Georgia, according to Warnock. "People need to know that before it was Martin's dream, it was Prathia's prayer."

Evelyn Brooks Higginbotham knew Hall and asked her about the dream. "She said, yes, it was true. He came to one of their rallies, and she led the prayer service, and she said when she was driving him to the airport, he said, 'I love the way you did that. I'm going to use that.' Now, she did not put all that content between 'I have a dream' and what he's saying, but just the motif, 'I have a dream; I have a dream today,' that was Prathia Hall."

Mahalia Jackson had heard King beginning to play with this metaphor in previous speeches. Midway through King's prepared remarks at the March on Washington for Jobs and Freedom on August 28, 1963, which drew a quarter million people to the nation's capital to bring attention to the crushing inequalities still endured by African Americans, Jackson called out from the stage behind him, "Tell them about the dream, Martin!" Like an interjection from the church pews, it spurred the preacher to his galvanizing but impromptu finale.

Hall's prayer and King's dream weren't merely sublimely rendered spiritual texts. They came to life because they were resonating expressions of the oppressive suffering African Americans experienced every day of their lives. Moving into the 1960s, some Black religious leaders would take up the prophetic mantle of the church to stand in the face of that suffering, whether through direct political action in the streets or in the halls of Congress. Perhaps no one personified this mix of the political and the pastoral more than Adam Clayton Powell, Jr., a Democrat who represented

Harlem in the U.S. House of Representatives. For him, religion and politics went hand in hand: "I belong to a group of people that God, omniscient, omnipresent God, God of all power said, 'You are my children, and you're the same as anyone else!' And with that kind of faith in me and courage in me, I know I'm as good, if not better, than anybody that walks the halls of Congress."

Powell would follow in his father's footsteps, but with his own signature swing. The younger preacher would not be fulfilled by a ministry that confined him to the walls of the Abyssinian Baptist Church. Young Powell saw the nation as his pulpit and social change as his calling and decided that his prophetic ministry could best be fulfilled within the larger political system.

Butts says of Powell, "He didn't believe in protest because he thought that protest would impede his ability to push through legislation. So he said, 'Keep 'em out of the street, and let me operate from the suites.' He knew his political strength, and he went forward with it. He used it in the New York City Council. He used it when he got to Congress, and he chased the segregationists around. That's the church." And that, says Pinn, was Powell. "Adam Clayton Powell, Jr., is not interested in any clear distinction between spiritual and secular."

MALCOLM X

Malcolm X emerged in the 1960s as one of the foremost religious critics of American society. Like King, Malcolm was the son of a Baptist minister, but he rejected his father's teachings and converted to Islam while in prison. Malcolm preached that Christianity was the religion of the white man and asserted that Black churches were complicit in the white power structure. He argued that the oppressed had a right to defend themselves "by any means necessary" and that Black separatism and self-determination were necessary for full equality. To Malcolm, religion needed to make an impact. "When you have a philosophy or gospel," he said, "I don't care whether it's the religious gospel or political gospel, an economic gospel or social gospel. If it's not going to do something for you and me right here right now, to hell with that gospel."

"Malcolm is as much a part of the Black religious experience as anybody else," Butts says. "He was a Muslim, but so what? He was a man empowered by God."

"Malcolm X is the greatest prophetic voice in the twentieth century to emerge out of the Black community, who's first and foremost a Muslim," argues the social critic and Harvard University professor Cornel West. "First and foremost a Muslim, with a Christian backdrop, but also a musical backdrop. He spent a whole lot of time in the club. He's deeply connected to Billie Holiday and the others, so he carries that cultural baggage. But he's first and foremost a Muslim." West insists that Malcolm X's religion must never be sidelined. "Malcolm is unintelligible without his Islamic faith. People tend to downplay that. He is a revolutionary Muslim in that way, and it sustained him."

Chan-Malik explains that King and Malcolm X had more in common than history has often led us to believe: "We see Malcolm X and Martin Luther King being portrayed as these two polar opposites in the press, and that's a kind of impression that lives on

Malcolm X Speaks, rally in New York City, July 27, 1963.

to this day. One was for integration and peace and love, and the other one was Black liberation by all means necessary, even if it means taking up arms. They want to portray Malcolm X as this firebrand, this insurgent that must be excised from the more liberal discourse of civil rights. While Malcolm and Martin started off in very different places, by the end of their lives, their thinking and their ways of engaging the issues of their time were really converging."[20]

When it came to civil rights legislation, Malcolm X, who left the Nation of Islam in 1964, came to agree with the goals of most southern civil rights activists, even as he agitated for revolution: "We want to make them pass the strongest civil rights bill they've ever passed," he said. "In order to do this, we're starting a voters' registration drive. . . . There won't be a door in Harlem that will not have been knocked on to see that whatever Black face lives behind that door is registered to vote."

And in the North, these voters could make a difference. "Between 1920 and 1960, African Americans have built real bastions of political power in the urban North so that they can actually demand a much higher level of accountability from the federal government," says the University of Florida professor of history Paul Ortiz, "so much so that Black voting strength begins to determine U.S. presidential elections. So if you're a person like John F. Kennedy or Lyndon B. Johnson, and you want to be elected president, suddenly the African American vote is a swing vote."

The right to vote was still a far-off dream for many African Americans in postwar America, especially in the former Confederate states of the Deep South. Jim Crow laws, poll taxes, literacy tests, and violent terror tactics blocked African Americans' access to full citizenship, despite the guarantees of the Fifteenth and Nineteenth Amendments, which barred discrimination by race or sex in the right to vote.

"African Americans believed that they had the opportunity to smash white supremacy," Ortiz says. "It's one of the most dramatic social movements in American history, and it's fueled at the base by Black churches, Black fraternal organizations, and Black labor unions."

Black church leaders, as well as members of their congregations

Ralph Abernathy and Wyatt Tee Walker Inspect Church, Leesburg, Georgia, August 15, 1962.
About twenty miles outside of Albany, Georgia, the Shady Grove Baptist Church had
been the site of a voter registration drive prior to the explosion that destroyed it.

who joined the struggle for civil rights, often suffered a violent and unrepentant backlash. As a result, Pierce explains, "There were plenty of Black churches that did not participate in the civil rights movement. They were afraid to be a part of it. They worried that their churches would be the next to be bombed. And so they refused to allow the leaders of the civil rights movement to even have services there."

Barber sympathizes with their concerns but still imagines the power of a unified Black Church. "I don't do a lot of judging of that, because you would get your church blown up. You would get your head shot off. But I often wonder what could have been if there was full unity. If there was a complete engagement, a total commitment of every Black denomination, could we have gone much further?"

"Again, it's about terrorism coming at Black people as a whole," West states. "And when the Black Church at its best is the public face of the witness of love and justice, it will be targeted."

The many church bombings that occurred during these years existed as part of a long history. "Church burnings in the twentieth and twenty-first centuries provide the same message that church burnings in the 1800s provided," Pinn says. "These church burnings are a way to reinforce white supremacy. If you are Black, there is no safe space."

September 15, 1963, was an ordinary morning in Birmingham, Alabama. Just three weeks after the massive March on Washington, African American children were studying the Bible during Sunday school at the Sixteenth Street Baptist Church. The lesson was from Matthew: "But I say unto you, Love your enemies, bless them that curse you, do good to them that hate you." That morning, prayers and lessons would be silenced as the church became the target of a horrific act of violence by white supremacists. A bomb planted in the church exploded, killing four Black girls: Carol Denise McNair, who was eleven years old, and Addie Mae Collins, Cynthia Wesley, and Carole Robertson, all age fourteen. Addie Mae's younger sister, Sarah, lived but lost an eye. The bombing was reminiscent of the savagery targeted at Black churches long before the Civil War. Coming on the heels of the March on Washington, it galvanized the struggle for the Civil Rights Act of 1964, which outlawed segregation in businesses and public places— including schools, finally enforcing the *Brown v. Board of Education* decision—and discrimination in employment. In the midst of an increasingly violent movement, from the bombing in Birmingham to 1964's Freedom Summer in Mississippi, which saw thirty-seven churches burned or bombed during a ten-week period, Martin Luther King, Jr., was awarded the Nobel Peace Prize.

On August 6, 1965, President Lyndon Baines Johnson signed the Voting Rights Act, safeguarding the sanctity of the vote for all Americans. To King, who attended the signing, the legislation was an essential and necessary step, but without proper implementation, he recognized that it was far from sufficient. African Americans had been waging the battle to secure and ensure the right to vote in the South since the collapse of Reconstruction and the drafting of the Mississippi Plan (1890), in which legislators rewrote the state constitution to exclude and disenfranchise Black voters; by 1910, seven other states of the former Confederacy had followed suit. With the passage of the Voting Rights Act, the promised land was within sight but not yet truly within reach.

The Reverend Otis Moss, Jr., a colleague of King who officiated at his wedding, speculates as to whether there would have been a civil rights movement had there not been a Martin Luther King. "Perhaps yes, but it would have been different," he says. "He brought into the movement a redemptive paradigm in harmony with the teachings of Jesus the Christ as a moral foundation and remained true to that principle." Or, as Dyson puts it, "This is the man who used the genius of the Gospel not to make this a Christian nation, but to use his Christianity to make this a just nation."

In the late 1960s, King radically expanded his civil rights activism, traveling tirelessly to spread his message. In 1967, he came out publicly against the Vietnam War. He argued that true power would come from strong coalitions of the most disenfranchised, no matter their color, gender, or denomination. "We are dealing with hard economic and social issues," King said that same year, "and it means that the job is much more difficult. It's much easier to integrate a lunch counter than it is to guarantee an annual income. It's much easier."

In the spring of 1968, King lent his support to sanitation workers striking in Memphis, who were demanding the city recognize their union, pay them a living wage, and guarantee the safety of their fellow employees. In his final public address, he said, "It's all right to talk about 'streets flowing with milk and honey,' but God has commanded us to be concerned about the slums down here, and his children who can't eat three square meals a day. . . . We are saying that we are determined to be men. We are determined to be people. We are saying that we are God's children." King preached these words at Mason Temple, the headquarters of the Church of God in Christ, where Bishop Charles Harrison Mason's body is entombed at what is the COGIC's most sacred shrine.

"Dr. King, the last night he was alive, when he preached, people call it 'I've Been to the Mountaintop,'" Barber says. "But again, that was the closing. Inside of that, he talked about there are a lot of people that want honey and milk over yonder, but people need some bread down here. And he was very clear. That night, he was challenging the church." And King knew the fight could not end with the rhetoric. "We have these mountaintop moments," says Simmons. "And then we have these moments where they'll get rid of us if they can. So we have to keep saying, here's why the word of God is important; here's why Black lives matter to God and to us."

The Memphis campaign was an early salvo in what SCLC called the Poor People's Campaign, which King hoped would culminate in another massive march on Washington, this time with a focus on economic security. King viewed it as "the beginning of a new co-operation, understanding, and a determination by poor people of all colors and backgrounds to assert and win their right to a decent life and respect for their culture and dignity." After King's assassination, the Reverend Ralph Abernathy took over the campaign, including Resurrection City, a shantytown of tents built on the Washington Mall. Despite the best efforts of the protesters living there, the program failed to gain traction, and the city of Washington forced Resurrection City to close on June 24, 1968.[21]

The assassination of Dr. King in Memphis brought the civil rights movement of the 1960s to a tragic and violent end, and the Black Church to a spiritual and political crossroads. Could Black churches continue to lead the fight for liberation onto new and changing battlefields? The forces of progressive change, both within the church and without, would soon become almost irreparably fractured. The next four decades would witness a battle for the soul of the Black Church, a fight not only over political tactics or God's true message, but for its very future.

Four

CRISIS OF FAITH

The Black people's leader . . . our Moses, the once-in-a-four-, five-hundred-year leader, has been taken from us by hatred and bitterness.

— THE REVEREND JESSE JACKSON

One of the great paradoxes of race in America is that the religion of the oppressor, Christianity, became the religion of the oppressed and the means of their liberation.

— THE REVEREND PETER J. GOMES, *The Good Book*

It's easy to hope when there are evidences all around of how good God is. But to have the audacity to hope when that love is not evident, . . . that is a true test. . . . To take the one string you have left and to have the audacity to hope—make music and praise God on and with whatever it is you've got left, even though you can't see what God is going to do.

— THE REVEREND JEREMIAH WRIGHT, "The Audacity to Hope"

D r. King's life had been violently cut short by an assassin's bullet. As cities across the country burned in protest, the title of his last book resonated: *Where Do We Go from Here: Chaos or Community?* With Black communities facing the greatest crisis since the collapse of Reconstruction, the traditional approaches to race, religion, and politics were under fire.

"With the killing of Martin Luther King, Jr.," Anthony B. Pinn says, "the ability of folks to see the Black Church as a strong force for transformation is brought into question."

In the years preceding King's death, young people had begun to split off from church-led activism, preferring organizations inspired by secular calls for a far more militant movement, most dramatically the Black Panther Party for Self-Defense, founded in October 1966 in Oakland, California, by Huey P. Newton and Bobby Seale. The Panthers criticized racial and economic injustice and embraced an aggressive form of self-defense and socialism. They emerged precisely as the Student Nonviolent Coordinating Committee began to distance itself from the nonviolent tactics that had defined much of the southern civil rights movement to that point. SNCC was the first Black political organization formally to embrace Black Power. In a dramatic speech delivered upon his emergence from jail on June 16, 1966, in Greenwood, Mississippi, twenty-four-year-old Stokely Carmichael (later Kwame Ture), who had succeeded John Lewis as SNCC's chairman a month earlier, gave the term its first national airing. The media splashed Carmichael's fiery rhetoric across the nightly news and front pages of national newspapers. Fear and alarm over its meaning gripped much of the white community, and African Americans were split as to whether Black Power represented the best path forward. In 1967 SNCC's chairman, H. Rap Brown, Carmichael's successor, declared, "Violence is a part of America's culture. It is as American as cherry pie. Americans taught the Black people to be violent. We will use that violence to rid ourselves of oppression if necessary." While some churches embraced this new movement only tentatively, others adopted it readily, and Black Power would cross the narthex and penetrate the nave of the church, its new language coloring the nature of sermons delivered from the pulpit.

According to Barbara Savage, Black Power advocates "bring a different kind of political assessment to the Christianity and the passivity that they associate with civil disobedience. They're looking for a much more nationalist approach to Black politics, and they're also looking to step away from the restrictions of church leadership."

To be sure, many Black members of white churches took Black Power to heart. In 1968, not two weeks after the assassination of Martin Luther King, Jr., Father Herman Porter founded the Black Catholic Clergy Caucus in Detroit. Its statement began, "The Catholic Church in the United States, primarily a white racist institution, has addressed itself primarily to white society and is definitely a part of that society." The priests called for local control of Catholic churches in Black neighborhoods and even stated that "the same principles on which we justify legitimate self-defense and just warfare must be applied to violence when it represents black response to white violence." Also in 1968, the National Black Sisters' Conference, founded by Sister Martin de Porres Grey, announced its plans to foster "a positive self-image among ourselves in our black folk, especially in our black youth" and to lead "community action aimed at the achievement of social, political, and economic Black power."[1]

Of course it was the predominantly African American churches that felt most deeply the ramifications of Black Power, as its advocates forced a reckoning with fundamental questions. Cornel West describes the way that Black Power affected the development of Black denominations and Black churches. "The Black Power movement was saying what? Black self-respect, Black self-determination, Black self-defense. That had to be integral to what it is to be a Black human being." And that, says West, was a good thing for the church. "The church needs to be challenged. If we're conformist, complacent, and cowardly, the best of the church will be lost. If Black Christians are courageous, compassionate, true to the best of what the Gospel is all about, then the spiritual awakening can be waiting for us."

After the stunning legislative victories of the civil rights movement, Black churches found themselves at a crossroads. They could retreat from the front lines, or they could try to remain relevant by incorporating this flood of Black nationalist thinking into their theology. A voice from the academy would create a new theology that fused the cultural, the political, and the spiritual, radically redefining the role of Black Christianity in a revolutionary new era.

BLACK THEOLOGY

In 1969, James Hal Cone, an AME minister and professor at Union Theological Seminary, published *Black Theology and Black Power*. In defining Black theology, he took on white theology. "White theology," Cone said, "basically is a theology which has defined the Christian faith in such a way that it has no relationship to black people." He argued that Jesus so strongly identified with the oppressed that he was metaphysically synonymous with this group. God is Black, Cone believed, updating Henry McNeal Turner's "God is a Negro" and bringing the 1960s Black pride movement inside the church walls. God was so intimately connected with struggle and against oppression that God, Cone stated, in effect, had been Black all along. "God is on the side of the oppressed," he said, "and since the oppressed are the ones who need be liberated, he must be identified with their condition."

Savage explains Cone's philosophy. "Black theology is a new way of looking at the relationship between Black religion and Black political struggle and an embrace of the tenets of 'Black Is Beautiful' and a comfort with African-inflected practices."

To Eddie S. Glaude, Jr., Cone's work is indebted to Martin Luther King: "King's witness is making its way into seminaries with James Cone, who's trying to figure out how to translate King's moral call to the nation and express it in a way that will speak to the rage of the moment." West says Cone reasoned that "if God makes us in God's image, as he does all human beings, then this must be something positive about Blackness. Blackness couldn't be solely negative, given the white supremacists' discourse. And Professor Cone hit that hard; he hit it strong."

Cone's work proved to be a game changer for African Americans like Kelly Brown Douglas. For her, Cone's ideas finally connected Christian theology to being African American, a specifically Black theology to counter the dominant, if unnamed, white narrative. "He said that God's story is the Black story," Douglas says, "and the Black story is God's story. And that, he said, is the Christian story. I said, Lord, Jesus, because I was ready to leave Christianity, because if I couldn't be Black and Christian, then I wasn't going to give up being Black. What I discovered when I discovered Dr. Cone's work was my own Black faith."

Douglas enrolled in Union Theological Seminary to study under Cone, and in 2017 her career came full circle when she became dean of the Episcopal Divinity School at the seminary. "There aren't that many degrees of separation," she says. "Any person who is doing Black theology today either studied with Dr. Cone or studied with somebody who studied with Dr. Cone. He's the tree of the Black theological narrative."

Cone's theology would soon move from the confines of the seminary into popular culture, such as on the network television show *Good Times* in 1974. The sitcom tackled topics rarely if ever presented to a largely white audience; on only the second episode of the long-running program, the characters discuss Black Jesus. When discovering a painting created by older brother J.J., which he calls *Black Jesus*, young Michael decides to replace the conventionally rendered portrait of a blond-haired, white-skinned Jesus hanging on the wall in the family's apartment with this one. "Since both are just symbols of Jesus," Michael explains, "a Black family should have a Black symbol." (Incidentally, mother Florida disagrees at first, and the episode explores the African American community's internal conflict between conventional white-centric Christianity and Cone's theology.)[2]

Cone's teachings would inspire a new generation of both Black clergy and feminist scholars to bring Black liberation theology to the people. In 1972, fresh from divinity school and full of ideas,

Black Madonna, church caretaker Beverly Williamson in foreground, Central United Church of Christ, Detroit, Michigan, March 16, 1968. A year earlier, the Reverend Albert Cleage had had the image installed and renamed the church the Shrine of the Black Madonna.

the young Reverend Jeremiah Wright arrived at Trinity United Church of Christ, on the impoverished South Side of Chicago. The eleven-year-old congregation had dwindled down to eighty-seven members, and the local community felt that the church wasn't addressing its cultural needs.

Wright recalls his interview with the chairman of the church's search committee: "I said, 'I'll tell you the truth. You guys say you wanted to be a Black church in the Black community. The question was, are we going to be a Black church serving the Black community, or are we going to continue to be a white church in black-face?' Well, the core group said, 'All we need to do is find a young fool to conduct the funeral for a dying congregation.' They found the fool, and here I am."

Over the next thirty-six years, Wright worked to transform Trinity from a middle-class church to one concerned with Black liberation and serving the poor. The church raised money for the homeless, helped the elderly find housing, hosted child care programs, and created a welcoming environment for the marginalized, including those addicted to drugs, serving prison sentences, and, later, suffering from AIDS.

Wright recalls some of the church's most important community programs. "Food co-op: not just showing up in people's lives Thanksgiving and Christmas, but every week feeding people. Reading: a tutorial program for all the kids in the local schools within a ten-block radius of the church. Those kinds of programs. Prison ministry did not just go into prison and have worship service: teaching GED skills, teaching computer skills in prison." Wright looks back on the church's history over the past decades. "We used to call ourselves in the seventies the Alphabet Soup Church," he says. "We had all the alphabets: AB, BS, MD, PhD, and ADC—which is welfare. Because the letters behind your name are how you make a living. The church is about how you make a life."

The son of a preacher and a veteran of the Marines, Wright put James Cone's Black theology into practice both culturally and politically. He articulated the theory in a sermon: "The culture says you are the wrong race. The Christ says I made your race and I ain't made no mistakes. The culture says your skin is Black. The Christ said so, and so was mine." The church's members were of the same mind, declaring themselves "unashamedly Black and unapologetically Christian." "We were practicing in the community where we sit," Wright says. "In the seventies, many Black churches moved to the suburbs where there was lots of land. This congregation made a decision: if we're going to be a Black church, we're staying right here, in the Black community, and make sure that our programs and ministries speak to what the community's needs are."

Savage has written that Trinity's work exemplifies precisely the kind of church that many had demanded during a time when Black communities had few resources. Likewise, Wright embodies many of the attributes of the highly educated, politically engaged clerical figure that was demanded by reformers such as W. E. B. Du Bois, Carter Woodson, Benjamin Mays, and Nannie Helen Burroughs. "Jeremiah Wright," Savage says, "is a combination of historical currents in one figure. This is a highly trained, prophetic, charismatic religious figure and someone who also has the political commitment as politically radical as King was in his day."[3]

Wright says that his church embraced Black liberation theology and put it into practice, "first in worship, [and] secondly, those kinds of ministry programs that took the principles of Black theology and made it Black practical theology. Black theology talks about all of us being the same, equal footing at the foot of the cross."

SEXISM AND SEXUALITY: THE CHURCH'S DOUBLE BIND

The Reverend Peter Gomes, a dear friend of mine, once remarked that the whole foundation of the Black Church was propped up by women and gay men, though the leadership of the church, he admitted, subjugated the former and was in denial about the latter. The issue of gender equality—or, more pointedly, gender inequality—had been an open wound for the Black Church since its inception. Change has been slow, but there is movement. The enrollment of Black women in seminary and divinity schools increased greatly in the 1980s, and Black women have risen to once unimaginable heights in the church, such as the appointment of Vashti Murphy McKenzie as a bishop in the AME Church in 2000.

But a focus on leadership obscures the sexism Black women continue to face in their congregations. Amid the struggle over Black Power and Black theology, other internal frustrations burst to the surface in the early seventies. "The Black Church has been the place where so many of us have come to know a God of justice and a God of love," says Eboni Marshall Turman. "But it has simultaneously been a place that has wounded so many of us."[4]

Douglas struggles with the contradictory message that comes

from many Black Church denominations. "How is it that a church that emerged out of a struggle for freedom would then indeed oppress its own members? If the Black Church is going to survive, it is going to have to be welcoming to the whole entire Black community, because otherwise, there's not going to be a church."

Douglas became a key theorist of womanist theology, which emerged in the 1980s as a critique of the blind spots of second-wave feminism. Black female theologians like Douglas and the Reverend Jacquelyn Grant built on the definition offered by Alice Walker, who is credited with inventing the term, and the writings of Black feminists and feminists of color to describe how white-dominated feminism had not fully considered the experience of Black women, who are triply oppressed by race, sex, and class, and whose oppression in broader society mirrors their oppression within the church. Douglas and her cohort put the experience of Black women at the center of a theology defined by Jesus's concern for the poor and oppressed. Womanist theology recalls the work of previous women religious scholars, such as the Reverend Pauli Murray, the first African American woman to be ordained a priest by the Episcopal Church, who wrote, "As patriarchy has distorted the race and function of women (and men), so has it distorted our perception of God."[5]

Issues of sexuality and culture have divided Black congregations. Many televangelists, for example, argue for what they call "traditional" gender norms and oppose gay marriage and a woman's right to choose. As Glaude puts it, "When we control for issues of race, African American Christians turn out to be among the most conservative Christians on so-called value questions in the country."[6]

The Edwin Hawkins Singers performing on *The Johnny Cash Show*, February 24, 1971.

On the West Coast in particular, those who felt marginalized within their own churches boldly broke with tradition and developed righteous new ways to express their beliefs. In 1968, the Edwin Hawkins Singers from Oakland, California, debuted their gospel song "Oh Happy Day." The group was one of several Pentecostal choirs emerging in the late sixties to bring a youthful energy back to the church, but this song was a dramatic break from the past. It not only became an international hit, it also won a Grammy, and the choir members were treated like rock stars. But Pentecostal church leaders criticized the singers, branding the song's crossover success as too worldly to be properly religious.

"I was so enthralled in the way that they presented the Gospel, Miss Shirley with her beautiful, regal-looking self," the gospel singer Yolanda Adams recalls, referring to the singer Shirley Miller. "And I'm like, oh, my gosh. This is what I can aspire to? And then to also look cool doing it."

But what about the tension between Saturday night and Sunday morning? Adams minimizes the distinction. "Entertainment shouldn't be in the church? What do you think the preacher does? But when the church makes the indictment that you don't serve God anymore, it hurts."

And sometimes that indictment can drive people away from the church. In 1972, building on the success of "Oh Happy Day," the Hawkins family opened a storefront church in Oakland. They called it Love Center. Unlike mainstream Pentecostal churches, Love Center adopted the Bay Area's counterculture approach to sexuality. Its choir and pews became a haven for gay and lesbian singers, among them the gospel musician Bishop Yvette Flunder, the daughter and granddaughter of Church of God in Christ pastors. Flunder felt deeply alienated from the Pentecostal church in which she'd been raised.

"I came from the church that was just—don't. You just don't," she says. "I never had to leave church to be a same-gender-loving woman. I didn't have to leave the church of my birth, because that's where I learned that I was a same-gender-loving woman. What made me an exile was because I decided to tell the truth. There's an awful price to pay. There are people who are very afraid. They're afraid to lose their churches. They're afraid to lose their positions. They don't want to harm their parents and their legacy. And so they remain deeply closeted."

Flunder left the Church of God in Christ and focused less on religion and more on her work with older people and HIV-positive people. She recalls with laughter the call she received from Love Center, asking her to fill in for Hawkins while he was away: "I said yes with my mouth, but my whole body said no. But I had said yes with my mouth by that time. I hung up the phone. I had to go find my Bible. I didn't know where it was. And I had my Bible. I rolled myself a joint and got a glass of red wine. So I want you to get that in your mind: a Bible, a joint, and a glass of red wine! I preached my own self free that day and joined the church."

What had been repressed would find a novel way to be expressed, when sacred, churchy vocals fused with secular club rhythms to form disco's gay anthems. The genre's divas, like Sylvester, anointed the "Queen of Disco" in the late 1970s, had all been raised in the church.

"Sylvester, who was raised in the Church of God in Christ, just like me," Flunder says, "had that tune, had those licks, had that sound, had that vibe"—and also that alienation from the church. "He said to me that the same people that turned me out turned him out. I'll never forget it. And I told him, I said, there's a lot of people that have that testimony. We didn't have to leave church to be sexualized. The truth of the matter is that sometimes the same atmosphere that sexualized you is the atmosphere that puts you out." Or, as West bluntly states, "Homophobia and transphobia are as evil as white supremacy, but most Black churches have not embraced this prophetic witness."

The arrival of HIV/AIDS in the early 1980s led to a range of disappointing responses from the Black religious community. Many initially dismissed the disease as a plague that affected only gay white men. Even as it ravaged the Black community, the AME Church maintained that the disease was contracted through sinful acts and promoted abstinence as its official position on the crisis.

Other denominations took a more sympathetic stance. In 1989, Pernessa Seele, an immunologist by profession who was raised in a Revivalist southern church, organized interdenominational communities in the first Harlem Week of Prayer to bring attention to the AIDS crisis and provide education for those who lacked it. She helped shift the Black community's response to HIV/AIDS and continued to mobilize the church community around public health issues.

Flunder responded by founding the City of Refuge in 1991. "During the dying years, the early years, as I call HIV, I was losing tons of people. I found myself trying to bridge the chasm between how to be a person of faith and also do work in the earth. The will of God is complicated, because sometimes God asks seemingly the most of you when you seem to have the least to contribute." The church was her answer to a calling. "I said, I feel called to start a church and to call it City of Refuge. In times like these, we need an anchor. What we don't have, we must create—a congregation that keeps the culture and the sound of the Black Church sans the homophobic and fragile patriarchy realities that exist in the churches that we came from was a risky experiment." In her church, Flunder provided a place for anyone who had ever been displaced, for those who had been treated disgracefully to find grace. "We were a worshipping community and a serving community and cross-pollinated."

HIV and AIDS have continued to disproportionately infect and kill Black people into the twenty-first century. But these recent years have also seen the growth of congregations that, like the City of Refuge, were willing to fight back and to accept people regardless of their sexual orientation. In March 2005 in Atlanta, Bishop O. C. Allen III founded the Vision Church in the living room he shared with his husband, Rashad Burgess. The in-home congregation that started with 12 congregants would grow to some 3,500, meeting in the massive Vision Cathedral in Atlanta's Grant Park neighborhood, sitting on the church's 28,000 square feet of property.[7] Through its nonprofit organization, the Vision Community Foundation, the church follows the model of serving and elevating its community that has so often been the mission of Black churches, feeding the homeless, offering GED training, and providing toys for poor children. In addition, it provides for HIV testing and participates in gay pride events. In 2015, President Barack Obama appointed Allen to the Presidential Advisory Council on HIV/AIDS.[8]

KEEPING HOPE ALIVE IN THE REAGAN ERA

The conservative politics of President Ronald Reagan dominated the 1980s. As federal and state policies of the era eroded the social safety net, and Reagan ignored the exploding AIDS crisis, the decade would demand a new kind of ministry to counter the growing influence of the Moral Majority, which overtly tied religion to race and political power. As the televangelist Jerry Falwell put it, "During the 1980s, preachers, we have a threefold primary responsibility. Number one, get people saved. Number two, get them baptized. Number three, get them registered to vote."

Black churches, as a result, played ever larger roles in their communities, providing safety nets and political bases. The crack epidemic in particular galvanized and polarized the Black Church, which in many ways was at the forefront of the "war on drugs," organizing anti-drug youth programs, conferences, and campaigns to tackle the crisis. But where some saw drug addiction as a problem of individual moral failing, others focused on the problematic policing and mass incarceration epidemic that followed.

"People were like sheep without a shepherd," Calvin O. Butts III says. "So the church had to try to maintain its balance, particularly in the urban areas, and [during] a heightened attack on affirmative action, civil rights. And we had to just give people—which is a very important part of the church—hope. Hope."

The Reverend Jesse Jackson, a protégé of C. L. Franklin and Martin Luther King, Jr., challenged the Reagan administration on affirmative action and other social justice issues, saying, "Reagan won when we were asleep. He won by the margin of despair." Born in 1941 in Greenville, South Carolina, Jackson honed his commitment to civil rights at the Agricultural and Technical College of North Carolina (now North Carolina A&T State University) in Greensboro, the epicenter of the sit-in movement, and to religion at the Chicago Theological Seminary. His work with the Southern Christian Leadership Conference brought him into contact with King, and, despite publicized differences, he became part of King's inner circle, present on the balcony of the Lorraine Motel in Memphis when King was assassinated.

A national civil rights leader in his own right, throughout the 1970s Jackson maintained an emphasis on economic equality while also entering the realm of Democratic politics. By 1984, with the Moral Majority mobilizing conservative white Christians to get out the vote, Jackson found ways to leverage the power of Black congregations to propel Martin Luther King's activist spirit directly into the political arena. He initially announced that he was seeking the Democratic presidential nomination at the House of the Lord in Brooklyn, New York, a historic Pentecostal church regarded as "a sterling example of faith in action," and whose pastor, the progressive Reverend Herbert Daughtry, served as an adviser to Jackson throughout the campaign.[9] During his campaign he embraced the role of the preacher politician, a legacy that stretched back to Reconstruction. "The logic is the same," Pinn says, "that the Black Church is prominent, the Black minister is a major symbol of leadership, and that this prominent symbol of leadership would then move into secular politics."

Black churches—those longtime organizing centers—made Jackson's campaign possible. As Glaude writes, "Sanctuaries continued to serve as organizing sites. Churches provided financial as well as human resources to the campaign as they worked diligently to challenge the rightward swing of the Democratic Party." As they did for politicians during the civil rights movement, churches bolstered Jackson's campaign on the local level by hosting rallies, leading voter registration drives, and making sure that new voters made it to the polling booth on Election Day.[10] Although he fell short of the nomination in 1984 and 1988, he set a remarkable precedent: that an African American could be taken seriously as a presidential candidate.[11]

Furthermore, Jackson also paved the way for a new generation

Jesse Jackson, then president of Operation PUSH, interviewed after his attendance at the first National Black Political Convention, Gary, Indiana, March 13, 1972.

of leaders both in the church and outside of it. Al Sharpton, initially wearing his signature tracksuit, gold medallion, and James Brown–influenced pompadour, dominated the headlines and the airwaves in New York City during the 1980s, in a period of intense racial strife. The minister was greatly influenced by Jackson: "He had swagger, and he didn't wear a suit and tie. He had a big 'fro. So I said, that's the kind of preacher I want to be, because he never pastored a church. He'd say, 'The whole country is my pulpit.'"

As the fallout from the war on drugs led to increased gang violence and police brutality in Black neighborhoods, Sharpton saw his form of crisis-driven activism as another way to keep King's civil rights legacy alive—with a roving, in-your-face preacher at center stage. "We're doing what Dr. King would have done," he says. "He'd be in the streets with the victim's mother."

HIP-HOP

In those same streets, a new kind of secular ministry began to emerge, with young Black people grabbing the mic for themselves. "Hip-hop is a judgment against silence and invisibility," Michael Eric Dyson says. "Hip-hop seizes the microphone to amplify the urgent drama of Black dispossession. These rappers are secular preachers."

West sees a global connection between hip-hop and religion: "Pentecostal is a religious globalized culture. Both are coming out of Black folk, coming out of American empire. There could be a parallel between the ways in which Black music in all of its forms, including hip-hop, is a more globalized culture than any other globalized culture that we know." Hip-hop, of course, is not a religion, but it exhibits something akin to a religious quality. "You've got to be able to connect your flow with somebody else's soul, you see," West continues. "In that way, there could be overlap, but it's not spiritual; the dominant forms are market-driven."

"The emergence of hip-hop creates a complicated moment for Black churches," Fredara Hadley explains. "The church, which is often run by older men in a lot of cases, had a real problem with what hip-hop represented. This tension boils over with the rise of 'gangsta rap': 'You don't understand what is happening in my life in this crack era'—and young people having to navigate through that.

It did the church no favors that their condemnation of hip-hop was swift and decisive." Butts, who in the early 1990s was one of the major religious figures to come out against gangsta rap, sees it differently. "We're not against rap," he counters. "We are not against those rappers. But we are against those who have absolutely nothing of redemptive value to offer."[12]

The emergence of hip-hop reflected a generational shift away from Black churches. The Reverend Brianna Parker, the CEO of the consulting firm Black Millennial Café, states plainly how her generation, millennials, relates to the church. "I think we're disenchanted with the Black Church," she says. "Black millennials don't want to walk into a fantasy world when they cross the threshold of a church. You have to include what is real."

Once again, a segment of the church tried to bridge that gap through music. In 1997, the gospel singer Kirk Franklin released the hit song "Stomp," featuring a cameo by the rapper Salt, of Salt-N-Pepa, and a sample from Funkadelic. "Stomp" became the first gospel song ever to top the Billboard R&B/hip-hop charts. Franklin says that "gospel music is not a sound; gospel music is a message," one that shares "the good news of Jesus Christ, that talks about the love, the beauty, and the majesty of Jesus." Not everyone heard beauty or majesty in "Stomp," though, and many Black Christians admonished him, saying, "You're bringing devil music into the church." Franklin views this lack of acceptance surrounding his song as part of a bigger issue: "I think that the hesitancy to embrace change has always been to our demise in the Black Church."

Today, some churches, such as the Hip Hop Church in Harlem,

incorporate hip-hop into their worship, and some of the genre's biggest stars have brought gospel into their mainstream albums, among them Kanye West in "Jesus Walks" (2004), "Ultralight Beam" (2016), and *Jesus Is King* (2019); Common in "Kingdom" (2014); and Chance the Rapper on his mixtape *Coloring Book* (2016).

A younger generation's growing frustration with what they saw as an increasingly conservative church leadership caused some African Americans to abandon the sacred spaces that had long stood at the heart of the Black community. "I still have a lot of reverence for the church and for the traditions that I grew up in," the singer John Legend says. "But I'm not actively religious now. For folks who are progressive, I think the church just doesn't connect on all the issues that we care about."

BUILDING COMMUNITY FOR THE BLACK MIDDLE CLASS

Since Martin Luther King's death, the Black middle class has doubled in size, and the Black upper-middle class has quadrupled.[13] The affluent sought a different kind of fulfillment from their church home, with a focus on the welfare, needs, and anxieties of the individual.

"Churches have to ask themselves," Pinn says, "what do you do with this new capacity for consumerism? What do you do with Black folks who now have economic means? On some level, a way to do that is what we've come to call the prosperity gospel."

Before there was the prosperity gospel, there was the New

Thought tradition, embodied by the ministry of the charismatic and complicated figure the Reverend Major Jealous Divine, best known as Father Divine. Glaude describes New Thought as an antecedent to the prosperity gospel, with the two philosophies bearing a "family resemblance" to each other.[14] Keeping the details of his birth and origins to himself, the self-named and self-styled Father Divine incorporated into his theology the power of the mind and of positive thinking to alter the world around us—and the teaching that he was God in a human body, come to usher in the kingdom of heaven on earth. In the midst of the Great Depression, Father Divine founded the International Peace Mission Movement, a group in which he preached celibacy and communal living, asking that his followers relinquish all their money and worldly possessions and pleasures. As a Black man in the Jim Crow era with prestige and a pulpit, he used his position to vehemently oppose segregation and lynching. Yet there was controversy. While his followers shared their resources with the poor, and the Peace Mission provided its adherents with food and clothing at a time of great suffering and deprivation for so many, Father Divine was accused of exploiting their labor, possessions, and wealth for his own personal gain. The allegations did little, however, to diminish his devout followers' faith in him. The Peace Mission was short-lived, but Father Divine, branded a charlatan by some and a savior by others, remains a compelling figure in twentieth-century church history.[15]

Decades later, the Reverend Frederick J. Eikerenkoetter II, popularly known as Reverend Ike, picked up what Sharpton calls "the strand in the Black religious world that would teach blessings

Father Divine's mission/grocery store, Denver, Colorado, March 31, 1937.

and prosperity." Promoting his mind-science philosophy, which built on some elements of New Thought theology, he moved in a much different direction from Father Divine's. "Reverend Ike was a larger-than-life personality that pulled people into his world of excess and riches," Jonathan L. Walton says. "For Reverend Ike, there was too much emphasis in the Black Church about poverty, about suffering." The southern-born, New York–based preacher and evangelist became the voice of the prosperity gospel. His weekly radio program drew millions of listeners, both Black and white, and his message peaked in popularity in the 1970s. Reverend Ike believed that the root of all evil could be traced to one source: the *lack* of money. "In the American economy," he said, "the only color of power is green. That's why I have never represented Black Power, only green power. If everybody can get some more green power, then there will be peace and love between the races." The comedian Richard Pryor parodied Reverend Ike in the 1976 film *Car Wash* as the character Daddy Rich, with the memorable line, "There's a good place in this world for money, and I know where it is. It's right here in my pocket." "Many people would laugh and disparage Reverend Ike, but his fan base was in the millions," Walton says.

"You've always had those who have said the most important thing is saving folks' souls," says Martha Simmons. "But if they can't eat, they don't have a decent place to live, what good did it do you to save their souls?"

The idea of building something new was also appealing to middle-class and upper-middle-class African Americans who were moving to the Sun Belt during the economic boom of the 1990s. Perhaps the key figure in this movement is Bishop Thomas Dexter Jakes, Sr., popularly known as T. D. Jakes, a dazzling preacher and theologian and founder of the Potter's House in Dallas. In addition to being a deeply committed spiritual leader, Jakes is a master of the uses of video and social media and an inventive entrepreneur. He preaches what Walton has called the "neo-Pentecostal perspective," meaning that he emphasizes deliverance and forgiveness, a God of love and grace, rather than hellfire and brimstone. Jakes's emphasis on the positive benefits of entrepreneurialism and wealth accumulation for all sectors of the Black community are quite distinct from standard accounts of the prosperity gospel, a label that has been erroneously applied to him. Jakes knows firsthand, through his parishioners, who represent all economic and social classes, what economists have pointed out: as Emily Badger reports in *The New York Times*, "Black families in America earn just $57.30 for every $100 in income earned by white families, according to the Census Bureau's Current Population Survey. For every $100 in white family wealth, black families hold just $5.04."[16] Jakes's focus is in line with that of progressive social programs: he feels that without narrowing the gap in wealth accumulation, the Black community is doomed. The difference between this theory and prosperity gospel advocates is crucial. As explained by Walton: "Luxury goods are not considered the guaranteed right of all Christians according to their faith. The neo-Pentecostal perspective retains a teleological blues sensibility that regards pain and suffering as having a perfecting role in the life of the believer."[17] Jakes has written, "Many millennials don't know the struggle that their parents and grandparents went through, so people in the current generation may be very familiar with the Prosperity Gospel and the way of thinking that goes along with it: it's easy to praise God when life is good and money is easy to come by. The struggle isn't real for some of them."[18]

Jakes built his ministry up from a storefront church in Charleston, West Virginia, to a massive enterprise that sits on more than four hundred acres on the outskirts of Dallas. "It was just something that God started," he explains. "And so since he started it, I had to trust him. Christ said, 'Upon this rock I build my church. The gates of hell should not prevail against it.'" The Potter's House, which Jakes says can hold up to fourteen thousand people, takes its name from the song "The Potter's House" by Tramaine Hawkins, which emphasizes the restorative power of God. In the art of preaching,

"The master, in my opinion, is T. D. Jakes," Oprah Winfrey says. "At first I was resistant to the big, massive church, because I grew up in this cocoon, but there's nothing like the community. So sometimes I will just get on my plane and fly to Dallas to the Potter's House and just sit in a service, and hearing those amens and mm-hmms and 'Preach, Bishop.'"

Like many contemporary megachurches, Jakes's eschews Christian symbolism, such as crosses, as unnecessary reminders of religious traditionalism. He believes strongly in the church adapting to suit the needs of the community it serves. "You can't feed people who are not hungry," he says. "If housing is not a problem, why build houses? And as the times have changed, the church has had to reinvent its focus to respond to the needs. I have taught entrepreneurship; I have taught home ownership; I have taught debt management. And yes, I believe God will bless you." He continues: "Everybody in the kingdom has the same responsibility. I don't care how many titles you've got. And I believe that there will always be a church." But, he concludes, "it may not be after the fashion of what its fathers thought it ought to be."

Jakes believes that his role as pastor is to stay out of politics: "Though the Black community was served well by ministers who doubled as political leaders in an era when the pulpit was often our only podium, today the African American community is no longer limited to the pulpit as our primary lecture post. We now have thousands of African American politicians elected to serve our interests, nonprofit leaders funded to lead our communal efforts, and academics educated to research our options and convey their findings to the world."[19]

The Potter's House, Dallas, Texas, May 14, 2006.

Today, scholars and preachers debate which model has become the dominant one in the Black Church as well as the ramifications of a divide difficult to bridge. "I don't know who won post-1968, Dr. King or Reverend Ike," Glaude says. "We claim Dr. King, but when we look at Black Christendom, it looks a lot like what Reverend Ike was doing."

William J. Barber II asks, "How did we go from 'I Have a Dream' to bling-bling? The Black Church has been very clear. To be a person of faith, to be a body of faith, is to be about the business of liberation. And if it's not, then what we are doing is just filling people with emotional fervor."

"The Gospel describes loving your neighbors as yourself, whatever that means, if it means to educate, to feed, to clothe, to house, to advocate, to fight for justice," Dwight Andrews says. "When the church stops doing that, the church has no reason for being. And I think many churches have now spent time paying for buildings and paying salaries and not doing ministry."

OBAMA REVEALS DIFFERENT SIDES OF THE BLACK CHURCH TO WHITE AMERICA

During his 2008 presidential campaign, Senator Barack Obama embraced the themes and the cadences of the activist Black Church. Of Obama, Sharpton says, "He knows how to talk in a way that we understand the message, like a minister, without being a minister. And he's very good at it and very sincere about it."

At a speech commemorating the voting rights campaign in Selma, Alabama, Obama cited the Old Testament story of Exodus and vowed to fulfill Dr. King's legacy and lead his people, at long last, to the promised land. "So don't tell me that I don't have a claim on Selma, Alabama," he said. "I'm here because somebody marched for our freedom."

Long before he was president, Obama's own spiritual journey brought him to Jeremiah Wright's Trinity United Church of Christ in Chicago, which had continued to put Black theology into practice. "There were benefits to involvement in Trinity that he embraced," Pinn says, "but the radical edge of this Black theology was not a part of the platform that Obama embraced."

The Obamas attended Trinity regularly; Wright officiated at Barack and Michelle Obama's wedding and baptized their children. But in March 2008, controversy erupted over the pastor's five-year-old sermon on the Iraq War. It went viral. "Where Governments lie, God does not lie," he said. "Where Governments change, God does not change. . . . When it came to treating her citizens of African descent fairly, America failed . . . then wants us to sing 'God Bless America.' No, no, no. Not 'God Bless America'; God Damn America! That's in the Bible, for killing innocent people. God Damn America for treating her citizens as less than human. God Damn America as long as she keeps trying to act like she is God and she is supreme!"

Wright ruminated on the amount of controversy the sermon generated. "I think they became controversial because they did not follow the 'We love this country,' 'My country right or wrong,' 'Make America Great Again' kind of thinking," he recently said. Savage describes the response to Wright's sermon this way: "It's an encapsulation of both a fear of African American religion and also the mystery of African American religion to people who don't attend Black churches or never have."

Desperate to put his campaign back on track, Obama delivered a speech in Philadelphia that he called "A More Perfect Union." It would become known as his "race" speech. "Like other predominantly Black churches across the country," he said, "the church [Trinity] contains in full the kindness and cruelty, the fierce intelligence and the shocking ignorance, the struggles and successes, the love and, yes, the bitterness and biases that make up the Black experience in America."[20]

Although his experiences at Trinity had a profound influence on his understanding of what it meant to be Black in America, Obama, according to his critics, weakened his ties to this church, to its theology, and especially to its pastor, all of which had played a part in launching him on his path to the White House.

Savage argues that when Obama renounced Wright at the end of April 2008, in response to further comments Wright made on TV, he attempted to confine Wright's Black liberationism to the past. "Obama succeeded, at least temporarily, by employing a politics of Black religion that deflected the politics of race threatening his presidential aspirations," she writes. "Later, when he explicitly renounced and rejected Wright, he relegated his mentor to a bygone era marked by racial division and pain. Obama erected a generational divide between himself and Wright, but his disavowal disregarded the longer historical narrative from which Wright and Trinity had emerged."[21]

By the time Obama formally resigned his membership in the church at the end of May, the Reverend Otis Moss III had taken over as Trinity's pastor. In a manner that he humbly acknowledges, Moss follows in Wright's footsteps, leading a church as active in community issues as in religious ones, supporting the Black Lives Matter movement, emphasizing HIV/AIDS outreach, and fighting gun violence, the mass incarceration of African American men, and police brutality.

If Obama's campaign exposed a more radical strain of the Black Church, his presidency exposed the church's conservative side. In 2012, he came out in support of gay marriage, and many African Americans furiously denounced him on religious grounds. The Coalition of African American Pastors (CAAP), a conference of more than four thousand ministers, issued a petition in opposition and organized protests around the country. Though in recent years more church leaders, like the Reverend Cedric Harmon, co-director of the nonprofit Many Voices, have shown leadership in support of LGBTQ rights, it remains a highly contentious issue in the Black Church, as it does in the larger Black community. The same can be said of women's reproductive health care and family planning decisions.

THE BLACK CHURCH IN THE ERA OF BLACK LIVES MATTER

Even with a Black president in the White House, police violence against unarmed Black men remained pervasive. But now the world was watching.

On July 17, 2014, an African American man named Eric Garner died when an officer from the New York Police Department put him in a chokehold in the midst of an arrest. The scene and Garner's repeated cries of "I can't breathe" were caught on video. On August 9, halfway across the country in Ferguson, Missouri, an unarmed eighteen-year-old African American man named Michael Brown was shot dead by a police officer in the middle of the street. "Our national field director called and said there's a man on the phone crying, saying that the police killed his grandson," Sharpton recalls. "I'm in the middle of the Eric Garner fight, just three weeks. And he told me, 'Are you near a computer?' Michael Brown was still laying on the ground in Ferguson. And I said, 'Sir, I'll be there day after tomorrow.'"

Protests following the murders inspired a political movement that deftly used social media hashtags like #handsupdontshoot and

#icantbreathe to encourage activism. The protests, on streets and on screens, led to great national recognition of the women-founded, member-driven Black Lives Matter movement. Black Lives Matter began in 2013 in response to the acquittal of George Zimmerman, who, in a largely white gated Florida community, shot and killed Trayvon Martin, an unarmed African American teenager whose hoodie and skin color were enough to spur the neighborhood watchman to take deadly aim. These new-school activists rejected old models of political leadership, including the role of the church. "Young women have been very important leaders in the movement for Black lives," says Barbara Ransby, the activist and historian who has written biographies of movement figures such as Ella Baker and Eslanda Robeson. "But it's not steeped in a religious institution, and it's certainly not steeped in a kind of patriarchal tradition that is often represented in the formal institutions of the Black Church."

Says Glaude, "Black Lives Matter forces the Black Church to return to one of its foundational claims: that we are all children of God and, because of that very fact, no matter the color of your skin we all matter. We are all sacred in the eyes of God." Some clergy hit the streets of Ferguson with the young protesters. The Reverend Traci Blackmon of the United Church of Christ led prayer vigils in front of police stations. "I scheduled a prayer vigil, and about halfway through, the young people said, 'That's enough praying.' So these young people, they abandoned the institution. They didn't necessarily abandon God. The Ferguson uprising was church."

In that moment, Blackmon believed that the presence of oppression and police brutality called for a different type of ministering. "I'm not an activist; I'm a pastor. One is called to be both priest and

The Reverend Traci Blackmon addressing demonstrators at the site where
Michael Brown was shot and killed by police, Ferguson, Missouri, August 14, 2014.

prophet. The prophet has to have the courage to speak truth to power, and the priest has to always care for those who are being harmed emotionally and physically. Yet the color of our skin still makes us a target."

On June 17, 2015, an avowed white supremacist named Dylann Roof entered Mother Emanuel AME Church in Charleston, South Carolina, under the guise of joining the Bible study happening at the time. There were thirteen African Americans studying and praying together. Within an hour, Roof would draw his pistol and kill nine of the parishioners, violently destroying the sanctity of this historic sanctuary. This was the church Denmark Vesey had built, Charleston's main Black church, and it was not the first time white people had destroyed it. After the Civil War, it was proudly rebuilt as Mother Emanuel AME Church. "It was the worst fears come alive again," Sharpton says. "It was the four girls bombed in the church in Birmingham again. This is in a Bible class, in the Black Church, historic Black church, Mother AME, the core of who we are. And if we couldn't protect ourselves there, what are we going to do?"

In the face of unthinkable racial violence, the man who had navigated the complex web of race, religion, and politics at the start of his administration became the pastor for the nation. "We do not know whether the killer of Reverend [Clementa] Pinckney and eight others knew all of this history," President Obama said during his eulogy. "But he surely sensed the meaning of his violent act, an act that he presumed would deepen divisions that trace back to our nation's original sin. Oh, but God works in mysterious ways." He used his time at the altar, in front of a primarily Black audience in the pews and a much vaster audience of all races watching at home, to implore the South Carolina legislature to once and for all remove the Confederate flag from the state capitol. "For many, Black and white, that flag was a reminder of systemic oppression and racial subjugation," he said. "By taking down that flag, we express God's grace." As has been true throughout the history of the Black Church, the lines between the political and the pastoral were blurred, this time by the African American man elected to the highest office in the land. And then, "in the presence of the full AME Church episcopacy," Cheryl Townsend Gilkes recalls, "Obama did what was Black tradition: he 'raised' 'Amazing Grace,' and the musicians picked him up, and the church stood with him. The kinesics of that moment were very significant and very traditional."[22]

President Obama delivering the eulogy at the funeral of the Reverend Clementa Pinckney, Charleston, South Carolina, June 26, 2015.

"That was the moment that this man who looked like us could stand up there and tell us, but remember 'Amazing Grace.' We needed that," Sharpton says.

The massacre was part of a resurgence of white supremacist activity that many of us thought we'd never see again. "Something has been let loose," the Episcopal bishop Michael Curry says, "and so religious folk must create a counternarrative to that. And I think the teachings of Jesus are just as clear that Christian folk and Christian leaders cannot abide or countenance anybody's supremacy over anybody else, white or anything, and cannot remain silent. Silence is consent."

Barber saw a chance to re-center questions of faith, freedom, and liberation in the church. "I'm a preacher, and I'm a theologically conservative liberal evangelical biblicist," he says. After right-wing politicians in the North Carolina legislature passed voter suppression laws and made cuts to health care in 2016, this son of a preacher reached back to the lessons of the prophets to inform his activism. "As clergy we came together and said, we don't need a left critique or a right critique or a conservative or liberal; we need a moral critique. And what we're going to do is, we're going to walk in the legislature with the Bible in one hand and the Constitution in the other."

A longtime member of the NAACP, Barber in 2013 introduced Moral Mondays, a series of protests in Raleigh against the increasingly rightward turn in North Carolina's government. The demonstrations involved prayer, speeches, and often mass arrests after protesters entered the statehouse.[23] "A lot of people came to Moral Monday and would say this to me: 'I had walked away from the church. At Moral Mondays, I found my faith again.' Because people know there's something wrong with a religion that has nothing to say about the oppressive realities that exist in life. God is the God of the oppressed."

Barber has called for a new Poor People's Campaign, arguing that, for Martin Luther King, the campaign of 1968 was tantamount to the Second Reconstruction. To Barber, the moment beginning with Donald Trump's election marked "the birth pangs of a Third Reconstruction," yet another cycle of progress and rollback. Echoing the Fusionist language that gripped his home state more than a century earlier, Barber argues that the Third Reconstruction can be won by an interracial coalition that is, among other things, antiracist, pro-justice, and transformative. "There's no shortcut around this. We must build a movement from the bottom up."[24]

Black churches have also mobilized to get out the vote—and to protect fair voting for African Americans in the midst of the ongoing rollback. The Black Church PAC formed in 2016 and tackles issues such as voter suppression, mass incarceration, and gun violence. In 2019 it held a forum where five Democratic presidential candidates argued why she or he deserved the support of Black voters. As the Reverend Leah Daughtry, a prominent Democratic strategist and national presiding prelate of the House of the Lord Churches, writes, "Gaining our vote requires gaining more than a cursory understanding of who we are as a people. Candidates will need to be able to speak to a full range of issues and concerns and, just as importantly, feel comfortable engaging directly with a range of African American people." In addition, in 2020, the Black Church Action Fund aligned with Vote.org to mount voter registration efforts among Black churchgoers.[25]

THE BLACK CHURCH AND THE CHALLENGES OF 2020

The year 2020 has proven to be an agonizing inflection point in our national story. African Americans especially have been devastated by a series of pandemics within pandemics. Our public health system, our economic futures, and the relationship among law, order, and our sacred bodies all are on the line at the very same time. And the lack of response from President Donald Trump and the federal government reeks of racist times past. Douglas notes this history by drawing upon a favorite saying of James Baldwin about African American loyalty to the government: "Baldwin said that there comes a time in every African American's life when they discover that the flag to which you have pledged allegiance and such loyalty has not pledged allegiance and loyalty to you."

Because of the spread of the novel coronavirus, sacred spaces across the nation have had to navigate strict physical-distancing rules, even shutdowns, while tending to the sick and dying, many of whom suffered profoundly lonely deaths as the pandemic worked its way through communities like a reaper. Tragically, some ministers defied the science, only to discover that their sanctuaries were "superspreader" sites, where gatherings from funerals to family weddings to prayer groups turned out to be lethal. As of this writing, the virus has infected more than 9 million people in the United States and killed at least 230,000.[26] Black, Indigenous, and Hispanic people have suffered disproportionately from COVID-19 across every variable, including age; location; and urban, suburban, or rural living. Astonishingly—or, sadly, perhaps not so astonishingly—the death rate among Black people as of October 2020 (108.4 deaths per 100,000 people) was double that of white people (54.4 deaths per 100,000). And I shudder to think what these numbers will look like by the time of publication.[27]

Churches, for both Black and white congregants, have proven to be incubators for the virus, and leaders have been in no way immune to its spread. COVID-19 has decimated the leadership of the Church of God in Christ. According to Anthea Butler, as many as thirty COGIC leaders had died of coronavirus by the middle of

April. "This will change the ecosystem of Black Church life," she states. "It's showing the inequities of health disparities and economic disparities in the Black community."[28]

How can Black churches respond when in many cases they can't even open their doors? Examples abound. In May, Friendship-West Baptist Church in South Dallas organized coronavirus testing in its parking lot.[29] Churches such as Light of the World in Indianapolis and Central Baptist in Pittsburgh have offered meals to those in need, all while trying to avoid physical contact. "The world is hearing a lot of rhetoric around canceling and shutdown, but the church never cancels, never shuts down," says the Reverend R. Janae Pitts-Murdock of Light of the World. "Even when we don't gather in physical space in the building, we are always open. We have to reconsider how we gather, how we minister, but as a pastor I am avoiding language that even exudes the idea that we could ever cancel."[30]

Still, Black churches struggle under the weight of the COVID-induced financial collapse. The Reverend Victor J. Grigsby of Central Baptist explains, "We have never been at this place before. The Black Church doesn't have endowments. We don't have trusts like other major white churches do to rely on. We are hand-to-mouth just like our parishioners."[31]

As the coronavirus rages, so, too, does white violence against African Americans, including highly publicized cases that have laid bare the vicious racism that sits at the center of American culture, particularly when it comes to policing. The Black Church, already reeling from a devastating public health crisis, is again asked to do what it has done before: fight a war, now on two fronts, that is literally robbing its people of life and breath.

The details of these cases have been seared into the national memory, but they must be retold. On February 23, Ahmaud Arbery went for a run in the Satilla Shores neighborhood of suburban Glynn County, Georgia. The twenty-five-year-old never made it home. Two white men, Gregory McMichael and his son Travis, pursued him in a truck, attempting to run him over; the scene was being video recorded by another white man, William Bryan, who had joined in the chase. Arbery couldn't escape. He was shot at least twice. The McMichaels later said that they believed Arbery was responsible for recent break-ins in the neighborhood. Bryan later testified that Travis McMichael called Arbery a "fucking nigger" after shots rang out.

"Later" was nearly three months later. Incredibly, local officials had passed on filing charges until the video of the event went viral on May 5. Finally, on May 7, the Georgia Bureau of Investigation arrested the father and son; two weeks later, on May 21, they arrested Bryan.[32]

With Memorial Day's kickoff-to-summer barbecues and festivities largely canceled because of the pandemic, May 25, 2020, should have been an unusually quiet day. Instead, the world erupted. First, on the morning of May 25, an African American man named Christian Cooper, a birding enthusiast, was on an expedition in New York's Central Park when he encountered a white woman named Amy Cooper (no relation) walking her dog unleashed, in violation of posted rules. He asked her to put her dog on a leash; she refused—and took out her phone, dialing 911 and warning him that she was "going to tell them there's an African American man threatening my life." He had taken out his phone as well, capturing the entire incident and phone call on video. She made good on her warning, her voice rising in hysteria: "I'm in the Ramble. There is a man, African American. He has a bicycle helmet and he is recording me and threatening me and my dog." He ended the video after her final plea to the operator: "I am being threatened by a man in the Ramble! Please send the cops immediately!"[33]

The video went viral, and fortunately for Christian Cooper, this encounter did not end the way it had so many times before. Such an accusation has always been the tried-and-true recipe for lynching. In 1955, Emmett Till was accused of whistling at a white woman in a grocery store in Money, Mississippi. In 1921, in Tulsa, Oklahoma, almost exactly ninety-nine years before the Cooper encounter in New York, a young Black man named Dick Rowland was accused of assaulting a white woman in an elevator. He may have inadvertently stepped on her toe. While Rowland was not lynched, and in fact charges against him were dismissed, the entire section of Tulsa called Greenwood, the "Black Wall Street," was burned to the ground, and as many as three hundred African Americans are thought to have died at the hands of a white mob out for justice in the name of protecting white womanhood. There are countless other examples of murder and mayhem, documented and undocumented, that followed the same script, perfected in the years following Reconstruction and during the Jim Crow era, and still in use in 2020.

But on the afternoon of May 25—four days after the last of

Ahmaud Arbery's murderers was finally charged in Georgia, hours after a phone call from a white woman falsely accusing a Black man of violence could have triggered a false arrest or worse in New York—what happened in Minneapolis, Minnesota, ignited some of the largest civil rights protests in U.S. history. On that day, a clerk at a Minneapolis convenience store called the police to report that a customer had tried to pass a counterfeit twenty-dollar bill to buy cigarettes. The customer's name, we would learn, was George Floyd. The police answered the call, and the horror that ensued—captured in an iPhone video—is far too familiar to all of us by now. A white police officer named Derek Chauvin, eyes fixed straight ahead, hands in his pockets, pinned Floyd facedown on the ground and drove his knee into Floyd's neck. Floyd repeatedly said he couldn't breathe and begged for help. He called for his mother. He cried out for his children. Out of breath, he said, "They'll kill me. They'll kill me." Onlookers pleaded with the officer to stop. Chauvin's three fellow officers did nothing. Floyd lost consciousness, but Chauvin kept his knee on his neck. He kept it there for over eight minutes, including the first minute and twenty seconds after paramedics arrived.

The Minneapolis police department fired the four officers the next day, but there was an outcry that the response wasn't strong enough. On June 3, a little over a week after Floyd's death, Minnesota attorney general Keith Ellison charged Chauvin with second-degree murder and the three other officers with aiding and abetting second-degree murder.[34]

Over the following days and nights, tens of thousands of Americans took to the streets to demonstrate against police brutality.

Many news reports focused on the alleged violence and looting of the protesters. President Trump blamed "thugs" and said, "When the looting starts, the shooting starts." In fact, police officers themselves often instigated violence. In Minneapolis, police used tear gas and rubber bullets. Police in Buffalo shoved a seventy-five-year-old white protester to the ground and walked past him, even though he suffered a head injury.[35]

Floyd's murder and the subsequent protests brought national attention to another police murder case that had happened in the early morning hours of March 13. In Louisville, Kentucky, three plainclothes police officers broke down the door of the home of an African American EMT named Breonna Taylor, on the false premise that her apartment was the hub of a drug-dealing ring. The officers later claimed that they identified themselves as police and that Taylor's boyfriend, Kenneth Walker, fired first. They also initially reported that Taylor suffered no injuries and that they faced no resistance entering the apartment. In reality, the police used a battering ram to break down the door and then shot Taylor eight times.[36]

On July 3, *The New York Times* declared, "Black Lives Matter May Be the Largest Movement in U.S. History." The authors suggested that as many as fifteen million to twenty-six million people participated in more than 4,700 protests, averaging 140 per day, following George Floyd's murder. By any measure, the numbers are staggering, and they cross the color line. "Unlike with past Black Lives Matter protests," the *Times* reported, "nearly 95 percent of counties that had a protest recently are majority white, and nearly three-quarters of the counties are more than 75 percent white." The change from protests past was noteworthy—and long overdue. As Stanford University professor emeritus Douglas McAdam put it, "Without gainsaying the reality and significance of generalized white support for the movement in the early 1960s, the number of whites who were active in a sustained way in the struggle were comparatively few, and certainly nothing like the percentages we have seen taking part in recent weeks."[37]

Observing the footage of the vicious murder of George Floyd on the streets of Minneapolis in late May was not only shocking, it was disorienting. So, too, was the lynching of Ahmaud Arbery while he was out jogging in a Georgia suburb, and the brutal, senseless killing of Breonna Taylor by police in Kentucky. Was this the year 2020, or 1968, or 1919, or 1876 all over again? In many ways, it was all those years at once, flashing before our eyes, as the pains of our ancestors echoed down to us in the horrifying images of a single Black brother, son, and father with the knee of the law crushing the life out of him. In these shattering times, with a rising generation demanding that their voices be heard, that the dehumanization of Black bodies end, that this be the last lynching, the Black Church once again has been challenged to respond with leadership and grace, resiliency and inspired action.

Setting a powerful example, Sharpton delivered the eulogy at George Floyd's funeral in Houston on June 9, his tribute to Floyd combined with a call for protest in the familiar language of the church.

God took an ordinary brother from the Third Ward,
from the housing projects, that nobody thought much about

but those that knew him and loved him. He took the rejected stone, the stone that the builder rejected. They rejected him for jobs. They rejected him for positions. They rejected him to play certain teams. God took the rejected stone and made him the cornerstone of a movement that's going to change the whole wide world. . . .

Oh, if you would have had any idea that all of us would react, you'd have took your knee off his neck. . . . If you had any idea that preachers, white and Black, was going to line up in a pandemic, when we're told to stay inside and we come out and march in the streets at the risk of our health, you'd have took your knee off his neck, because you thought his neck didn't mean nothing. But God made his neck to connect his head to his body. And you have no right to put your knee on that neck.[38]

Sharpton also recognized the family members of other slain African Americans in the audience, relatives of Trayvon Martin, Eric Garner, Botham Jean, Pamela Turner, Michael Brown, and Ahmaud Arbery—all of whom perished either at the hands of police or, in the case of Trayvon Martin and Ahmaud Arbery, whose deaths were the result of blatant racist acts by white killers who found a measure of sanctuary in the arms of the law. "They wanted to be here to be part of this," Sharpton said of the families, "because they understand the pain better than anyone, because they've gone through the pain."[39]

Barber, the architect of Moral Mondays and the faith leader calling for the new Poor People's Campaign, also played a visible role in the response. "What made that cop think he could do that to George is still a part and parcel of society, where too many people think they can use their power to crush people rather than lift people. If poor and low-wealth people organize around an agenda and vote, they can fundamentally shift politics."[40]

As the crosses carried by the civil rights generation are passed on to the shoulders of the Black Lives Matter generation, churches and their leaders must evolve with the faithful and, in so doing, strengthen the bedrock foundation on which so much of our people's freedom struggle has stood tall. We've come this far—and must go farther still—by the faith our ancestors taught us so that we, too, might survive this life and ascend to the next.

A s I pointed out in the first chapter of this book, the foundation of the African American spiritual journey was formed out of fragments of faith that our ancestors brought with them to this continent starting five hundred years ago, and from those fragments has grown the powerful institution that we fondly call the Black Church. But, as Jason Young reminds us, "It's important in thinking about the 'Black Church' to define it as a plural rather than a singular. There are storefront urban churches in the North, there are now, increasingly, megachurches around the country, and all of that contributes to the broader fabric of Black religiosity in the country."

"The Black Church is fundamental to the African American experience," Paul Harvey says. "The African American experience is fundamental to American history. Therefore, Black churches are fundamental to American history." As W. E. B. Du Bois put it in his seminal essay "Of the Faith of the Fathers" in *The Souls of Black Folk*, "It is thus clear that the study of Negro religion is not only a vital part of the history of the Negro in America, but no uninteresting part of American history."

"There will always be moments that push us back to our faith," Jakes believes, "because life has a way of reminding you that you need something bigger than you to get through a season."

"The Black Church for me still remains the strongest demonstration of God with us that we have," Blackmon says. "And it is those small Black churches that have made the difference in our communities. It is that strength that I want the church to tap back into."

EPILOGUE

On the Holy Ghost:
The Beautiful and the Sublime,
the Vision and the Trance

It was out in the country, far from home, far from my foster
home, on a dark Sunday night. The road wandered from our
rambling log-house up the stony bed of a creek, past wheat and
corn, until we could hear dimly across the fields a rhythmic
cadence of song,—soft, thrilling, powerful, that swelled and
died sorrowfully in our ears. I was a country schoolteacher
then, fresh from the East, and had never seen a Southern
Negro revival. To be sure, we in Berkshire were not perhaps as
stiff and formal as they in Suffolk of olden time; yet we were
very quiet and subdued, and I know not what would have
happened those clear Sabbath mornings had some one
punctuated the sermon with a wild scream, or interrupted the
long prayer with a loud Amen! And so most striking to me, as I
approached the village and the little plain church perched aloft,
was the air of intense excitement that possessed that mass of
black folk. A sort of suppressed terror hung in the air and
seemed to seize us,—a pythian madness, a demoniac possession,
that lent terrible reality to song and word. The black and
massive form of the preacher swayed and quivered as the words
crowded to his lips and flew at us in singular eloquence. The
people moaned and fluttered, and then the gaunt-cheeked
brown woman beside me suddenly leaped straight into the air
and shrieked like a lost soul, while round about came wail and
groan and outcry, and a scene of human passion such as I had
never conceived before.

Those who have not thus witnessed the frenzy of a Negro
revival in the untouched backwoods of the South can but dimly
realize the religious feeling of the slave; as described, such

scenes appear grotesque and funny, but as seen they are awful.
Three things characterize this religion of the slave,—the
Preacher, the Music, and the Frenzy.

—W. E. B. DU BOIS, *The Souls of Black Folk*, 1903

Some folks get happy, they run
Others speak in an unknown tongue
Some cry out in a spiritual trance;
I get happy and do the Holy Dance!

—SANCTIFIED CHURCH FOLK SAYING

On January 13, 1972, Aretha Franklin performed a concert that would soon be released as the best-selling record of her career, *Amazing Grace*. At the request of the
Reverend James Cleveland, the legendary Reverend C. L. Franklin
took the stage to introduce his legendary daughter and recounted
a story of an encounter with a neighborhood woman in Detroit
that testified to his feelings about Aretha's decision to embark on a
career recording secular music. It goes like this:

I went in the cleaners one day in Detroit, to pick up
some clothes.
And Aretha had appeared on a recent television show,
and she told me, "I saw your daughter, Aretha, last night."
She said, "It was all right."
Said, "But I'll be glad when she comes back to the
church."

How did her wise father respond? Let's let him tell it:

I said, "Listen, baby, let me tell you something. If you want to know the truth, Aretha has never *left* the church! All you have to do is have . . . the ability to hear and the ability to feel, and you will know that Aretha is still a gospel singer! And the way she sings in this church she sings anywhere she sings."

Aretha's father was right. The distance between the structures of Black sacred and secular music was often the distance between the juke joint and the choir behind the pulpit, the few hours between late Saturday night and eleven o'clock on Sunday morning. We can think of these two forms of Black music, which were mutually exclusive for the person C. L. Franklin met in the dry cleaners, as symbolic of the nature of African American culture itself: Janus-faced; flip sides of a musical form; joined together and inseparable, "in one black body," as W. E. B. Du Bois wrote in *The Souls of Black Folk*. In other words, Aretha had never left the church, because the church had never left her.

I suppose no one who was raised in the church ever fully leaves it. But I can safely say that after so many years of watching it from a distance, not as a member but as an avid spectator—especially in summers at Union Chapel on Martha's Vineyard or at the Memorial Church in Harvard Yard—making our PBS series and writing this book have allowed me to understand more fully, both intellectually and emotionally, the meaning and the magic of the Black Church, its centrality to the history of the African American people, and the seminal role it continues to play some five hundred years after our captors violently uprooted and forcibly relocated our African ancestors to these shores.

Throughout our childhood, from as early as I can remember, my brother, Paul, and I attended the church that my mother's family attended, the Waldon Methodist Church on Water Street in Piedmont, West Virginia. We never missed church on Sunday mornings, we sang in the choir, but we were not saved. That is, we had not joined the church, that moment when a person stands before the congregation and answers set questions posed by the minister, effectively giving their life to Christ, which means obeying the rules set by the church for Christlike behavior. Within my mother's family, the Coleman family, only my grandmother, Big Mom, was saved. The rest of us were voyeurs, of a sort.

Everything changed for me on one very sad Sunday evening.*

I was twelve years old. My brother and I were watching TV. My mother hadn't been herself lately, and out of the blue, my father solemnly informed us that he was taking her to the hospital. She bent over and hugged me. Then she kneeled down and, crying, told me she was going to die. I should be a "good boy" to my father after she was gone, she said, and I should "listen to him." And then they left. I was inconsolable. I have never felt more alone.

I went upstairs to my bedroom. I kneeled by my bed and prayed to Jesus. I told him that if he let my mother live, I would give my life to Christ; I would join the church. I prayed that prayer over and over, begging Jesus to let my mother come home alive. Exhausted with grief, I eventually fell asleep.

Judging from the expression on my father's face when we had

---

* This is a story that has stayed with me and shaped me in more ways than I can count. I've explored this incident before, in my 1994 memoir, *Colored People*.

breakfast early the next morning, the odds didn't look good. I didn't tell anybody what I had done.

But about three days later, I was told that Mom had gotten better, and she was coming home that evening. I went up to my bedroom and looked in the mirror and thought, Uh-oh. I had made a deal with Jesus. You can't make a deal with Jesus and then go back on your word. You can mess with a lot of people, but you can't mess with God.

Because the size of the Black population in our county in West Virginia was so small, one minister serviced the two local Black Methodist churches, one in our hometown of Piedmont, the other five miles away in the county seat, Keyser. Service in Keyser took place on Saturday afternoon, around five o'clock; service in Piedmont was at eleven o'clock the following Sunday morning. I'm not sure why, but I came to the decision that I would join the church, as we still call it, at the Saturday service in Keyser, away from the gaze and the complications of my family and friends. That's where I would publicly commit my life to Christ. I got dressed, left the house without telling anyone where I was going, and hitchhiked to Keyser.

At the end of the service, the minister made his usual call to the altar, the invitation for anyone who has been sufficiently moved to join the church. Every person in that church knew this part of the service by heart, because it meant that church was almost over, since in my recollection, hardly anyone ever responded to the call. At the appointed time, trembling, I rose from my seat in the pew. The minister assumed that I had to go to the bathroom and simply said, "Skippy, the toilet is behind the door to the right of the pulpit." I was so surprised that, for a second, I didn't know what to say. Then I blurted out, "I want to join the church!" The minister and the few people in attendance were just as shocked as I was to hear those words come tumbling out of my mouth. I walked up to the altar. All gathered around me in a semicircle. The minister read the questions of commitment, I whispered the correct answers, and when it was over, everyone there hugged me, and they and I burst into tears. I hitchhiked back home to Piedmont.

That night, as we sat around our little black-and-white TV following dinner, I told my parents what I had done. "You did what?" my father, a devout Episcopalian, sputtered in frustration and disappointment. He thought such emotional rituals as joining the church were unseemly. My mother just looked at me strangely. "Why did you do that and not tell us?" Not only did I not tell them *then* why I had done what I did, I never, ever told them. We all sat around that night in stunned silence. The last thing I remember my father telling me before I went to bed was now that I had made this crazy decision, it was my duty to keep my word. He had no idea that no one was more keenly aware of that than I was.

So, for the next two years, I didn't play cards, I didn't attend basketball games, I didn't go to movies or dances (I loved movies and I loved to dance as much as I loved to play cards), and I did my best not to lust in my heart. I sang in the choir, I attended prayer meetings, I took Communion, and I never missed church. Everyone said that I would be a minister one day, and though I'd been raised to be a doctor, I wondered if the ministry might be my true calling. Maybe I could combine medicine with missionary work in Africa, like my hero of the moment, Albert Schweitzer.

I was saved, but I never underwent the deeply emotional experience of possession by the Holy Ghost (also known, of course, as the Holy Spirit), which, though rare in our small Methodist church, did occasionally occur. Miss Sarah Russell, a leader of our church, frequently emoted during services, not in a loud or dramatically demonstrative way, but with enough outward expression that we nicknamed her Sister Holy Ghost. But this was not the norm among our congregants, like it was for those who had been saved in the Church of God in Christ across the street.

In my heart of hearts, I was relieved and thankful that I did not receive the Holy Ghost. You see, it was one thing to give my life to Christ by pledging various forms of abstinence; it was quite another to be entirely swept away in an emotional outpouring with several manifestations that took oneself not only out of one's body, but out of one's senses as well. This at least was how my classmate, Woody Green, described his own experience receiving the Holy Ghost during a summer church service at a revival meeting sponsored by the COGIC. (By the way, some people say the *Holy* Ghost, others the Holy *Ghost*. I'm not sure why, but when I hear the name spoken in the former way, God's third and most dynamic and mysterious manifestation is somehow more powerful, more full of awe and terror.)

At the age of fourteen I migrated my faith to the Episcopal Church, my father's church, the church of his parents, his grandparents, and his great-grandmother, who had been enslaved. But before that, I had basically spent two years gripped by the fear that what had happened to Woody would happen to me.

To tell the truth, to say I was terrified of being possessed by the Holy Ghost wasn't too strong a word. It may not even be strong enough. Here's how bad it was: There were two churches on Water Street, so named because it ran parallel to the barrier that protected the flat section of Piedmont from the mighty Potomac River, which had a tendency to flood. It didn't happen frequently, but frequently enough so that major floods, such as the devastating one from Hurricane Hazel in 1954, were used as occasions to mark significant historic events, like Armistice Day or VJ Day. Since this wasn't exactly prime real estate and flood insurance was expensive and hard to come by, and since it marked the border between "downtown" and the river, people nicknamed it Back Street, which was quickly rebranded Black Street. Mostly Black people lived on Water Street, and also on the street that ran parallel to it, Paxton Street. One of my mother's sisters and one of her brothers lived on Paxton Street, and we all attended the Methodist church on Back Street.

The vigorously animated Church of God in Christ occupied a large multistory building in the middle of the right side of Water Street. (We called it Holiness and Pentecostal interchangeably, even though by that time in church history it would have been part of the Pentecostal denomination. I'm going to refer to it as the Holiness Church in my retelling, simply because in my memory, that was our usual description of it.) Sleepy Waldon Methodist Church—Big Mom's church, the church in which my brother and I and all of our many cousins had been christened—sat about a hundred yards farther down from the Holiness Church, on the left side of Water Street. On Sundays and at prayer meetings on Wednesday nights, the Holiness Church *rocked*. That was the only word for it. First of all, Mr. Les Clifford held court there with his saxophone. He was a master of that thing, and he was legendary throughout the Potomac valley. He and his band had played every Saturday night in the area juke joints—before he got saved, anyway, people said; before the devil himself came up out of the floor of the smoke-filled room in which he and his band were jamming and chased him by foot all the way back to his house, about twenty miles or so away. After outracing the devil himself, Mr. Les continued to jam, but only in the Holiness Church. No more juke joints for him.

Second, that church rocked because you could hear every amen and hallelujah and "Thank you, Jesus" from its small but determined congregation halfway to Keyser. And third, well, over the blare of Mr. Les's holy saxophone and the thundering chorus of amens, sometimes you heard the strangest sounds, people doing the Holy Dance, shouting or whooping or moaning the oddest phrases and sentences, unfathomable to the unconverted and untranslatable even to the faithful. People called it speaking in tongues, which, to our ears, only added to its strangeness.

Everyone knew that what made the Holiness Church special, even fearsome, was what the scholar Gastón Espinosa calls "the outpouring and leading of the Holy Ghost," a "*release* and longing for hope, though perhaps just out of reach," and "not due to speaking in tongues per se."[2] While I can see that now, try telling that to a bunch of adolescents. Quite honestly, there was no question that the most dramatic aspect of this experience for us was *exactly* that moment when people started to exhort in that elusive language that only God could understand, signifying that they had been possessed by the Holy Ghost. A phenomenon also known as glossolalia, or "the unknown tongue," it is practiced today by Pentecostal and charismatic Christians.

In chapter 2, where I discuss "the Frenzy," the most mysterious of Du Bois's triad of the three key elements that constitute the Black Church (the Music and the Preacher are the other two), he *seems* to be including speaking in tongues in his description—"the stamping, shrieking, and shouting, the rushing to and fro and wild waving of arms, the weeping and laughing, the vision and the trance"—yet he doesn't mention it by name. He wrote of the frenzy in 1903. In terms of doctrine, speaking in tongues wasn't "officially" part of the history of the Pentecostal Church until 1906, when the Azusa Street Revival in Los Angeles—what today we would call a diverse, multicultural event—introduced the denomination to the world.[3]

The practice of speaking in tongues was decidedly controversial at the beginning of the century, Cheryl Townsend Gilkes tells me. In fact, when William Joseph Seymour, the African American man who ultimately oversaw the Azusa Street Revival, preached in a Holiness church in California that full holiness required speaking in tongues, the pastor padlocked the door to keep him out. But, Gilkes says, Seymour captured the attention of some congregants, and as their numbers grew wildly, so, too, did their fervor. By spring, in Los Angeles, "a small group followed Seymour to a house on Bonnie Brae Street, where they proceeded to have a good old-fashioned Black Church worship—'the frenzy'—until the house collapsed," she explains. "They counted it as a miracle that no one was hurt and moved into a former AME church that was also a former horse stable at 312 Azusa Street in Los Angeles." It was here, she says, in this event that attracted both Black and white people and that captivated the press, that the Pentecostal movement got started, when speaking in tongues went from being a feature of ecstatic worship to a central part, even a doctrinal requirement, of sanctification.[4]

This was in 1906, three years after Du Bois had written about "the faith of our fathers." Why does it concern me whether he included speaking in tongues on his list of elements that defined the frenzy? He certainly marveled at the ring shout in his masterwork of sociological analysis, *The Philadelphia Negro*, published in 1899.[5] Although his take on the singing he heard was not particularly flattering—he referred to "the weird witchery of those hymns sung rudely"—he possessed a scholar's interest in the ring shout's link to the past, noting its connection to "the methods of worship in Africa and the West Indies."[6] I possess the same sort of fascination regarding the historical origins of speaking in tongues within African American experience.

Were those ancestors coming out of slavery and their descendants speaking in tongues as well? Perhaps not in so many words—there was no formalization or routinization of the practice prior to 1906—but Cheryl J. Sanders believes so. "My short answer is yes," she wrote to me. "I am not certain that Du Bois witnessed glossolalia in the backwoods of Tennessee, but the 'wail and groan and outcry' he notes could signify speaking in tongues. He clearly states that Negroes in the southern revivals experienced spirit possession, and he readily relates 'The Frenzy' to the unmistakable manifestation of the presence of God."[7]

After speaking with these scholars, I can only conclude that speaking in tongues was implicit in Du Bois's notion of the frenzy based on his own observations of the religious culture in the rural African American South.

But Du Bois, like me, intuited something much more ancient than what he was observing in his own times. He ends his description of the frenzy with two stunning declarations, the first about the relation of possession by the Holy Ghost to other forms of possession: "All this is nothing new in the world, but old as religion, as Delphi and Endor."[8] We know quite a lot about the mysteries of the oracle at Delphi, but Endor is a more obscure reference. In our modern era, *Star Wars* fans may recognize Endor as the home of the Ewoks. Clearly not what Du Bois was referring to! Bible scholars know that the Witch of Endor is summoned by King Saul in the first book of Samuel. Du Bois's point is that spirit possession is as old as the Greeks and the Hebrews, as old as civilization itself. One way to think about the Holy Ghost, to extend Du Bois's analogy, is to think of it, in broad metaphorical terms, as the *messenger* of God, much as Hermes was in Greek mythology, as Esu-Elegbara is today in Yoruba religion. Possession is the "language" through which God expresses God's self to the faithful, and "unknown tongues" or "speaking in tongues" is the "language" in which the faithful respond to and communicate with God, and God alone, since no one else can translate.

Speaking in tongues has many sources in the Bible, among them "And these signs shall follow them that believe . . . they shall speak with new tongues" (Mark 16:17); "And they were all filled with the Holy Ghost, and began to speak with other tongues, as the Spirit gave them utterance" (Acts 2:4); and "And when Paul had laid [his] hands upon them, the Holy Ghost came on them; and they spake with tongues, and prophesied" (Acts 19:6). The Christian Bible portrays speaking in tongues as a gift bestowed upon believers, and it is this sense that defines the Holy Spirit in the Black Church, especially in Pentecostal denominations, Gilkes notes, "such as the Church of God in Christ and the Church of Our Lord Jesus Christ, sometimes lovingly referred to as 'cool Jay Cee,' to name two of many."[9]

And it is this gift that is the greatest gift of all, as Du Bois makes clear in his second point about the frenzy: that the visible, audible manifestation represents the degree of *authenticity* within the larger Black Church of one's genuine religious conversion and direct relation to God; indeed, that one has been and is "saved." "And so firm a hold did it have on the Negro," Du Bois continues, "that many generations firmly believed that *without this visible manifestation of the God there could be no true communion with the Invisible*" (emphasis mine).

After two years of filming in every sort of Black house of worship and denomination conceivable, I would say unequivocally that Du Bois's observation about possession by the Holy Ghost remains just as true to Protestant believers in the second decade of the twenty-first century as it was at the turn of the century when he published his stunningly perceptive analysis of the church, the chapter of *The Souls of Black Folk* titled "Of the Faith of the Fathers."

When Du Bois writes of the frenzy, his language conveys both awe and condescension. I like to think that awe won out in the end, but I'm not so sure. We certainly saw the latter in Bishop Daniel Payne's proud recollection of his intervention in a southern rural church service's rites that, for him, bordered dangerously close to the satanic. It is evident in the writing of both that possession by the Holy Ghost has been to some a distasteful, and at times controversial, subject in the history of the Black Church, certainly since the end of the Civil War. (Remember that William Joseph Seymour's arrival in Los Angeles was inspiring to some but alienating to others.) In *Black Gods of the Metropolis*, Arthur Huff Fauset reported on the "Holiness cult," in which "it is not sufficient for one that he be converted. After conversion one must be sanctified, and besides, he must be filled with the Holy Spirit." It is akin to a "graduate church," where, "like the university it may be said to offer a master's and a doctor's degree in addition to the bachelor's degree. To become one of the elect you must have experienced all three."[10] Barbara Savage writes in the foreword to Fauset's brilliant exploration of the diversity of African American religion, "The construct that Fauset could not escape and that framed his entire book [was] the debate about the presence of African retentions in African-American religious practices, and the related notion that black people were by nature overly and primitively religious."[11] Alexander Crummell—the first Black graduate of the University of Cambridge, an ordained Episcopal priest, a missionary for twenty years in Liberia, the co-founder of the American Negro Academy, and Du Bois's hero—said that the Black Church far too often "substituted rhapsody and hallucinations for spiritual service and moral obligation." Crummell traced this tendency in African American congregations to their African origins: African religion, he wrote, could be characterized by a certain "race peculiarity," by which he meant what he called its "warm, emotional, and impulsive energy, which was both its failing and its virtue." This "failing," he lamented, far exceeded its virtues, requiring "a strong corrective, or, otherwise, the flame of religious life, however intense for a time [would] blaze with unhealthy violence, or else soon burn itself out." The ultimate danger—Crummell confessed what others deeply feared but merely whispered—was "a reversion to heathenism."[12]

A reversion to heathenism.

This was the barely repressed fear at the heart of debates about being saved by the Holy Ghost, performing the Holy Dance under the spirit, and speaking in tongues. This so-called heathenism, of course, would trace back to the pre-Christian origins of our people, straight to our ancestral African cultural origins. It was this relationship to the African past that, by any means necessary, for the Black middle class, both during Reconstruction and following its collapse, must be repressed. In this sense, the Holy Ghost—for well over a century and a half—was a pawn in a complicated class war over culture in the Black community.

Espinosa makes an ingenious connection between the mission of the group of Black intellectuals and leaders that Du Bois famously dubbed "the Talented Tenth"—those who objected most strenuously to the practice of charismatic religion—and William Joseph Seymour's mission for his followers, pointing out with stunning insight that both the theory of the Talented Tenth and the manifestation of glossolalia at the Azusa Street Revival occurred virtually simultaneously. "Du Bois," Espinosa argues, "writes that this 'Talented Tenth' were called on to be the 'missionaries of culture' who exercise the 'vision of seers.' He believed they would 'leaven the lump' of Black society and 'inspire the masses.'" Seymour "turned this reference to the Black lump of masses bottom side up and instead saw the lump of Spirit-filled Black masses—rather than the Talented Tenth—as providing leaven for the Black community and American society." Espinosa concludes, "Seymour—though never a part of the Talented Tenth—nonetheless was and ended up being a 'missionary of culture' that had the 'vision of seers.'" Espinosa also argues that it's clear that Seymour's language sometimes echoes Du Bois's. Both Du Bois and Seymour saw elite groups within the Black community as having true "saving power" to redeem America from its original sins, be they those of slavery or those of the flesh, though their definitions of "elite" were surely not aligned.[13] Could Du Bois's and Seymour's theories have been flip sides of the same coin?

Espinosa believes that "from Seymour's perspective, the Holy Spirit baptism enables marginalized people to reimagine their debilitating identities and frees them up to express their hitherto unrealized hopes, expectations, and dreams," precisely when Jim Crow racism had robbed the freedmen and freedwomen and their descendants of those very things. To Sanders, too, that timing is critical. She concludes that the interracial outbreak of speaking in tongues at the Azusa Street Revival in 1906, and its massive spread thereafter, is evidence that the phenomenon "may signify the move of God to rescue us at 'The Nadir,'" the lowest point in American race relations since the fall of Reconstruction and the rise of the ex-Confederacy's Redemption, the period of the Lost Cause and the legislation of Jim Crow segregation. When Du Bois was writing of the Talented Tenth in 1903 and organizing, first, in 1905, the African American civil rights group the Niagara Movement, followed by, in 1909, the interracial National Association for the Advancement of Colored People, it is doubtful that he would have seen his mission and Seymour's as similar in the least. But their seemingly contrary ideas were both formulations of deliverance from the devils that were torturing our people, and both emerged within the same decade.

During my months of filming for this PBS series, in Black churches large and small, North, South, East, and West, Sunday after Sunday, having watched as carefully as I could people falling out in the aisles of churches or collapsing in their pews or at the altar, and hearing and recording a legion of believers just as spontaneously speaking an ocean of mutually unintelligible tongues, I have arrived at a different theory about the role and function of the Holy Ghost and its dazzling linguistic multiplicity.

Possession by the Holy Ghost, which I so feared as a boy, is perhaps the most vibrant, complex, and mysterious vestige of the African cultural past retained by African Americans—even as it is to some observers, such as Bishop Payne and the Reverend Crummell and Dr. Du Bois, the most "embarrassing." Other retentions and reinventions of the African cultural past include myriad sacred and secular forms of dance; call-and-response in music and oratory; polyrhythms (the interplay of primary and secondary beats, reflecting a generating principle of cross-rhythms); and structures of sermonizing that the scholar Gerald Davis calls "the circular mode" in his study *I Got the Word in Me and I Can Sing It, You Know*, and Otis Moss III calls "blue note preaching," which he defines as "a unique cultural narrative and theological enterprise where African motifs meet diverse Western influences of North America." These are celebrated as seminal examples of the magic of cultural continuity between the Old World of Africa and the New World of Black America that survived the horrors and ravages of the Middle Passage and the scattering and fragmentation of ethnic cultures during the slave regime.[14] I think it's fair to say that, in general, speaking in tongues and the spontaneous eruptions of the Holy Dance are *not* proudly celebrated as African retentions, despite their having survived the same horrific journey as the cultural crossovers. In fact, Black Christian spirit possession as practiced in the Black Church seems to be one of the most obvious examples of how the symbolic practices of the fifty or so most commonly represented African ethnic groups in the cultural and genetic DNA of the African American people blended together into peculiarly African American forms.

Speaking in tongues and spirit possession might be considered, for some African Americans, the troublesome African retention.[15] Somehow these elements slipped through that mysterious portal through which other Pan-African cultural legacies (along with other "Africanisms") were transmitted and took root solidly in Black American cultural soil, mutating under Christianity into the possession by the Holy Ghost that manifests in evangelical services. Jean Toomer coined a name for this portal in 1923, in his novel *Cane*: "the Dixie Pike," which "has grown from a goat path in Africa." He also said quite perceptively that in the Black

214

tradition at its best, a "body is a song," a principle that we witness in the greatest of Black preaching and Black Church singing. Du Bois somewhat demeaned sacred spirit possession by describing it with the term "trance." And it was my own fear of succumbing to it, or more accurately being captivated or taken over by it, that led me to walk down Water Street on the left side of the road, to Waldon Methodist, rather than on the right side, by the Church of God in Christ, where, I was convinced, the Holy Ghost lived.

Why was I so afraid of the Holy Ghost as a boy? Well, maybe because Victor Clay, my brother's friend, was leaving a revival meeting, walking up the aisle and heading out the door, when all of a sudden, he told us, something grabbed him, turned him around, and drove him straight back down the aisle to altar, in the grip of the Holy Ghost and speaking in tongues. Even in Waldon Methodist, the Holy Spirit made its shadowy way from the Holiness Church down the street a couple hundred feet and grabbed my father's friend, Mr. Stanley Fisher, who dropped to all fours, began barking like a dog, and in that posture made his way to the altar to confess, join the church, and speak in tongues. The man was on all fours. Maybe that's why I was terrified of the Holy Ghost.

Why did African spirit possession translate itself into the Black Church in these ways? I think it's because the church is a concentrated, consecrated theater where the Word and the Song can combine as a site of conjuration, the space where the Spirit (Du Bois's "Frenzy") can be conjured each Sunday, recapitulating the journey that our ancestors' spiritual practices undertook as they trod that Dixie Pike out of Africa. Throughout this project, I watched a plethora of individuals get the Holy Spirit. Sometimes I felt the experience seemed forced, but not often. Mostly, in fact, I felt that I was witnessing a miracle of soul transformation, something full of wonder and mystery and terror—and realness—that I didn't have the language to explain. During interviews, I routinely asked preachers, soloists, musicians, and congregants if they had experienced the Holy Ghost. John Legend, who graduated from the University of Pennsylvania after turning Harvard down, answered matter-of-factly: "I spoke in tongues. It's a rite of passage in the Pentecostal Church. Folks shout, dance in the aisles. I was raised in that tradition, and I wouldn't be an artist today if I hadn't grown up in that tradition."

For me, part of the magic, part of the irresistible fascination of the Black Church is that it is Black culture's site of the beautiful and the sublime. Today, we think of the sublime, according to the dictionary, as "of such excellence, grandeur, or beauty as to inspire great admiration or awe." Certainly Black sacred music and classical Black preaching fall into that category. But the sublime, in eighteenth-century aesthetic thought, as put forth by Immanuel Kant and Edmund Burke, connoted something terrifying. The Yale University professor David Bromwich argues, however, that "once you see the strange enactment of passion as a usual thing and taken for granted in churches, your experience of it turns habitual. Then the surprise or shock is removed and the sense of sublimity diminished. As Burke notes, 'Custom reconciles us to every thing.'"[16] In other words, Holy Ghost possession retains its enormous power but has lost its capacity to terrify, as it did a twelve-year-old Black boy in Piedmont, West Virginia.

The Holy Ghost is the Black sublime, beyond the control of our will, in an experience equally astonishing, strange, and beautiful at once. It is the most haunting, unsettling, mystical, fascinating, terrifying—indeed, the most sublime—remnant of our African past, and it comes alive at a large portion of churches in the Black community each and every Sunday. For many of us, its manifestation remains novel, despite infinite repetitions, retaining its characteristics of shock and, to some extent, fear at this visible, miraculous manifestation of the Spirit of God.

My wife, Marial Iglesias Utset, is a Cuban citizen and a historian of slavery and the slave trade to Cuba. Her parents were deeply committed to the Cuban Revolution and raised their three children not only outside of the Catholic Church, but as staunch atheists. (Marial's grandmother remained a devout Catholic and spirited the kids away one day to the church just down the street so the priest could baptize them, incurring the wrath of her son.) At least a dozen times, Marial has asked me, out of genuine curiosity, "Why did the Black people get in love with this white Jesus that they inherited from the people who enslaved them?" When we compare the large number of Black people in Cuba and Brazil who practice Santeria and Candomblé with the vastly smaller numbers of practitioners of Obeah or Hoodoo or "Voodoo" in the United States, it is reasonable to ask what "work" Protestant Christianity, and especially evangelical Christianity, was performing for the African American people, both enslaved and free.

I once asked my friend Dr. Francis Collins, the director of the National Institutes of Health and the former head of the Human Genome Project, why he was a devout Christian. He told me that he decided to convert as he observed that believing Christians faced death with more ease than nonbelievers did. Two of my mother's nine brothers founded their own churches, both evangelical churches, when they turned sixty. Another brother graduated from divinity school at Boston University in 1960 and is a semi-retired Methodist minister. Big Mom never missed a Sunday. My father loved the liturgy of the Episcopal Church, especially its bells and whistles, its incense and repeated formality, until the day he died, and I found those things quite attractive myself when I left the church of my mother and underwent confirmation in the Episcopal Church of my father at the age of fourteen. To my surprise, my mother was confirmed as well.

The rigidly literal interpretations of the Bible among my fellow Waldon Methodists was clashing with the growth of my studies in biology, physics, and chemistry, fitting me like a girdle, as Zora Neale Hurston put it in another context. Once I knew that the world couldn't have been created in seven days, and that there couldn't have been an Adam and Eve, and that so much of the Bible was cast in allegory and analogy, simile and metaphor, that it was a text to be interpreted and not holy writ, I found the openness of the Episcopal Church to my expanding intellect and relentless teenage questioning a relief, and quite refreshing. I could retain my religious beliefs and not have to put my intellect on hold. Plus, I didn't have to worry about the Holy Ghost taking possession of me at any point in the service. Not a chance!

So why the persistence and growth of the Black Church? Why are so many of my friends, who, truth be told, are at best agnostic and more probably atheist, drawn to the sermons of T. D. Jakes or Otis Moss III or Calvin O. Butts III either in person or online? How is it that these worldly men and women won't miss Black church on a Sunday? Why is Union Chapel in Oak Bluffs on Martha's Vineyard, surely one of the most highly educated and economically comfortable Black congregations in the world, literally packed, standing room only, Sunday after Sunday for the ten o'clock morning service each week in July and August? Of course there are those who are true believers, but for the lot of us who wouldn't be included in that category, it's because of what I think of as the racial comfort of this cultural space, the familiarity with the rituals, with all of the elements, as Jennifer Hudson put it in our interview, that contribute to the Black Church as "theater," where Du Bois's three key structural elements, the Preacher, the Music, and the Frenzy, meet.

The Black Church is the space where our direct cultural ties to Africa come to life in new and mutated but still recognizable form. It's that cultural space in which we can bathe freely in the comfort of our cultural heritage, and where everyone knows their part, and where everyone can judge everyone else's performance of their part, often out loud with amens, with laughter, with clapping, or with silence. It's the space that we created to find rest in the gathering storm. It's the place where we made a way out of no way. It's the place to which, after a long and wearisome journey, we can return and find rest before we cross the river. It's the place we call, simply, the Black Church. As Miss Toot Marshall expressed it in the refrain to her rendition of "The Prodigal Son," the gold standard of hymns sung regularly by the choir at Waldon Methodist and, without doubt, my favorite gospel song:

Oh, I believe, I believe

I will go back home.

Well, I believe, I believe

I will go back home.

I believe, I believe

I will go back home

And be a servant for the Lord.

APPENDIX

Great Voices in the
African American Preaching Tradition

I heard it time and again when I was working on this film and book: the power of the Black Church is not just in the words delivered from the pulpit; it's in the way those words are spoken or sung. I was curious: Who did the people who know the church best, the spiritual leaders and scholars and activists and musicians I interviewed for this project, find most inspirational, most electrifying? I asked them, and what follows is their list of the men and women who helped shape their beliefs and their views of Christianity, Islam, and religion, broadly construed, and the world. Some of the names are widely known, and their voices have been heard around the world; others had no less of an impact, even if not on the national stage. Several people on this list have passed, among them men and women with resonant voices that were never recorded, yet their words continue to leap off the page and into our hearts and souls. Many have addressed slavery, anti-Black racism, women's rights, and civil rights, have spoken against homophobia, anti-immigrant prejudice, and ethnic hatred of all kinds. All have fostered self-worth and self-determination in the African American community. Because of the history of patriarchy in organized religion, it is unavoidable that more men are represented here than women, but all have left an indelible mark on their parishioners, their students, their followers.

Charles Gilchrist Adams

Cameron M. Alexander

Barbara Amos

E. K. Bailey

Willie Barrow

Traci Blackmon

J. A. Blake

William Holmes Borders, Sr.

Audrey Bronson

Walter Henderson Brooks

Jo Ann Browning

Cecelia Williams Bryant

John Richard Bryant

Nannie Helen Burroughs

E. Anne Henning Byfield

Juanita Bynum

Leslie D. Callahan

Katie Geneva Cannon

Arlene Churn

C. A. W. Clark

Clarence Henry Cobbs

Johnnie Colemon

Suzan Johnson Cook

Claudette Copeland

Marcus D. Cosby

Michael Curry

Sarah Davis

Frederick Douglass

Clay Evans

Tony Evans

Louis Farrakhan

Elaine Flake

Yvette Flunder

James A. Forbes, Jr.

C. L. Franklin

Teresa L. Fry Brown

Cheryl Townsend Gilkes

Morris E. Golder

Peter J. Gomes

Jacquelyn Grant

Francis J. Grimké

Carolyn Tyler Guidry

Neichelle R. Guidry

Cynthia L. Hale

Prathia Hall

E. E. Hamilton

Barbara C. Harris

Frederick D. Haynes III

APPENDIX

Alice M. Henderson

H. Beecher Hicks, Jr.

Ruby Holland

Rosa A. Horn

Charles Shepherd Henry Hunter, Jr.

Charles Shepherd Henry Hunter, Sr.

Jessica Kendall Ingram

Alvin O'Neal Jackson

T. D. Jakes

John Jasper

Courtney Clayton Jenkins

Vernon Johns

Mordecai Johnson

Noel Jones

Ozro Thurston Jones, Jr.

William Augustus Jones, Jr.

Bernice King

D. E. King

Martin Luther King, Jr.

Cheryl Kirk-Duggan

Carolyn A. Knight

Raquel S. Lettsome

Ann Lightner-Fuller

Brenda Williams Piper Little

Iona Locke

Nicole Massie Martin

James Earl Massey

APPENDIX

Benjamin Elijah Mays

Jackie McCullough

Vashti Murphy McKenzie

Wilbert S. McKinley

Ella Pearson Mitchell

Ed Montgomery

Otis Moss, Jr.

Otis Moss III

Huford Norwood

Joan S. Parrott

Donald Parsons

J. O. Patterson

Carlton Pearson

Samuel DeWitt Proctor

Sandy Frederick Ray

Theodore A. Richardson

Eugene F. Rivers III

Frederick G. Sampson II

Cheryl J. Sanders

Manuel L. Scott, Sr.

William J. Shaw

Fred Shuttlesworth

Amanda Berry Smith

E. Dewey Smith

Lucy Turner Smith

Gina M. Stewart

Maria Stewart

Gardner C. Taylor

Hycel B. Taylor II

Rafe Taylor

Howard Thurman

Emilie Townes

Harriet Tubman

Eboni Marshall Turman

Henry McNeal Turner

Norman Wagner

Raphael G. Warnock

William Watley

Renita J. Weems

Ralph Douglas West

Gloria White-Hammond

Alfreda L. Wiggins

Delores Williams

Jasper Williams, Sr.

Smallwood E. Williams

C. Dexter Wise III

Maceo L. Woods

Jeremiah Wright

Malcolm X

Andrew Young

Johnny Ray Youngblood

Participants in the survey were Yolanda Adams; Dwight Andrews; William J. Barber II; Traci Blackmon; Charles Blake; James Bryson, Jr.; Calvin O. Butts III; Michael Curry; Kelly Brown

Douglas; Michael Eric Dyson; Walter Fluker; Yvette Flunder; Kirk Franklin; Marla Frederick; Cheryl Townsend Gilkes; Victor J. Grigsby; Evelyn Brooks Higginbotham; Charlayne Hunter-Gault; T. D. Jakes; Vernon Jordan; John Legend; Vashti Murphy McKenzie; Otis Moss, Jr.; Otis Moss III; Brianna Parker; Yolanda Pierce; Stephen G. Ray; Eugene F. Rivers III; Cheryl J. Sanders; Al Sharpton; Martha Simmons; Thurmond N. Tillman; Eboni Marshall Turman; Jonathan L. Walton; Raphael G. Warnock; Oprah Winfrey; Jeremiah Wright; and Andrew Young.

ACKNOWLEDGMENTS

For the purposes of the four-hour PBS documentary of which this book is an extension, I had the honor to discuss the history and the religious and political implications of the Black Church as well as the significance of religion in African American history with dozens of accomplished preachers, pastors, musical artists, church members, deacons, auxiliary members, choirmasters, and scholars, many of whom are quoted in the preceding pages. Additionally, the scholarly literature on Black religion is both sophisticated and enormous. My debt to these scholars, ministers, musicians, and practitioners cannot be overstated and is acknowledged in the preceding appendix and in the notes at the conclusion of this book. Interviewing this amazing cohort and reading their scholarly works about these very issues also made clear the role the church has played and continues to play, above all else, in fostering dignity in the African American people, who, still today, are often denied the opportunity to see their own reflections or hear their own voices in so very many aspects of the broader American society.

For helping me so fully to realize the awesome significance of the Black Church and Black religious beliefs in my own life and in the lives of our people, I thank the following:

ACKNOWLEDGMENTS

This film and book would not exist if not for the remarkable series advisers, who generously shared their time and knowledge with me: Steve Bracey, Anthea Butler, Marla Frederick, Fredara Hadley, Paul Harvey, Linda Heywood, the Reverend Otis Moss III, Larry G. Murphy, Anthony B. Pinn, Barbara Savage, the Reverend Martha Simmons, John Thornton, and Judith Weisenfeld. Another group of brilliant scholars was there for me literally around the clock, answering my every question and leading me down new paths of investigation and inquiry. The companion book allows me a bit more room to roam, shall we say, and these people helped me explore topics that I could only touch on briefly in the film. I express my gratitude to David Blight, David Bromwich, Michael Eric Dyson, David Eltis, Gastón Espinosa, Cheryl Townsend Gilkes, Eddie S. Glaude, Jr., Jorge Felipe Gonzalez, Randall Kennedy, Jane Landers, Ingrid Monson, Eugene F. Rivers III, Cheryl J. Sanders, and Laurence Tribe. Evelyn Brooks Higginbotham and Cornel West are brilliant scholars as well as beloved friends who continue to educate me and inspire me, both at Harvard and at home. I have long known Dwight Andrews; this brilliant scholar was a tremendous resource for the film, but to me he will always be first and foremost the dear friend who baptized my children. And to Oprah Winfrey I owe a debt of gratitude not only for helping me pick the title of the series, but for so generously sharing her thoughts and feelings on the role of the church in her own life and in the history of the African American people.

This is my second book for Penguin Press, and once again I had the pleasure of working with my editor, Scott Moyers, whose support for my vision for this project is unsurpassed, and with his team at Penguin Random House, Mia Council and Toby Greenberg.

Then there's my research team, the three people with whom I've been blessed to work on multiple projects over the years. I am indebted to Dr. Kevin Burke for his leadership (on both book and film) and to Dr. Robert Heinrich for his meticulousness; their combined passion for American history is rivaled only by their extraordinary breadth of knowledge and outstanding research skills. Julie Wolf's editorial skills and attention to detail are unmatched. I cannot acknowledge enough the tireless efforts of this team.

The PBS documentary served as the foundation for this book, and I thank the production team at McGee Media for presenting my beloved Black Church so beautifully to a wide audience, some of whom already know its glory and others of whom are experiencing it for the first time. My heartfelt appreciation goes to my dedicated production partner and devoted friend, Dyllan McGee, and the entire production team, including John Legend, Ty Stiklorius, Mike Jackson, Stacey L. Holman, Shayla Harris, Christopher Bryson, Deborah Porfido, Kevin Burke, Robert Yacyshyn, Mark Weigel, Jennifer Weigel, Christine Fall, Chinisha Scott, Eric Thielman, Edward Bishop, Sandra Christie, Adriana Pacheco, Jason Pollard, Christine Allen, Barry Cole, Megan Graham, Matt Head, Ben Howard, Branden Janese, Nikki Junda, Gabrielle Koehler, Madeleine Lawrence, Veronica Leib, Reena Mangubat, Julia Marchesi, Nicholas Mastrangelo, Gracie Markland, James Rohan, Tony Rossi, Emily Schkolnick, Graham Smith, Katherine Swiatek, and David Raphael. Special thanks go to Caroline Bliss, who curated the most dazzling, dynamic images for both the film and the book.

ACKNOWLEDGMENTS

Funding for the PBS series was generously provided by the following: Johnson & Johnson, Lilly Endowment, the Ford Foundation, the Corporation for Public Broadcasting (CPB), and CBS. I also want to thank Sharon Percy Rockefeller, president and CEO of WETA; John Wilson, executive producer for WETA; Paula Kerger, president and CEO of PBS; Perry Simon, former chief programming executive and general manager of PBS; Bill Gardner, vice president of programming and development for PBS; Patricia de Stacy Harrison, president and CEO of CPB; Michael Levy, executive vice president and COO of CPB; and Kathryn Washington, vice president of television programming for CPB. I cannot measure the gratitude that Dyllan McGee and I have for their support of this project and all those that came before.

The film *The Black Church* was completed before the coronavirus upended the world and this nation; the book was my steady companion in the strange months that followed. In this difficult time, we have been asked to keep our distance even from those we love. To my family and friends and colleagues who sustain me, I promise you that the distance from some of you may be physical, but I always hold you close in my heart: my daughters, Maggie and Liza Gates; my son-in-law, Aaron Hatley; and my beautiful granddaughter, Ellie; as well as my literary attorney, Bennett Ashley, and my literary agents, David Kuhn and Nate Muscato. And for their support of my work in so many ways, I would like to thank my friends Elizabeth Alexander; James Basker; Larry Bobo and Marcyliena Morgan; Lonnie Bunch; Sarah Colamarino; Velma Dupont; the late Richard Gilder; my meticulous, well-organized executive assistant, Amy Gosdanian; Charlayne Hunter-Gault;

232

ACKNOWLEDGMENTS

Glenn H. Hutchins; Jamaica Kincaid; Earl Lewis; Howard and Abby Milstein; Louise Mirrer; Steven J. Niven; Terri Oliver; Braxton Shelley; Michael Sneed; Jim and Susan Swartz; Richard Taylor; Darren Walker; the Reverend Jonathan Walton; and the unflappable and brilliant administrator Dr. Abby Wolf, the executive director of Harvard's Hutchins Center. But nobody's opinions and thoughts are more important to my work than those of my wife, the historian Dr. Marial Iglesias Utset, my most faithful and careful reader and critic.

Notes

Preface

1. Darryl Pinckney, "'We Must Act Out Our Freedom,'" *New York Review of Books*, August 20, 2020, 58.
2. The quotation comes from Marx's introduction to *Critique of Hegel's Philosophy of Right*, published in 1844. See the translation by Joseph J. O'Malley (Cambridge, UK: The Press Syndicate of the University of Cambridge, 1970).
3. David Blight, email to author, August 18, 2020; David W. Blight, *Frederick Douglass: Prophet of Freedom* (New York: Simon and Schuster, 2018), 97; Robert B. Stepto, *From Behind the Veil: A Study of Afro-American Narrative* (Urbana: University of Illinois Press, 1991).
4. Thom Chandler, "John Lewis: In His Own Words," *The Georgia Sun*, https://www.thegeorgiasun.com/2020/07/18/john-lewis-in-his-own-words/.
5. Jorge Felipe Gonzalez, email to author, August 9, 2020.
6. James Weldon Johnson, *The Book of American Negro Spirituals* (New York: Viking Press, 1925), 15.
7. Henri Giles, dir., *Reflect, Reclaim, Rejoice: Preserving the Gift of Black Sacred Music* (Nashville, TN: The United Methodist Church and General Board of Discipleship, 2014), film available online at https://www.vimeo.com/84870076.

Introduction

1. "Religious Composition of Blacks," Religious Landscape Study, Pew Research Center, https://www.pewforum.org/religious-landscape-study/racial-and-ethnic-composition/black/.

Chapter One: The Freedom Faith

1. It is important to note that many Africans who were transported to North America had likely been baptized as Christians on the continent before their enslavement. The scholars Linda Heywood and John Thornton explain that in 1619, in what appears to be a rebuke of the transatlantic slave trade, the bishop of Angola, Manuel Soares, wrote a letter to the King of Portugal protesting Black Catholics being "captured and sold as slaves" in "what he saw as an illegal and very harmful military campaign conducted by the governor Luis Mendes de Vasconcellos with the support of Imbangala (Jaga) mercenaries." Linda Heywood and John Thornton, email to author, September 7, 2020; David Daniels III, "1619 and the Arrival of African Christianity," McCormick Theological Seminary, September 3, 2019, https://www.mccormick.edu/news/1619-and-arrival-african-christianity.

2. Jane Landers, *Black Society in Spanish Florida* (Urbana: University of Illinois Press, 1999), 9; Jane Landers, email to author, July 15, 2020.

3. Landers, email to author, July 15, 2020.

4. African American Heritage and Ethnography, National Park Service Park Ethnography Program, https://www.nps.gov/ethnography/aah/aaheritage/SpanishAmC.htm.

5. Linda Heywood and John Thornton, email to author, October 2, 2020.

6. W. E. B. Du Bois, *The Souls of Black Folk*, ed. Henry Louis Gates, Jr., and Terri Hume Oliver, Norton Critical Editions (New York: W. W. Norton, 1999), 123.

7. For more on the practice of Islam among African Americans, see Sylviane A. Diouf, *Servants of Allah: African Muslims Enslaved in the Americas* (New York: New York University Press, 1998); see also Diouf, *Dreams of Africa in Alabama: The Slave Ship Clotilda and the Story of the Last Africans Brought to America* (New York: Oxford University Press, 2007).

8. Albert J. Raboteau, *Slave Religion: The "Invisible Institution" in the Antebellum South* (New York: Oxford University Press, 2004), 46.

9. The interviews with men and women born in slavery that make up the Slave Narrative Collection in the Manuscript Division at the Library of Congress were conducted almost entirely by white interviewers who were instructed to transcribe their Black subjects' speech phonetically. By the late 1930s, "white representations of black speech already had an ugly history of entrenched stereotypes dating back at least to the nineteenth century. What most interviewers assumed to be 'the usual' patterns of their informants' speech was unavoidably influenced by preconceptions and stereotypes." "A Note on the Language of the

Narratives," Born in Slavery: Slave Narratives from the Federal Writers' Project, 1936 to 1938, Library of Congress Digital Collections, https://www.loc.gov/collections/slave-narratives-from-the-federal-writers-project-1936-to-1938/articles-and-essays/note-on-the-language-of-the-narratives/.

10. Melissa L. Cooper, *Making Gullah: A History of Sapelo Islanders, Race, and the American Imagination* (Chapel Hill: University of North Carolina Press, 2017), 112–13.

11. This article contains a useful timeline regarding gun ownership and the laws inhibiting it among African Americans: Steve Ekwall, "The Racist Origins of US Gun Control: Laws Designed to Disarm Slaves, Freedmen, and African-Americans," Sedgwick County, KS, website, https://www.sedgwickcounty.org/media/29093/the-racist-origins-of-us-gun-control.pdf.

12. Cooper, *Making Gullah*, 22–25; Allan D. Austin, "Salih Bilali (c. 1765–c. 1855)," *African American National Biography*, ed. Henry Louis Gates, Jr., and Evelyn Brooks Higginbotham, Oxford African American Studies Center, https://doi.org/10.1093/acref/9780195301731.013.35923.

13. Michael A. Gomez, *Black Crescent: The Experience and Legacy of African Muslims in the Americas* (Cambridge, UK: Cambridge University Press, 2005), 154–55; Allan D. Austin, *African Muslims in Antebellum America: Transatlantic Stories and Spiritual Struggles* (New York: Routledge, 1997), 5–6, see also all of chapter 5; Austin, "Salih Bilali."

14. David Eltis, email to author, April 23, 2019; "How the Autobiography of a Muslim Slave Is Challenging an American Narrative," *PBS NewsHour*, April 23, 2019; John Thornton, email to author, April 27, 2019.

15. Gomez, *Black Crescent*, 152–53, 156–57; C. Eric Lincoln and Lawrence H. Mamiya, *The Black Church in the African American Experience* (Durham, NC: Duke University Press, 1990; reprint 2003), Kindle loc. 6210; Austin, *African Muslims in Antebellum America*, 98.

16. Austin, *African Muslims in Antebellum America*, 53–54, see also all of chapter 3; Allan D. Austin, "Jallo, Job ben Solomon (1702?–1773)," *African American National Biography*, ed. Henry Louis Gates, Jr., and Evelyn Brooks Higginbotham, Oxford African American Studies Center, https://doi.org/10.1093/acref/9780195301731.013.37188; David J. Peavler, "Solomon, Job Ben," *Encyclopedia of African American History, 1619–1895: From the Colonial Period to the Age of Frederick Douglass*, ed. Paul Finkelman, Oxford African American Studies Center, https://doi.org/10.1093/acref/9780195301731.013.45038; Gomez, *Black Crescent*, 167.

17. Austin, *African Muslims in Antebellum America*, 54–56; Austin, "Jallo, Job ben Solomon"; Gomez, *Black Crescent*, 167; Peavler, "Solomon, Job Ben."

18. Gomez, *Black Crescent*, 168; Austin, *African Muslims in Antebellum America*, 8, see also all of chapter 7; Allan D. Austin, "Said, Umar ibn (c. 1770–1863)," *African American National Biography*, ed. Henry Louis Gates, Jr., and Evelyn Brooks Higginbotham, Oxford African American Studies Center, https://doi.org/10.1093/acref/9780195301731.013.37799; Omar Ibn Said Collection, Library of Congress, https://www.loc.gov/collections/omar-ibn-said-collection/about-this-collection/; John Franklin Jameson, ed., "Autobiography of Omar ibn Said, Slave in North Carolina, 1831," *The American Historical Review* 30, no. 4 (July 1925): 787–95, https://docsouth.unc.edu/nc/omarsaid/omarsaid.html.

19. Katharine Gerbner, *Christian Slavery: Conversion and Race in the Protestant Atlantic World* (Philadelphia: University of Pennsylvania Press, 2018), Kindle loc. 54–84, 1761; Randall Kennedy, email to author, September 12, 2020; Laurence Tribe, email to author, September 12, 2020.

20. Gerbner, *Christian Slavery*, Kindle loc. 84–99.

21. Gerbner, *Christian Slavery*, Kindle loc. 1253–77; Paul Harvey, *Through the Storm, Through the Night: A History of African American Christianity* (Lanham, MD: Rowman and Littlefield, 2011), Kindle loc. 636.

22. Morgan Godwyn, "Proposals for the Carrying on the Negro's Christianity," 1681, http://www.swarthmore.edu/SocSci/bdorsey1/41docs/58-goo.html.

23. Harvey, *Through the Storm, Through the Night*, Kindle loc. 636.

24. Gerbner, *Christian Slavery*, Kindle loc. 3826–30.

25. Gomez, *Black Crescent*, 152–53, 156–57; Lincoln and Mamiya, *The Black Church in the African American Experience*, Kindle loc. 6210; Austin, *African Muslims in Antebellum America*, 98.

26. Harvey, *Through the Storm, Through the Night*, Kindle loc. 636; Eddie S. Glaude, Jr., *African American Religion: A Very Short Introduction* (New York: Oxford University Press, 2014), 34.

27. Harvey, *Through the Storm, Through the Night*, Kindle loc. 729–72; Thomas E. Carney, "Catholic Church and African Americans," *Encyclopedia of African American History, 1619–1895: From the Colonial Period to the Age of Frederick Douglass*, ed. Paul Finkelman, Oxford African American Studies Center, https://doi.org/10.1093/acref/9780195301731.013.44613.

28. Raboteau, *Slave Religion*, 212.

29. These and more than 2,300 other WPA narratives are transcribed at Born in Slavery: Slave Narratives from the Federal Writers' Project, 1936 to 1938, Library of Congress Digital Collections, https://www.loc.gov/collections/slave-narratives-from-the-federal-writers-project-1936-to-1938/about-this-collection/.

30. Harvey, *Through the Storm, Through the Night*, Kindle loc. 1096–111.
31. Paul Harvey, email to author, August 8, 2020.
32. Lincoln and Mamiya, *The Black Church in the African American Experience*, Kindle loc. 671–85.
33. Harvey, *Through the Storm, Through the Night*, Kindle loc. 1096–111; Edward A. Hatfield, "First African Baptist Church," *New Georgia Encyclopedia*, https://www.georgiaencyclopedia.org/articles/arts-culture/first -african-baptist-church; Milton C. Sernett, "Bryan, Andrew," *Africana: The Encyclopedia of the African and African American Experience*, 2nd ed., ed. Kwame Anthony Appiah and Henry Louis Gates, Jr., Oxford African American Studies Center, https://doi.org/10.1093/acref/9780195301731 .013.40510.
34. Hatfield, "First African Baptist Church"; Leslie Hildreth, "Missionaries You Should Know: George Liele," International Mission Board, June 26, 2018, https://www.imb.org/2018/06/26/missionaries-you-should-know -george-liele/; Sernett, "Bryan, Andrew."
35. Richard Newman, *Freedom's Prophet: Bishop Richard Allen, the AME Church, and the Black Founding Fathers* (New York: New York University Press, 2009), 48, 169–75.
36. Peter Hudson, "African Methodist Episcopal Zion Church," *Africana: The Encyclopedia of the African and African American Experience*, 2nd ed., ed. Kwame Anthony Appiah and Henry Louis Gates, Jr., Oxford African American Studies Center, https://doi.org/10.1093/acref/9780195301731 .013.39876; Newman, *Freedom's Prophet*, 180; Glaude, *African American Religion*, 49.
37. Jarena Lee, *Religious Experience and Journal of Mrs. Jarena Lee, Giving an Account of Her Call to Preach the Gospel*, rev. ed. (Philadelphia: Printed and published for the author, 1849), 11.
38. Lee, *Religious Experience and Journal*, 17.
39. "African Methodist Episcopal Church Posthumously Ordains Woman Preacher," First Friday Letter: World Methodist Council (April 2016), http://firstfridayletter.worldmethodistcouncil.org/2016/04/african -methodist-episcopal-church-posthumously-ordainsfirst-womp/.
40. Carney, "Catholic Church and African Americans."
41. Carney, "Catholic Church and African Americans"; Stephen Smith and Kate Ellis, "Shackled Legacy: History Shows Slavery Helped Build Many U.S. Colleges and Universities," *American Public Media Reports*, September 4, 2017, https://www.apmreports.org/episode/2017/09 /04/shackled-legacy; Rachel L. Swarns, "272 Slaves Were Sold to Save Georgetown. What Does It Owe Their Descendants?" *New York*

Times, April 16, 2016, https://www.nytimes.com/2016/04/17/us/george
town-university-search-for-slave-descendants.html; Adam Rothman,
"Georgetown University and the Business of Slavery," *Washington History* 29, no. 2 (Fall 2017): 18.

42. "Trans-Atlantic Slave Trade-Estimates," Slave Voyages, https://slave
voyages.org/estimates/liyiPFPK.

43. David Eltis, email to author, July 16, 2020.

44. Eltis, email to author, July 16, 2020.

45. The scholar Michael P. Johnson has cast doubt on whether Vesey planned
an uprising at all. See especially Michael P. Johnson, "Denmark Vesey
and His Co-Conspirators," *The William and Mary Quarterly* 58, no. 4
(2001): 915–76 and "Reading Evidence," *The William and Mary Quarterly*
59, no. 1 (2002): 193–202. For more on Johnson's work see Dinitia Smith,
"Think Tank; Challenging the History of a Slave Conspiracy," *New
York Times*, February 23, 2002, https://www.nytimes.com/2002/02/23
/arts/think-tank-challenging-the-history-of-a-slave-conspiracy.html;
and Olivia Waxman, "The Most Important Slave Revolt That Never
Happened," *Time*, March 15, 2017, http://time.com/4701283/denmark
-vesey-history-charleston-south-carolina/.

46. "The Confessions of Nat Turner," *Africans in America*, PBS, http://www
.pbs.org/wgbh/aia/part3/3h500t.html.

47. Eddie S. Glaude, Jr., *Exodus!: Religion, Race, and Nation in Early Nineteenth-
Century Black America* (Chicago: University of Chicago Press, 2000), 167.

48. Frederick Douglass, "Men of Color, To Arms!" broadside, Rochester,
NY, March 21, 1863.

Chapter Two: A Nation within a Nation

1. Adam McNeil, "Black Women's Anti-Colonizationist Political Thought,"
Black Perspectives, African American Intellectual History Society
(AAIHS), February 22, 2019, https://www.aaihs.org/black-womens-anti
-colonizationist-political-thought/.

2. Steven Mintz, "Historical Context: Black Soldiers in the Civil War,"
History Resources, The Gilder Lehrman Institute of American History,
https://www.gilderlehrman.org/history-resources/teaching-resource
/historical-context-black-soldiers-civil-war.

3. Henry McNeal Turner, Chaplain Letters: 1864–1865, *The Christian Recorder*, September 24, 1864, online at The #HMTProject, http://www
.thehenrymcnealturnerproject.org/2017/07/army-correspondence
-september-24-1864.html; see also Jean Lee Cole, ed., *Freedom's Witness:*

NOTES

The Civil War Correspondence of Henry McNeal Turner (Morgantown: West Virginia University Press, 2013).

4. Phyl Garland, *The Sound of Soul: The Story of Black Music* (Chicago: Henry Regnery Company, 1969), 86; Robert Darden, *People Get Ready!: A New History of Black Gospel Music* (New York: Continuum, 2004), 7.

5. W. E. B. Du Bois, *The Souls of Black Folk*, ed. Henry Louis Gates, Jr., and Terri Hume Oliver, Norton Critical Editions (New York: W. W. Norton, 1999), 120.

6. Angela M. Nelson, "Spirituals," *Encyclopedia of African American History, 1619–1895: From the Colonial Period to the Age of Frederick Douglass*, Oxford African American Studies Center, https://doi.org/10.1093/acref/9780195301731.013.45045.

7. Thomas Wentworth Higginson, "Negro Spirituals," *The Atlantic Monthly*, June 1867, https://www.theatlantic.com/past/docs/issues/1867jun/spirit.htm.

8. Paul Harvey, *Through the Storm, Through the Night: A History of African American Christianity* (Lanham, MD: Rowman and Littlefield, 2011), Kindle loc. 1379–1405.

9. Ingrid Monson, email to author, July 17, 2020.

10. James Weldon Johnson, *The Book of American Negro Spirituals* (New York: Viking Press, 1925), 20; Harvey, *Through the Storm, Through the Night*, Kindle loc. 1416–37; Nelson, "Spirituals."

11. Calvin Reid, "Albert Murray: Conditioned to Deal with the Blues," *Publishers Weekly*, February 26, 1996, https://www.publishersweekly.com/pw/by-topic/authors/profiles/article/71085-albert-murray-conditioned-to-deal-with-the-blues.html.

12. Vincent Harding, *There Is a River: The Black Struggle for Freedom in America* (San Diego, CA: Harvest, 1981), 262–63; interview with Garrison Frazier, "Minutes of an Interview between the Colored Ministers and Church Officers at Savannah with the Secretary of War and Major-Gen. Sherman," January 12, 1865, as reported in *The New York Daily Tribune*, February 13, 1865, http://www.freedmen.umd.edu/savmtg.htm.

13. Eric Foner, *Reconstruction: America's Unfinished Revolution, 1863–1877*, updated ed. (New York: Harper Perennial, 2014), Kindle loc. 1754–75; Russell Duncan, "Tunis Campbell (1812–1891)," *New Georgia Encyclopedia*, https://www.georgiaencyclopedia.org/articles/arts-culture/tunis-campbell-1812-1891.

14. Oliver Vernon Burton with Wilbur Cross, *Penn Center: A History Preserved* (Athens: University of Georgia Press, 2014), 16–17, 21, 24–25.

NOTES

15. Martin Luther King, Jr., interview on *Meet the Press*, April 17, 1960, The Martin Luther King Papers, http://okra.stanford.edu/transcription/document_images/Vol05Scans/17Apr1960_InterviewonMeetthePress.pdf.

16. Harvey, *Through the Storm, Through the Night*, Kindle loc. 1817–52; James Sellman, "Turner, Henry McNeal," *Africana: The Encyclopedia of the African and African American Experience*, 2nd ed., ed. Kwame Anthony Appiah and Henry Louis Gates, Jr., Oxford African American Studies Center, https://doi.org/10.1093/acref/9780195301731.013.43703.

17. Daniel Alexander Payne, *Recollections of Seventy Years* (Nashville, TN: Publishing House of the AME Sunday School Union, 1888), 19, 27, 41–46, 72, 108, https://docsouth.unc.edu/church/payne70/payne.html; "Daniel Payne," *This Far by Faith*, PBS, https://www.pbs.org/thisfarbyfaith/people/daniel_payne.html; Thomas E. Carney and Sylvia Frey, "African Methodist Episcopal Church," *Encyclopedia of African American History, 1619–1895: From the Colonial Period to the Age of Frederick Douglass*, Oxford African American Studies Center, https://doi.org/10.1093/acref/9780195301731.013.44522.

18. Reginald F. Hildebrand, *The Times Were Strange and Stirring: Methodist Preachers and the Crisis of Emancipation* (Durham, NC: Duke University Press, 1995), 50, 55.

19. Charles Rosenberg, "Broughton, Virginia E. Walker," *African American National Biography*, ed. Henry Louis Gates, Jr., and Evelyn Brooks Higginbotham, Oxford African American Studies Center, https://doi.org/10.1093/acref/9780195301731.013.38534.

20. Evelyn Brooks Higginbotham, "Women and the Black Baptist Church," *Africana: The Encyclopedia of the African and African American Experience*, 2nd ed., ed. Kwame Anthony Appiah and Henry Louis Gates, Jr., Oxford African American Studies Center, https://doi.org/10.1093/acref/9780195301731.013.43924.

21. Payne, *Recollections of Seventy Years*, 253–54.

22. William Francis Allen, Charles Pickard Ware, and Lucy McKim Garrison, *Slave Songs of the United States* (New York: A. Simpson and Co., 1866), esp. iii, https://docsouth.unc.edu/church/allen/allen.html; Nelson, "Spirituals."

23. Gayle Murchison, "Work, John Wesley, Jr. (1873–1925)," *Africana: The Encyclopedia of the African and African American Experience*, 2nd ed., ed. Kwame Anthony Appiah and Henry Louis Gates, Jr., Oxford African American Studies Center, https://doi.org/10.1093/acref/9780195301731.013.36602.

24. Eric Foner, *Freedom's Lawmakers: A Directory of Black Officeholders during Reconstruction* (New York: Oxford University Press, 1993), xxi.

25. Evelyn Brooks Higginbotham, *Righteous Discontent: The Women's Movement in the Black Baptist Church, 1880–1920* (Cambridge, MA: Harvard University Press, 1994), 6, 65.
26. Du Bois, *The Souls of Black Folk*, 120.
27. Cheryl Townsend Gilkes, email to author, September 28, 2020.
28. Zora Neale Hurston, *The Sanctified Church* (New York: Marlowe & Company, 1981), 104.
29. Cheryl Townsend Gilkes, email to author, October 5, 2020.
30. Estrelda Y. Alexander, *Black Fire: One Hundred Years of African American Pentecostalism* (Downers Grove, IL: InterVarsity Press, 2011), Kindle loc. 122–31, 139–43.
31. Alexander, *Black Fire*, Kindle loc. 139–41; Robert Mapes Anderson, *Vision of the Disinherited: The Making of American Pentecostalism* (New York: Oxford University Press, 1979).
32. Cheryl Townsend Gilkes, email to author, July 21, 2020.
33. Gilkes, email to author, October 5, 2020.
34. Cheryl J. Sanders, email to author, July 23, 2020.
35. Tinney had a varied career, establishing himself as a pastor, a journalist, a speechwriter, and a professor. A gay man, he founded the Pentecostal Coalition for Human Rights and was excommunicated from the Temple Church of God in Christ, where he served as a lay minister, after staging a Lesbian-Gay Revival in 1982. He went on to establish the nondenominational Faith Temple in Washington, D.C., with a congregation consisting primarily of gay and lesbian Black men and women. In 1988, at age forty-six, Tinney died of complications related to AIDS. "Dr. James S. Tinney, Profile," LGBTQ Religious Archives Network, www.lgbtqreligiousarchives.org/profiles/james-s-tinney.
36. James S. Tinney, "William Seymour: Father of Modern-Day Pentecostalism," in *Black Apostles: Afro-American Clergy Confront the Twentieth Century*, ed. Randall K. Burkett and Richard Newman (Boston: G. K. Hall, 1978), 213–14. The author wishes to express his gratitude to the Reverend Sanders for bringing Tinney's work to his attention.

Chapter Three: God Will Make a Way

1. Lerone A. Martin, *Preaching on Wax: The Phonograph and the Shaping of Modern African American Religion* (New York: New York University Press, 2014), 103; Lerone A. Martin, "Selling to the Souls of Black Folk: Atlanta, Reverend J. M. Gates, the Phonograph, and the Transformation of African American Protestantism and Culture, 1910–1945," M.Div. Diss., Princeton Theological Seminary, 2005, 150.

2. Robert Darden, *People Get Ready!: A New History of Black Gospel Music* (New York: Continuum, 2004), 1.

3. Cheryl Townsend Gilkes, email to author, September 28, 2020.

4. Wallace D. Best, *Passionately Human, No Less Divine: Religion and Culture in Black Chicago, 1915–1952* (Princeton, NJ: Princeton University Press, 2013), 40–43; Christopher Robert Reed, *The Rise of Chicago's Black Metropolis, 1920–1929* (Urbana: University of Illinois Press, 2011), 197–98; Hans A. Baer and Merrill Singer, *African American Religion: Voices of Protest and Accommodation*, 2nd ed. (Knoxville: University of Tennessee Press, 2002), 189–90; St. Sukie de la Croix, *Chicago Whispers: A History of LGBT Chicago before Stonewall* (Madison: University of Wisconsin Press, 2012), 155–56; First Church of Deliverance, City of Chicago Landmark Designation Reports (Chicago: City of Chicago, 1981), 10–11, https://ia800702.us.archive.org/5/items/CityOfChicagoLandmarkDesignation Reports/FirstChurchOfDeliverance.pdf.

5. de la Croix, *Chicago Whispers*, 156–57; First Church of Deliverance, City of Chicago Landmark Designation Reports, 11.

6. de la Croix, *Chicago Whispers*, 156–58.

7. "Noted Chicago Pastor, Clarence Cobbs, 71, Dies," *Jet*, July 19, 1979.

8. First Church of Deliverance, City of Chicago Landmark Designation Reports, 12–16; Best, *Passionately Human*, 189.

9. Geoffrey Himes, "Shout It! Gospel according to Shirley Caesar," *Washington Post*, April 3, 1987, https://www.washingtonpost.com/archive/life style/1987/04/03/shout-it-gospel-according-to-shirley-caesar/9bf81ba8 -1d9e-400a-8500-1bb1ea4ee5ac/?utm_term=.0e8f0969eade.

10. Marshanda Smith, "Caesar (Williams), Shirley Ann," *Black Women in America*, 2nd ed., ed. Darlene Clark Hine, Oxford African American Studies Center, https://doi.org/10.1093/acref/9780195301731.013.44059; Gayle Murchison, "Caesar, Shirley Ann," *African American National Biography*, ed. Henry Louis Gates, Jr., and Evelyn Brooks Higginbotham, Oxford African American Studies Center, https://doi.org/10 .1093/acref/9780195301731.013.36354.

11. Shirley Caesar, "Fighting the Good Fight" (2013), AZLyrics, https://www.azlyrics.com/lyrics/shirleycaesar/fightingthegoodfight.html.

12. Darden, *People Get Ready!*, 131, 182; James Sellman, "Gospel Music," *Africana: The Encyclopedia of the African and African American Experience*, 2nd ed., ed. Kwame Anthony Appiah and Henry Louis Gates, Jr., Oxford African American Studies Center, https://doi.org/10.1093/acref/9780195 301731.013.41490; Robert Darden, *Nothing But Love in God's Water*, vol. 1, *Black Sacred Music from the Civil War to the Civil Rights Movement* (University Park: Pennsylvania State University Press, 2014), 1, 88–91.

NOTES

13. Warren C. Platt, "The African Orthodox Church: An Analysis of Its First Decade," *Church History* 58, no. 4 (1989): 474–88.
14. Peniel E. Joseph, *The Sword and the Shield: The Revolutionary Lives of Malcolm X and Martin Luther King Jr.* (New York: Basic Books, 2020), 33.
15. For many Americans, for the last several decades, the public face of the Nation of Islam has been Louis Farrakhan. A polarizing figure, he is lauded for his exceptionally powerful organizational abilities and calls for Black political self-determination but is held at arm's length by many religious and political leaders, both Black and white, for his virulently anti-Semitic rhetoric. For more on Black-Jewish history and relations in the United States, see Marc Dollinger, *Black Power, Jewish Politics: Reinventing the Alliance in the 1960s*, Brandeis Series in American Jewish History, Culture, and Life (Waltham, MA: Brandeis University Press, 2018); Cheryl Lynn Greenberg, *Troubling the Waters: Black-Jewish Relations in the American Century*, Politics and Society in Modern America (Princeton, NJ: Princeton University Press, 2006); and Jack Salzman and Cornel West, *Struggles in the Promised Land: Towards a History of Black-Jewish Relations in the United States* (Cary, NC: Oxford University Press, 1997).
16. "Ebenezer Baptist Church," *King Encyclopedia*, https://kinginstitute .stanford.edu/encyclopedia/ebenezer-baptist-church-atlanta-georgia. Notably, Martin Luther King, Sr., was born Michael King, and he passed the name Michael to his oldest son. In 1934 King, Sr., traveled to Germany and bore witness to the rise of Nazism. But Germany was also the birthplace of Protestantism. Explains King's biographer, Clayborne Carson: "Daddy King himself said he changed the name because he had an uncle named Martin and an uncle named Luther, and he was following his father's wishes to change the name. But it seems likely he was affected by the trip to Berlin because that would have brought him in the land of Martin Luther. I think the obvious reason is Martin Luther sounded more distinguished than Mike King." That same year, sometime after his return home, he changed both his name and his son's to Martin Luther. Deneen L. Brown, "The Story of How Michael King Jr. Became Martin Luther King Jr.," *Washington Post*, January 15, 2019.
17. "Taylor, Gardner C.," *King Encyclopedia*, https://kinginstitute.stanford .edu/encyclopedia/taylor-gardner-c; "Progressive National Baptist Convention (PNBC)," *King Encyclopedia*, https://kinginstitute.stanford.edu /encyclopedia/progressive-national-baptist-convention-pnbc; "Jackson, Joseph Harrison," *King Encyclopedia*, https://kinginstitute.stanford.edu /encyclopedia/jackson-joseph-harrison; Sarah Pulliam Bailey, "Civil Rights Leader, Friend of MLK and Iconic Preacher Gardner C. Taylor

NOTES

Has Died," *Washington Post*, April 5, 2015, https://www.washingtonpost
.com/news/acts-of-faith/wp/2015/04/05/dean-of-americas-preachers
-and-civil-rights-leader-gardner-c-taylor-has-died/.

18. "Freedom Singers," SNCC Digital Gateway, https://snccdigital.org
/inside-sncc/sncc-national-office/freedom-singers/; Robert Darden,
Nothing But Love in God's Water, vol. 2, *Black Sacred Music from Sit-Ins
to Resurrection City* (University Park: Pennsylvania State University
Press, 2016), Kindle loc. 2809, 4151; "The Freedom Singers," *American
Roots Music*, PBS, https://www.pbs.org/americanrootsmusic/pbs_arm_saa
_freedomsingers.html.

19. "Baker, Ella Josephine," *King Encyclopedia*, https://kinginstitute.stanford
.edu/encyclopedia/baker-ella-josephine; "Ella Baker," SNCC Digital
Gateway, https://snccdigital.org/people/ella-baker/.

20. For an excellent analysis of the converging paths of these two iconic figures, see Joseph, *The Sword and the Shield*.

21. "Poor People's Campaign, May 12, 1968–June 24, 1968," *King Encyclopedia*,
https://kinginstitute.stanford.edu/encyclopedia/poor-peoples-campaign.

Chapter Four: Crisis of Faith

1. Matthew J. Cressler, "The History of Black Catholics in America," *Smith-
sonian Magazine*, June 7, 2018, https://www.smithsonianmag.com/history
/history-black-catholics-in-america-180969271/; Matthew J. Cressler,
*Authentically Black and Truly Catholic: The Rise of Black Catholicism in the
Great Migration* (New York: New York University Press, 2017), 131.

2. *Good Times*, "Black Jesus," February 1974, https://www.youtube.com
/watch?v=UPguBFKcxRQ. For more on the fascinating history of this
episode, see James Hill, "The Breakdown: Black Jesus on *Good Times*,"
September 2, 2016, https://tvone.tv/38322/the-breakdown-black-jesus
-on-good-times/; Robin R. Means Coleman and Novotny Lawrence,
"FIX IT BLACK JESUS: The Iconography of Christ in *Good Times*,"
Religions 10, no. 7 (2019): 410, https://doi.org/10.3390/rel10070410.

3. Barbara Dianne Savage, *Your Spirits Walk beside Us: The Politics of Black
Religion* (Cambridge, MA: The Belknap Press of Harvard University
Press, 2008), Kindle loc. 2927–28, 2957, 2978.

4. Eddie S. Glaude, Jr., *African American Religion: A Very Short Introduction*
(New York: Oxford University Press, 2014), 85–86.

5. Beretta E. Smith-Shomade, "Womanist Theology," in *Black Women in
America*, 2nd ed., ed. Darlene Clark Hine, Oxford African American
Studies Center, https://doi.org/10.1093/acref/9780195301731.013.44487.

6. Glaude, *African American Religion*, 86.

7. O. C. Allen Biography, Vision Church of Atlanta, http://www.thevision
church.org/bishop-o-c-allen-iii/; "Our History," Vision Church of Atlanta, http://www.thevisionchurch.org/our-history/; Joicelyn Dingle,
"The Coolest Black Family in America, No. 10: The Burgess-Allens,"
Ebony, April 1, 2013, https://www.ebony.com/life/the-coolest-black
-family-in-america-no-10-393/; Darian Aaron, "The Vision Church
of Atlanta: Moving from Vision to Victory," *The Georgia Voice*, January
21, 2016, https://thegavoice.com/faith/the-vision-church-of-atl-moving
-from-vision-to-victory/.

8. Aaron, "The Vision Church of Atlanta"; O. C. Allen Biography, Vision
Church of Atlanta.

9. Cornel West, email to author, October 21, 2020; "The History of the
House of the Lord & Church on the Mount: Official Orientation Material," 6, 9, https://www.readkong.com/page/the-history-of-the-house
-of-the-lord-4664236?; Nathan Carpenter, "In Bittersweet Move, House
of the Lord Fellowship Finds New Space," *The Oberlin Review*, December 13, 2019, https://oberlinreview.org/20121/arts/in-bittersweet-move
-house-of-the-lord-fellowship-finds-new-space/; Henry Louis Gates, Jr.,
and Kevin M. Burke, *And Still I Rise: Black America since MLK, an Illustrated Chronology* (New York: HarperCollins, 2015), 108–9.

10. Paul Harvey, *Through the Storm, Through the Night: A History of African
American Christianity* (Lanham, MD: Rowman and Littlefield, 2011),
Kindle loc. 2892; Glaude, *African American Religion*, 85; Albert J. Rabo-
teau, *Canaan Land: A Religious History of African Americans* (New York:
Oxford University Press, 2001), Kindle loc. 1212.

11. Savage, *Your Spirits Walk beside Us*, Kindle loc. 2839.

12. For a brief account of an aborted protest against gangsta rap staged by
Butts in Harlem, see Clifford J. Levy, "Harlem Protest of Rap Lyrics
Draws Debate and Steamroller," *New York Times*, June 6, 1993, https://
www.nytimes.com/1993/06/06/nyregion/harlem-protest-of-rap-lyrics
-draws-debate-and-steamroller.html.

13. I wrote about income inequality and how the continuing fight for racial
justice manifested itself on college campuses in "Black America and the
Class Divide," *New York Times*, February 1, 2016, https://www.nytimes
.com/2016/02/07/education/edlife/black-america-and-the-class-divide
.html.

14. Eddie S. Glaude, Jr., email to author, August 7, 2020.

15. For a comprehensive biography of Father Divine, see Jill Watts, *God,
Harlem U.S.A.: The Father Divine Story* (Berkeley: University of California Press, 1992).

16. Emily Badger, "Whites Have Huge Wealth Edge over Blacks (but Don't Know It)," *New York Times*, September 18, 2017, https://www.nytimes.com/interactive/2017/09/18/upshot/black-white-wealth-gap-perceptions.html.
17. Jonathan L. Walton, *Watch This!: The Ethics and Aesthetics of Black Televangelism* (New York: New York University Press, 2009), 81.
18. T. D. Jakes, "What Is the Prosperity Gospel?" TDJakes.com, https://www.tdjakes.com/posts/what-is-the-prosperity-gospel.
19. Walton, *Watch This!*, 113–14.
20. Gates and Burke, *And Still I Rise*, 237.
21. Savage, *Your Spirits Walk beside Us*, Kindle loc. 2957–58.
22. Cheryl Townsend Gilkes, email to author, September 28, 2020.
23. William J. Barber II, "We Are Witnessing the Birth Pangs of a Third Reconstruction," *ThinkProgress*, December 15, 2016, https://thinkprogress.org/rev-barber-moral-change-1ad2776df7c/.
24. Barber, "We Are Witnessing the Birth Pangs of a Third Reconstruction."
25. Black Church Political Action Committee website, https://www.blackchurchpac.org/; Leah Daughtry, "As Democrats Vie for African American Votes, the Black Church Is Paying Attention," *Religion News Service*, August 20, 2019, https://religionnews.com/2019/08/20/as-democrats-vie-for-african-american-votes-the-black-church-is-paying-attention/; Mariel Turner, "Black Church Action Fund, Vote.org Launch Digital Vote-by-Mail Campaign for Black Faith Voters," *The Grio*, May 29, 2020, https://thegrio.com/2020/05/29/black-church-action-fund-vote-org-campaign/.
26. "Covid in the U.S.: Latest Map and Case Count," *New York Times*, https://www.nytimes.com/interactive/2020/us/coronavirus-us-cases.html.
27. Jeremy A. W. Gold, et al., "Race, Ethnicity and Age Trends in Persons Who Died from COVID-19, United States, May–August, 2020," *Centers for Disease Control and Prevention Morbidity and Mortality Weekly Report*, October 16, 2020; David Williams, email to author, October 28, 2020; APM Research Lab Staff, "The Color of Coronavirus: COVID-19 Deaths by Race and Ethnicity in the U.S.," October 15, 2020, https://www.apmresearchlab.org/covid/deaths-by-race.
28. Michelle Boorstein, "Covid-19 Has Killed Multiple Bishops and Pastors within the Nation's Largest Black Pentecostal Denomination," *Washington Post*, April 19, 2020, https://www.washingtonpost.com/religion/2020/04/19/church-of-god-in-christ-pentecostal-coronavirus-kills-bishops/.
29. "To Combat Disparities, Black Churches in Dallas Offer Coronavirus Testing," NPR, June 13, 2020, https://www.npr.org/sections/health-shots

/2020/06/13/874950245/to-combat-disparities-black-churches-in-dallas -offer-coronavirus-testing/.

30. Andre Kimo Stone Guess, "In the Age of the Coronavirus, Touching and Reaching Souls Is Different Now for the Black Church," *The Undefeated*, March 23, 2020, https://theundefeated.com/features/in-age-of -the-coronavirus-touching-and-reaching-souls-is-different-now-for-the -black-church/.

31. Guess, "In the Age of the Coronavirus."

32. Richard Fausset, "Two Weapons, a Chase, a Killing and No Charges," *New York Times*, April 26, 2020, https://www.nytimes.com/2020/04/26 /us/ahmed-arbery-shooting-georgia.html; Eliott C. McLaughlin, "Ahmaud Arbery Was Hit with a Truck Before He Died, and His Killer Allegedly Used a Racial Slur, Investigator Testifies," CNN, June 4, 2020, https://www.cnn.com/2020/06/04/us/mcmichaels-hearing-ahmaud -arbery/index.html.

33. Sarah Maslin Nir, "White Woman Is Fired after Calling Police on Black Man in Central Park," *New York Times*, May 26, 2020, https://www.ny times.com/2020/05/26/nyregion/amy-cooper-dog-central-park.html.

34. Evan Hill, Ainara Tiefenthäler, Christiaan Triebert, et al., "How George Floyd Was Killed in Police Custody," *New York Times*, May 31, 2020, updated July 8, 2020, https://www.nytimes.com/2020/05/31/us/george -floyd-investigation.html; Nicholas Bogel-Burroughs, "8 Minutes, 46 Seconds Became a Symbol in George Floyd's Death. The Exact Time Is Less Clear," *New York Times*, June 18, 2020, updated June 20, 2020, https://www.nytimes.com/2020/06/18/us/george-floyd-timing.html.

35. Bogel-Burroughs, "8 Minutes, 46 Seconds Became a Symbol in George Floyd's Death."

36. Richard A. Oppel, Jr., and Derrick Bryson Taylor, "Here's What You Need to Know about Breonna Taylor's Death," *New York Times*, July 9, 2020, https://www.nytimes.com/article/breonna-taylor-police.html; Kay Jones, Carma Hassan, and Leah Asmelash, "A Kentucky EMT Was Shot and Killed during a Police Raid of Her Home. The Family Is Suing for Wrongful Death," CNN, May 13, 2020, https://www.cnn.com/2020/05/13/us /louisville-police-emt-killed-trnd/index.html; Theresa Waldrop, Ray Sanchez, and Elizabeth Joseph, "Officer Fired in Shooting Death of Breonna Taylor, Louisville Police Say," CNN, June 23, 2020, https://www.cnn .com/2020/06/23/us/breonna-taylor-shooting-officer-fired/index.html.

37. Larry Buchanan, Quoctrung Bui, and Jugal K. Patel, "Black Lives Matter May Be the Largest Movement in U.S. History," *New York Times*, July 3, 2020, https://www.nytimes.com/interactive/2020/07/03/us/george -floyd-protests-crowd-size.html.

38. "Reverend Al Sharpton George Floyd Funeral Eulogy Transcript June 9," Rev Transcripts, June 9, 2020, https://www.rev.com/blog/transcripts /reverend-al-sharpton-george-floyd-funeral-eulogy-transcript-june-9.

39. Stuart Emmrich, "The Most Moving Moment of Al Sharpton's Eulogy for George Floyd," *Vogue*, June 10, 2020, https://www.vogue.com/article /al-sharpton-george-floyd-funeral-eulogy.

40. Madeleine Carlisle, "Reverend William Barber: George Floyd Protests Represent Call to Address Systemic Racism and Poverty in U.S.," *Yahoo! News*, June 4, 2020, https://news.yahoo.com/rev-william-barber-george -floyd-004019598.html.

Epilogue: On the Holy Ghost: The Beautiful and the Sublime, the Vision and the Trance

1. Gastón Espinosa, email to author, July 25, 2020.

2. Cheryl Townsend Gilkes, email to author, July 21, 2020.

3. Cheryl Townsend Gilkes, email to author, July 22, 2020. See chapter 2 for more on the birth of Pentecostalism.

4. Gilkes, email to author, July 22, 2020.

5. W. E. B. Du Bois, *The Philadelphia Negro: A Social Study* (Philadelphia: Published for the University, 1899), 220–21.

6. Cheryl J. Sanders, email to author, July 23, 2020.

7. W. E. B. Du Bois, *The Souls of Black Folk*, ed. Henry Louis Gates, Jr., and Terri Hume Oliver, Norton Critical Editions (New York: W. W. Norton, 1999), 120.

8. Cheryl Townsend Gilkes, email to author, September 28, 2020.

9. Arthur Huff Fauset, *Black Gods of the Metropolis: Negro Religious Cults of the Urban North* (Philadelphia: University of Pennsylvania Press, 1971), 82.

10. Barbara Dianne Savage, foreword to Fauset, *Black Gods of the Metropolis*, x.

11. Quoted in Wilson Jeremiah Moses, *Alexander Crummell: A Study of Civilization and Discontent* (New York: Oxford University Press, 1989), 182, 212.

12. Espinosa, email to author, July 25, 2020.

13. For more on the link between African traditions and spirit possession, see Albert Raboteau, *Slave Religion: The "Invisible Institution" in the Antebellum South* (New York: Oxford University Press, 2004), 55–75; see also Cheryl J. Sanders, *Saints in Exile: The Holiness-Pentecostal Experience in African American Religion and Culture* (New York: Oxford University Press, 1996), esp. 58–63.

14. See Henry Louis Gates, Jr., "Foreword: The Politics of 'Negro Folklore,'" in *The Annotated African American Folktales*, ed. Henry Louis Gates, Jr., and Maria Tatar (New York: Liveright, 2018).

15. David Bromwich, email to author, July 25, 2020, referencing Edmund Burke, *A Philosophical Enquiry into the Origin of Our Ideas of the Sublime and Beautiful*, part 4, section 18.

Recommended Reading

Alexander, Estrelda Y. *Black Fire: One Hundred Years of African American Pentecostalism*. Downers Grove, IL: InterVarsity Press, 2011.

Allen, William Francis, Charles Pickard Ware, and Lucy McKim Garrison. *Slave Songs of the United States*. New York: A. Simpson and Co., 1866, esp. iii. https://docsouth.unc.edu/church/allen/allen.html.

Anderson, Robert Mapes. *Vision of the Disinherited: The Making of American Pentecostalism*. New York: Oxford University Press, 1979.

Andrews, William L. *Sisters of the Spirit: Thee Black Women's Autobiographies of the Nineteenth Century*. Religion in North America. Bloomington: Indiana University Press, 1986.

Angell, Stephen Ward. *Bishop Henry McNeal Turner and African-American Religion in the South*. 1st ed. Knoxville: University of Tennessee Press, 1992.

Austin, Allan D. *African Muslims in Antebellum America: Transatlantic Stories and Spiritual Struggles*. New York: Routledge, 1997.

Baer, Hans A., and Merrill Singer. *African American Religion: Voices of Protest and Accommodation*. 2nd ed. Knoxville: University of Tennessee Press, 2002.

Barber, William J., II, with Jonathan Wilson-Hartgrove. *The Third Reconstruction: How a Moral Movement Is Overcoming the Politics of Division and Fear*. Boston: Beacon Press, 2016.

Best, Wallace D. *Langston's Salvation: American Religion and the Bard of Harlem*. New York: New York University Press, 2017.

RECOMMENDED READING

————. *Passionately Human, No Less Divine: Religion and Culture in Black Chicago, 1915–1952*. Princeton, NJ: Princeton University Press, 2013.

Blight, David W. *Frederick Douglass: Prophet of Freedom*. New York: Simon & Schuster, 2018.

Blum, Edward J., and Paul Harvey. *The Color of Christ: The Son of God and the Saga of Race in America*. Chapel Hill: University of North Carolina Press, 2012.

Born in Slavery: Slave Narratives from the Federal Writers' Project, 1936 to 1938. Library of Congress Digital Collections. https://www.loc.gov/collec tions/slave-narratives-from-the-federal-writers-project-1936-to-1938/about -this-collection/.

Branch, Taylor. *At Canaan's Edge: America in the King Years, 1965–68*. New York: Simon & Schuster, 2006.

————. *Parting the Waters: America in the King Years, 1954–63*. New York: Simon & Schuster, 1989.

————. *Pillar of Fire: America in the King Years, 1963–65*. New York: Simon & Schuster, 1999.

Brooks, Walter H. *The Silver Bluff Church: A History of Negro Baptist Churches in America*. Ann Arbor: University of Michigan Library, 2009.

Burroughs, Nannie Helen. *Nannie Helen Burroughs: A Documentary Portrait of an Early Civil Rights Pioneer, 1900–1959*. Edited by Kelisha B. Graves. African American Intellectual Heritage Series. Notre Dame, IN: University of Notre Dame Press, 2019.

Burton, Oliver Vernon, with Wilbur Cross. *Penn Center: A History Preserved*. Athens: University of Georgia Press, 2014.

Butler, Anthea D. *Women in the Church of God in Christ: Making a Sanctified World*. Chapel Hill: University of North Carolina Press, 2012.

Campbell, James T. *Songs of Zion: The African Methodist Episcopal Church in the United States and South Africa*. New York: Oxford University Press, 1995.

Cannon, Katie G., and Anthony B. Pinn. *Oxford Handbook of African American Theology*. Oxford Handbooks. Cary, NC: Oxford University Press, 2014.

RECOMMENDED READING

Chappell, David L. *A Stone of Hope: Prophetic Religion and the Death of Jim Crow*. Chapel Hill: University of North Carolina Press, 2009.

Cole, Jean Lee, ed. *Freedom's Witness: The Civil War Correspondence of Henry McNeal Turner*. Morgantown: West Virginia University Press, 2013.

Cone, James H. *God of the Oppressed*. Rev. ed. Maryknoll, NY: Orbis Books, 1997.

Cone, James H., and Gayraud S. Wilmore. *Black Theology: A Documentary History*. Vol. 1: 1966–1979. Maryknoll, NY: Orbis Books, 1993.

———. *Black Theology: A Documentary History*. Vol. 2: 1980–1992. Maryknoll, NY: Orbis Books, 1993.

Cooper, Melissa L. *Making Gullah: A History of Sapelo Islanders, Race, and the American Imagination*. Chapel Hill: University of North Carolina Press, 2017.

Creel, Margaret Washington. *A Peculiar People: Slave Religion and Community-Culture among the Gullahs*. The American Social Experience Series, 7. New York: New York University Press, 1988.

Cressler, Matthew J. *Authentically Black and Truly Catholic: The Rise of Black Catholicism in the Great Migration*. New York: New York University Press, 2017.

Curry, Michael B. *Songs My Grandma Sang*. New York: Morehouse Publishing, 2016.

Darden, Robert. *Nothing But Love in God's Water*. Vol. 1: *Black Sacred Music from the Civil War to the Civil Rights Movement*. University Park: Pennsylvania State University Press, 2014.

———. *Nothing But Love in God's Water*. Vol. 2: *Black Sacred Music from Sit-Ins to Resurrection City*. University Park: Pennsylvania State University Press, 2016.

———. *People Get Ready!: A New History of Black Gospel Music*. New York: Continuum, 2004.

Day, Keri. *Unfinished Business: Black Women, the Black Church, and the Struggle to Thrive in America*. Maryknoll, NY: Orbis Books, 2012.

RECOMMENDED READING

de la Croix, St. Sukie. *Chicago Whispers: A History of LGBT Chicago before Stonewall.* Madison: University of Wisconsin Press, 2012.

Diouf, Sylviane A. *Dreams of Africa in Alabama: The Slave Ship Clotilda and the Story of the Last Africans Brought to America.* New York: Oxford University Press, 2007.

———. *Servants of Allah: African Muslims Enslaved in the Americas.* New York: New York University Press, 1998.

Dollinger, Marc. *Black Power, Jewish Politics: Reinventing the Alliance in the 1960s.* Brandeis Series in American Jewish History, Culture, and Life. Waltham, MA: Brandeis University Press, 2018.

Douglas, Kelly Brown. *The Black Christ.* The Bishop Henry McNeal Turner Studies in North American Black Religion. Vol. 9. Maryknoll, NY: Orbis Books, 1994.

———. *Sexuality and the Black Church: A Womanist Perspective.* Maryknoll, NY: Orbis Books, 1999.

Du Bois, W. E. B. *The Negro Church.* Alton B. Pollard, series ed. Eugene, OR: Cascade Books, 2011.

———. *The Philadelphia Negro: A Social Study.* Philadelphia: Published for the university, 1899.

———. *Prayers for Dark People.* Edited by Herbert Aptheker. Amherst: University of Massachusetts Press, 1980.

———. *The Souls of Black Folk.* Edited by Henry Louis Gates, Jr., and Terri Hume Oliver. Norton Critical Editions. New York: W. W. Norton, 1999.

Dyson, Michael Eric. *Between God and Gangsta Rap: Bearing Witness to Black Culture.* New York: Oxford University Press, 1996.

Elaw, Zilpha. *Memoirs of the Life, Religious Experience, Ministerial Travels and Labours of Mrs. Zilpha Elaw.* London: Published by the authoress; Mr. B. Taylor, 1846.

RECOMMENDED READING

Elmore, Charles J. *Savannah, Georgia.* Black America Series. Charleston, SC: Arcadia Publishing, 2002.

Evans, Curtis J. *The Burden of Black Religion.* New York: Oxford University Press, 2008.

Fauset, Arthur Huff. *Black Gods of the Metropolis: Negro Religious Cults of the Urban North.* Philadelphia: University of Pennsylvania Press, 1971.

Floyd-Thomas, Juan M., and Anthony B. Pinn. *Religion in the Age of Obama.* London: Bloomsbury Academic, 2018.

Fluker, Walter. *The Ground Has Shifted: The Future of the Black Church in Post-Racial America.* Religion, Race, and Ethnicity, Book 6. New York: New York University Press, 2016.

Foner, Eric. *Reconstruction: America's Unfinished Revolution, 1863–1877.* Updated ed. New York: Harper Perennial, 2014.

Frazier, E. Franklin, *The Negro Church in America,* and C. Eric Lincoln, *The Black Church since Frazier.* New York: Schocken Books, 1977.

Garland, Phyl. *The Sound of Soul: The Story of Black Music.* Chicago: Henry Regnery Company, 1969.

Gates, Henry Louis, Jr. *Colored People: A Memoir.* 1st ed. New York: Knopf, 1994.

Gates, Henry Louis, Jr., and Kevin M. Burke. *And Still I Rise: Black America since MLK, an Illustrated Chronology.* New York: HarperCollins, 2015.

George, Carol V. R. *Segregated Sabbaths: Richard Allen and the Emergence of Independent Black Churches, 1760–1840.* New York: Oxford University Press, 1973.

Georgia Writers' Project. Savannah Unit. *Drums and Shadows: Survival Studies among the Georgia Coastal Negroes.* New ed. of 1940 ed. Athens: University of Georgia Press, 1986.

Gerbner, Katharine. *Christian Slavery: Conversion and Race in the Protestant Atlantic World.* Philadelphia: University of Pennsylvania Press, 2018.

Gilkes, Cheryl Townsend. *If It Wasn't for the Women: Black Women's Experience and Womanist Culture in Church and Community.* Maryknoll, NY: Orbis Books, 2001.

Glaude, Eddie S., Jr. *African American Religion: A Very Short Introduction.* New York: Oxford University Press, 2014.

―――. *Exodus!: Religion, Race, and Nation in Early Nineteenth-Century Black America.* Chicago: University of Chicago Press, 2000.

Godwyn, Morgan. *The Negro's [and] Indians Advocate, Suing for Their Admission into the Church: Or A Persuasive to the Instructing and Baptizing of the Negro's and Indians in Our Plantations. Shewing, That as the Compliance Therewith Can Prejudice No Mans Just Interest; so the Wilful Neglecting and Opposing of It, Is No Less than a Manifest Apostacy from the Christian Faith. To Which Is Added, a Brief Account of Religion in Virginia.* London: Printed by J[ohn] D[arby], 1680.

Gomez, Michael A. *Black Crescent: The Experience and Legacy of African Muslims in the Americas.* Cambridge, UK: Cambridge University Press, 2005.

Greenberg, Cheryl Lynn. *Troubling the Waters: Black-Jewish Relations in the American Century.* Politics and Society in Modern America. Princeton, NJ: Princeton University Press, 2006.

Griffith, R. Marie, and Barbara Dianne Savage. *Women and Religion in the African Diaspora: Knowledge, Power, and Performance.* Lived Religions. Baltimore: Johns Hopkins University Press, 2006.

Harding, Vincent. *There Is a River: The Black Struggle for Freedom in America.* San Diego: Harvest, 1981.

Harvey, Paul. *Freedom's Coming: Religious Culture and the Shaping of the South from the Civil War through the Civil Rights Era.* Chapel Hill: University of North Carolina Press, 2005.

―――. *Through the Storm, Through the Night: A History of African American Christianity.* Lanham, MD: Rowman and Littlefield, 2011.

Heilbut, Anthony. *The Fan Who Knew Too Much: Aretha Franklin, the Rise of the Soap Opera, Children of the Gospel Church, and Other Meditations.* New York: Knopf, 2012.

———. *The Gospel Sound: Good News and Bad Times.* New York: Simon and Schuster, 1971.

Heywood, Linda M., and John K. Thornton. *Central Africans, Atlantic Creoles, and the Foundation of the Americas, 1585–1660.* New York: Cambridge University Press, 2007.

Higginbotham, Evelyn Brooks. *Righteous Discontent: The Women's Movement in the Black Baptist Church, 1880–1920.* Cambridge, MA: Harvard University Press, 1994.

Hildebrand, Reginald F. *The Times Were Strange and Stirring: Methodist Preachers and the Crisis of Emancipation.* Durham, NC: Duke University Press, 1995.

Hurston, Zora Neale. *The Sanctified Church.* New York: Marlowe & Company, 1981.

Johnson, James Weldon. *The Book of American Negro Spirituals.* New York: Viking Press, 1925.

———. *God's Trombones: Seven Negro Sermons in Verse.* New York: Viking Press, 1927.

Jones, Martha S. *All Bound Up Together: The Woman Question in African American Public Culture, 1830–1900.* The John Hope Franklin Series in African American History and Culture. Chapel Hill: University of North Carolina Press, 2007.

Jordan, Vernon E., Jr., with Annette Gordon-Reed. *Vernon Can Read!: A Memoir.* New York: Public Affairs, 2009.

Joseph, Peniel E. *The Sword and the Shield: The Revolutionary Lives of Malcolm X and Martin Luther King Jr.* New York: Basic Books, 2020.

Knecht, Sharon C. *Oblate Sisters of Providence: A Pictorial History.* Brookfield, MO: Donning Company, 2007.

Landers, Jane. *Black Society in Spanish Florida.* Urbana: University of Illinois Press, 1999.

RECOMMENDED READING

Lee, Jarena. *Religious Experience and Journal of Mrs. Jarena Lee, Giving an Account of Her Call to Preach the Gospel.* Philadelphia: Printed and published for the author, 1849.

Lincoln, C. Eric, and Lawrence H. Mamiya. *The Black Church in the African American Experience.* Durham, NC: Duke University Press, 1990; reprint 2003.

Martin, Lerone A. *Preaching on Wax: The Phonograph and the Shaping of Modern African American Religion.* Religion, Race, and Ethnicity. New York: New York University Press, 2014.

Mays, Benjamin E., and Joseph William Nicholson. *The Negro's Church.* New York: Arno Press, 1969.

McFeely, William S. *Sapelo's People: A Long Walk into Freedom.* 1st ed. New York: W. W. Norton, 1994.

McNeil, Genna Rae, et al. *Witness: Two Hundred Years of African-American Faith and Practice at the Abyssinian Baptist Church of Harlem, New York.* Grand Rapids, MI: William B. Eerdmans Publishing Company, 2013.

Mitchell, Ella Pearson, ed. *Those Preachin' Women: Sermons by Black Women Preachers.* Vol. 1. Valley Forge, PA: Judson Press, 1985.

———. *Those Preachin' Women: More Sermons by Black Women Preachers.* Vol. 2. Valley Forge, PA: Judson Press, 1988.

Moses, Wilson Jeremiah. *Alexander Crummell: A Study of Civilization and Discontent.* New York: Oxford University Press, 1989.

Moss, Otis III, and Otis Moss, Jr. *Preach!: The Power and Purpose behind Our Praise.* Cleveland: Pilgrim Press, 2012.

Murphy, Larry G., J. Gordon Melton, and Gary L. Ward. *Encyclopedia of African American Religions.* Religious Information Systems. London: Routledge, 1993.

Newman, Richard S. *Freedom's Prophet: Bishop Richard Allen, the AME Church, and the Black Founding Fathers.* New York: New York University Press, 2009.

Pace, Courtney. *Freedom Faith: The Womanist Vision of Prathia Hall.* Athens: University of Georgia Press, 2019.

Payne, Daniel Alexander. *History of the African Methodist Episcopal Church*. Reprint of 1891 ed. The American Negro, His History and Literature. New York: Arno Press, 1969.

———. *Recollections of Seventy Years*. Nashville, TN: Publishing House of the AME Sunday School Union, 1888.

Pierce, Yolanda. *Hell without Fires: Slavery, Christianity, and the Antebellum Spiritual Narrative*. History of African-American Religions. Gainesville: University Press of Florida, 2005.

Pinn, Anthony B. *The Black Church in the Post–Civil Rights Era*. Maryknoll, NY: Orbis Books, 2002.

———. *Terror and Triumph: The Nature of Black Religion*. Minneapolis, MN: Augsburg Fortress, 2003.

Powell, Adam Clayton, Jr. *Keep the Faith, Baby!* New York: Trident Press, 1967.

Raboteau, Albert J. *Canaan Land: A Religious History of African Americans*. New York: Oxford University Press, 2001.

———. *Slave Religion: The "Invisible Institution" in the Antebellum South*. New York: Oxford University Press, 2004.

Ransby, Barbara. *Ella Baker and the Black Freedom Movement: A Radical Democratic Vision*. Gender and American Culture. Chapel Hill: University of North Carolina Press, 2003.

Reed, Christopher Robert. *The Rise of Chicago's Black Metropolis, 1920–1929*. Urbana: University of Illinois Press, 2011.

Rouse, Carolyn Moxley, et al. *Televised Redemption: Black Religious Media and Racial Empowerment*. New York: New York University Press, 2016.

Said, Omar ibn, and A. Alryyes. *A Muslim American Slave: The Life of Omar ibn Said*. Translated and edited by Ala Alryyes. Wisconsin Studies in Autobiography. Madison: University of Wisconsin Press, 2011.

Salvatore, Nick. *Singing in a Strange Land: C. L. Franklin, the Black Church, and the Transformation of America*. 1st ed. New York: Little, Brown, 2005.

Salzman, Jack, and Cornel West. *Struggles in the Promised Land: Towards a History of Black-Jewish Relations in the United States.* Cary, NC: Oxford University Press, 1997.

Sanders, Cheryl J., ed. *Living the Intersection: Womanism and Afrocentrism in Theology.* Minneapolis, MN: Augsburg Fortress Publishers, 1995.

Sanders, Cheryl J. *Saints in Exile: The Holiness-Pentecostal Experience in African American Religion and Culture.* New York: Oxford University Press, 1996.

Savage, Barbara Dianne. *Your Spirits Walk beside Us: The Politics of Black Religion.* Cambridge, MA: The Belknap Press of Harvard University Press, 2008.

Sernett, Milton C., ed. *African American Religious History: A Documentary Witness.* The C. Eric Lincoln Series on the Black Experience. Durham, NC: Duke University Press, 2000.

Sernett, Milton C. *Bound for the Promised Land: African American Religion and the Great Migration.* The C. Eric Lincoln Series on the Black Experience. Durham, NC: Duke University Press, 1997.

Shelby, Tommie, and Brandon Terry, eds. *To Shape a New World: Essays on the Political Philosophy of Martin Luther King, Jr.* Cambridge, MA: The Belknap Press of Harvard University Press, 2018.

Simmons, Martha, and Frank A. Thomas, eds. *Preaching with Sacred Fire: An Anthology of African American Sermons, 1750 to the Present.* 1st ed. New York: W. W. Norton, 2010.

Smith, J. Alfred, ed. *Outstanding Black Sermons.* Valley Forge, PA: Judson Press, 1976.

Smith, Suzanne E. *To Serve the Living: Funeral Directors and the African American Way of Death.* Cambridge, MA: Harvard University Press, 2010.

Taylor, Robert L. *Thomas A. Dorsey: Father of Black Gospel Music: An Interview.* Genesis of Black Gospel Music. Bloomington, IN: Trafford Publishing, 2013.

Thompson, Charles. *Biography of a Slave, Being the Experiences of Rev. Charles Thompson, a Preacher of the United Brethren Church, While a Slave in the South,*

Together with Startling Occurrences Incidental to Slave Life. Dayton, OH: United Brethren Publishing House, 1875. Project Gutenberg, http://www.gutenberg.org/files/9941/9941-h/9941-h.htm.

Thurman, Howard. *Jesus and the Disinherited.* New York: Abingdon-Cokesbury Press, 1949.

———. *Sermons on the Parables.* Edited by David B. Gowler and Kipton E. Jensen. Maryknoll, NY: Orbis Books, 2018.

———. *With Head and Heart: The Autobiography of Howard Thurman.* 1st ed. New York: Harcourt Brace Jovanovich, 1979.

Tinney, James S. "William Seymour: Father of Modern-Day Pentecostalism." In *Black Apostles: Afro-American Clergy Confront the Twentieth Century,* edited by Randall K. Burkett and Richard Newman. Boston: G. K. Hall, 1978.

Truth, Sojourner. *Narrative of Sojourner Truth; a Bondswoman of Olden Time, Emancipated by the New York Legislature in the Early Part of the Present Century; with a History of Her Labors and Correspondence, Drawn from Her "Book of Life."* Boston: Published by the author, 1875. https://docsouth.unc.edu/neh/truth75/truth75.html.

Turman, Eboni Marshall. *Toward a Womanist Ethic of Incarnation: Black Bodies, the Black Church, and the Council of Chalcedon.* 1st ed. Black Religion/Womanist Thought/Social Justice. New York: Palgrave Macmillan, 2013.

Walker, Wyatt Tee. *"Somebody's Calling My Name": Black Sacred Music and Social Change.* Valley Forge, PA: Judson Press, 1979.

Walton, Jonathan L. *A Lens of Love: Reading the Bible in Its World for Our World.* Louisville, KY: Presbyterian Publishing, 2018.

———. *Watch This!: The Ethics and Aesthetics of Black Televangelism.* New York: New York University Press, 2009.

Warnock, Raphael G. *The Divided Mind of the Black Church: Theology, Piety, and Public Witness.* Religion, Race, and Ethnicity. New York: New York University Press, 2013.

RECOMMENDED READING

Watts, Jill. *God, Harlem U.S.A.: The Father Divine Story*. Berkeley: University of California Press, 1992.

Weisenfeld, Judith. *New World A-Coming: Black Religion and Racial Identity during the Great Migration*. New York: New York University Press, 2016.

Weisenfeld, Judith, and Richard Newman, eds. *This Far by Faith: Readings in African-American Women's Religious Biography*. New York: Routledge, 1996.

West, Cornel, and Eddie S. Glaude, Jr. *African American Religious Thought: An Anthology*. 1st ed. Louisville, KY: Westminster John Knox Press, 2003.

Wiggins, Daphne C. *Righteous Content: Black Women's Perspectives of Church and Faith*. Religion, Race, and Ethnicity. New York: New York University Press, 2004.

Woodson, Carter G. *The History of the Negro Church*. Washington, DC: The Associated Publishers, 1921.

Young, Andrew. *A Way Out of No Way: The Spiritual Memoirs of Andrew Young*. Nashville, TN: Thomas Nelson, Inc., 1996.

Young, Jason R. *Rituals of Resistance: African Atlantic Religion in Kongo and the Lowcountry South in the Era of Slavery*. Baton Rouge: Louisiana State University Press, 2007.

Illustration Credits

ILLUSTRATION CREDITS

p. 172: Bettmann/Getty Images

p. 176: Jill Johnson/*Fort Worth Star-Telegram*/Tribune News Service via Getty Images

p. 182: AP Photo/Jeff Roberson

p. 184: Wikimedia Commons

Gallery

p. 2, top left: The Picture Art Collection/Alamy Stock Photo

p. 2, top right: Southern Baptist Historical Library and Archives, Nashville, Tennessee

p. 2, bottom left: National Portrait Gallery

p. 2, bottom right: Schomburg Center for Research in Black Culture, Manuscripts, Archives, and Rare Books Division, The New York Public Library

p. 3, top left: Courtesy of Richard J. Watson, watsonartforyou.com

p. 3, top right: Library of Congress Prints and Photographs Division

p. 3, bottom: Thomas Haller Buchanan

p. 4, left: Library of Congress Prints and Photographs Division

p. 4, top right: Library of Congress Prints and Photographs Division

p. 4, bottom right: Valentine Museum, Virginia Commonwealth University

p. 5, top left: National Portrait Gallery

p. 5, bottom left and right: Library of Congress Prints and Photographs Division

p. 6, top left: Moorland Spingarn

p. 6, bottom left: Flower Pentecostal

p. 6, top right: HathiTrust Digital Library

p. 6, bottom right: Internet Archive

p. 7, top left: George Rinhart/Corbis via Getty Images

p. 7, bottom left and right: Library of Congress Prints and Photographs Division

p. 8, top: Bettmann/Getty Images

p. 8, bottom: © CORBIS/Corbis via Getty Images

p. 9, bottom: AP Photo/*Atlanta Journal-Constitution*, Joe Benton

p. 10, top: The Center for African American Church History and Research, Inc./Glenda Williams Goodson

p. 10, bottom: Mark Kauffman/The LIFE Picture Collection via Getty Images

p. 11, top: Bettmann/Getty Images

p. 11, bottom: AP Photo/Jacob Harris

p. 12, top: AP Photo

p. 12, bottom: University of Michigan

p. 13, top: Thomas Michael Alleman/Liaison via Getty Images

p. 13, bottom: Ted Thai/The LIFE Picture Collection via Getty Images

p. 14, top: John Dominis/The LIFE Picture Collection via Getty Images

p. 14, center: Daily Reflector Negative Collection (Manuscript Collection

741, Box 25, Folder B, Image 31). Carolina Manuscript Collection of J. Y. Joyner Library

p. 14, bottom: Lee Lockwood/The LIFE Images Collection via Getty Images/Getty Images

p. 15: Time Life, Richard Saunders via Getty Images

p. 16: Dozier Mobley/Getty Images

p. 17, top: AP Photo/Peter Southwick

p. 17, bottom: Ellisphotos/Alamy Stock Photo

p. 18, top: Atlanta University Center Robert W. Woodruff Library

p. 18, bottom: Getty Images

p. 19, top: Taylor Hill/Getty Images for Big Hassle Media

p. 19, bottom: AP Photo/*Detroit News*, David Coates

p. 20, top: Union Theological Seminary

p. 20, bottom: Magnum Photos

p. 21: Ken Hawkins/Alamy Stock Photo

p. 22, top: Tim Sloan/AFP/Getty Images

p. 22, bottom: Evan Richman/*The Boston Globe* via Getty Images

p. 23, top: Office of the General Secretary/CIO-AMEC

p. 23, bottom: Enid Alvarez/*NY Daily News* Archive via Getty Images

p. 24, top: John Leyba/*The Denver Post* via Getty Images

p. 24, bottom: Lady Parchment Photography

p. 25, top: Keith Bedford/*The Boston Globe* via Getty Images

p. 25, bottom: Photo by Pete Muller

p. 26, top: Photograph by Philip McCollum, courtesy of First Congregational Church, UCC, of Altanta

p. 26, center: AP Photo/Taimy Alvarez, AJC

p. 26, bottom: Ralph Basui Watkins, MFA, PhD

p. 27: John Chapman/Alamy Stock Photo

p. 28, top: Photograph by Brian Baker/www.deanbaker.org

p. 28, center right: Daniel Dubois/Vanderbilt University

p. 28, bottom: Office of the General Secretary/CIO-AMEC

p. 29, top: Erik S. Lesser/Getty Images

p. 29, bottom left: Photograph by Benjamin Perry/Courtesy of Union Theological Seminary

p. 29, bottom right: AP Photo/Ric Feld

p. 30, top: Brian Killian/WireImage

p. 30, bottom: Courtesy of Pablo Jones/www.pablojones.org

p. 31, top: Nikki Kahn/*The Washington Post* via Getty Images

p. 31, bottom: Angelo Merendino/Getty Images

p. 32, top: Erin Scott/ZUMA Wire/Alamy Live News

p. 32, bottom: AP Photo/David Goldman

Index

Page numbers in *italics* refer to photographs.

INDEX

INDEX

INDEX

INDEX

INDEX

INDEX